Experience Machines

Experience Machines

The Philosophy of Virtual Worlds

Edited by Mark Silcox

ROWMAN & LITTLEFIELD
INTERNATIONAL

London • New York

Published by Rowman & Littlefield International, Ltd.
Unit A, Whitacre Mews, 26-34 Stannary Street, London SE11 4AB
www.rowmaninternational.com

Rowman & Littlefield International, Ltd. is an affiliate of Rowman & Littlefield
4501 Forbes Boulevard, Suite 200, Lanham, Maryland 20706, USA
With additional offices in Boulder, New York, Toronto (Canada), and London (UK)
www.rowman.com

British Library Cataloguing in Publication Information Available
A catalogue record for this book is available from the British Library

ISBN: HB 978-1-78660-067-7
ISBN: PB 978-1-78660-068-4

Library of Congress Cataloging-in-Publication Data

Names: Silcox, Mark, editor.
Title: Experience machines : the philosophy of virtual worlds / edited by Mark Silcox.
Description: Lanham : Rowman & Littlefield International, 2017. | Includes bibliographical refer-
    ences and index.
Identifiers: : LCCN 2017012206 (print) | LCCN 2017016913 (ebook) | ISBN 9781786600691 (Elec-
    tronic) | ISBN 9781786600677 (cloth : alk. paper) | ISBN 9781786600684 (pbk. : alk. paper)
Subjects: LCSH: Experience. | Reality. | Virtual reality. | Computer simulation.
Classification: LCC B105.E9 (ebook) | LCC B105.E9 E9425 2017 (print) | DDC 128/.4--dc23
LC record available at https://lccn.loc.gov/2017012206

∞™ The paper used in this publication meets the minimum requirements of American
National Standard for Information Sciences—Permanence of Paper for Printed Library
Materials, ANSI/NISO Z39.48-1992.

Printed in the United States of America

Contents

Introduction: The Experience Machine

From Thought Experiment to (Virtual) Reality

Mark Silcox

Robert Nozick, in his 1974 book *Anarchy, State, and Utopia*, described the experience machine as a wondrous, but purely hypothetical, piece of technology:

> Suppose there was an experience machine that would give you any experience you desired. Superduper neuropsychologists could stimulate your brain so that you would think and feel you were writing a great novel, or making a friend, or reading an interesting book. All the time you would be floating in a tank, with electrodes attached to your brain. (Nozick 1974, 42)

The question that Nozick's thought experiment was designed to provoke in his readers was a simple one: "Should you plug into this machine for life, preprogramming your life's experiences?"

It is less than entirely clear from the book itself exactly what broader philosophical conclusions Nozick was personally inclined to draw from this imaginative exercise. But he certainly did think it was obvious that most of us would answer his question strongly in the negative. He also described at least one inference he thought that anyone could draw upon becoming aware of this inclination. "By imagining an experience machine and then realizing that we would not use it," he claimed, "we learn that *something matters to us in addition to experience*" (Nozick 1974, 44).

Over the subsequent four decades, Nozick's brief argument has been invoked in a wide variety of contexts to defend a startlingly diverse array of philosophical claims. It has also become a staple of college classrooms, internet discussion threads, and energetic late-night bull sessions, both inside and outside the walls of the academy. Philosophers who have shared Nozick's intuitions about the experience machine's fundamental unattractiveness have appealed to them to criticize various species of *hedonism* (the view that all we ultimately value—or that all we should so value—is pleasure), as well as to defend the widespread but often rather inchoately formulated intuition that what matters above all else to human beings is *autonomy*. Some, however, have also expressed doubts that the lessons to be learned from Nozick's scenario have anything whatsoever to do with the value of pleasure. And still others have raised questions about the very rationality of our aversion to plug in, or simply denied that Nozick is correct in anticipating how most people would behave if they were presented with the real-life prospect of lifelong dependence upon the machine.

All of this rich and provocative philosophical discussion, however, has thus far been carried out more or less haphazardly. There has been very little effort made to compare or synthesize reactions to the thought experiment that appear to be in tension with one another. And perhaps even more puzzlingly, few philosophers have attempted (at least in print) to compare intuitions about the machine's possible appeal to the attractions of actual, real-life experiences provided by new technologies that have arisen in the wake of the 1980s' personal computer revolution.

Here, for the first time, Nozick's experience machine is made the explicit focus of sustained, concerted scrutiny from a multiplicity of philosophical perspectives. The authors of the chapters in this volume explore (in arguably unprecedented depth) all of the hypotheses about the philosophical significance of the experience machine already mentioned, as well as lots of others. The conclusions that they reach do not by any means represent the achievement of some grand consensus. Any reader who makes it to the end of the book will doubtless be struck above all else by the remarkable diversity of opinions that the Nozickian *gedankenexperiment* is capable of provoking. The only shared presupposition in evidence here is that, by thinking carefully about why (and whether) we might prefer to avoid the sort of life in which more of our experiences are products of human artifice, new insights can be gained into the deeper sources of value and obligation for which philosophers always are searching.

The authors whose work is collected here have also paid sustained attention to the real-world significance of such investigations for the inhabitants of technologically advanced societies—implications of his thought experiment that Nozick might not himself have been in a position to anticipate. The enormous cultural and technological changes that occurred near the end of the twentieth century, thanks mainly to the sudden cheap availability of powerful computers, and later on to the growth of the internet, have made his argument seem considerably more imbued with immediate practical significance.

The types of activities in which people engage when they play computer games, interact via social media, and build computer simulations of real-world phenomena for research or entertainment all produce the sorts of experiences that one can perfectly well imagine being attractive to anybody at least willing to *consider* plugging into Nozick's machine. But these technologies also impose a kind of structure upon the experiences (or, indeed, the whole lives) of their users that adds a dimension of complexity to any attempt to assess their value. Habitual players of *Second Life*, *World of Warcraft*, or *League of Legends*, as well as anyone who has ever taken an online "tour" of a distant city, an art gallery, or a famous building, have all (however briefly) chosen to inhabit a *virtual world*, presumably out of a sense that their ordinary, real-world environments were at least in some way temporarily inadequate. Several of the contributors to the present volume have thought very carefully about what such decisions might show about how recent technological developments have *already* affected our conceptions of what's truly valuable—within our own lives as well as others'—and how they might be expected to in the future.

AXIOLOGIES OF THE REAL

Nozick's own explanation for why at least *many* people would refuse the offer of a permanent connection to the experience machine is quite well known. He proposes that, in the first place, as human inhabitants of the "real" world "we want to *do* certain things, and not just have the experience of doing them." And in the second place, each of us also wants "to *be* a certain way, to be a certain sort of person," rather than just an "indeterminate blob" hooked up to a machine. "Why should we be concerned with how our time is filled, but not with what we are?" (Nozick 1974, 43).

Such considerations cannot be the whole of the story about what makes us so averse to plugging in, however, given that (as Nozick himself helpfully observes) many of us would be equally disinclined to plug into what he calls a *transformation machine* or a *results machine*. The former hypothetical device would have the capacity to change an individual into whatever type of person she most wanted to be; the latter would produce any outcome whatsoever in the world that one's own activities would have produced anyway. Such instruments are perhaps a little harder to envisage than a machine that simply changed one's inner states. But if, to the extent that we *can* imagine them, we would also reject the offer to make use of them, then the default set of values we would be relying on would become even more inscrutable to ordinary reflection.

The third reason that Nozick gives for not plugging in is perhaps his most provocative. The problem with the experience machine isn't just explicable in terms of what determinate opportunities it might rob us of, but additionally (he claims) its very status as a human *artifact*. The machine "limits us to a man-made reality, to a world no deeper or more important than that which people can construct" (Nozick 1974, 43). One might be tempted to think of the experience machine as analogous to a dose of some extremely potent, persistently efficacious hallucinogen. But many avid drug users, he suggests, would actually be *revolted* by the prospect of plugging into the experience machine, because it would leave them closed off to a "plumbing of deeper significance." A similar ambiguity besets traditional conceptions of eternal bliss embraced by the religious, many of whom hope earnestly for a heavenly reward but would vigorously reject even a 100 percent guaranteed technological simulacrum (Nozick 1974, 43).

Because his main topic in *Anarchy, State, and Utopia* is the legitimacy of political authority rather than more abstract ethical considerations, Nozick never develops any of these rather tentative suggestions into a full account of what human beings either do or should value "more than experience." Instead, he merely suggests that there should be certain inviolable, public constraints upon the use of any one person (or animal) by another to increase a society's overall level of happiness.[1]

In the years since Nozick's book was published, some other philosophers have provided more fully developed accounts of the ultimate sources of value in human life that might plausibly be regarded as consonant with the motivations behind his elliptical remarks. The idea that human autonomy has a peculiarly fundamental and non-negotiable type of value over that of any of our occurrent psychological states, for example, has always been favored by moral philosophers working in the Kantian tradition, and has recently received some powerful new defenses.[2] And elsewhere, among the small cadre of contemporary philosophers still sympathetic to hedonism, it has become popular to think of what they call "attitudinal" pleasure as the most valuable kind. Such pleasure consists of certain types of second-order attitudes that agents take toward their discrete affective states, rather than those states themselves: one is happy (in the relevant sense) *that* one enjoys pizza, or the respect of one's colleagues, rather than because of the feelings one gets from eating pizza or from being respected. The possibility of cultivating such attitudes might require one to have a type of agency that one simply cannot attain when plugged into the experience machine.[3]

Nozick's remarks about the importance of keeping oneself open to the "deeper significance" of one's experiences suggest that certain types of *knowledge* might also possess an autonomous type of value unconnected to the way that it merely *feels* to know something. Of course, there is no reason to deny that at least some types of knowledge might be available to agents in the experience machine.[4] But it seems plausible to conclude that one's knowledge of the external world, at least, would have to be available only indirectly, and that at least some first-person knowledge about one's own *connection* to reality (including, of course, the very knowledge that one is hooked up to the experience machine) would be completely inaccessible. To the extent that the possession of such knowledge may be attributed a nonderivative kind of value, this might also help to justify an aversion to plugging in.[5]

Yet in spite of the availability of all these philosophical buttresses to Nozick's peremptory attack on the experience machine, certain doubts remain. Are the sorts of preferences Nozick identifies as the basis of an aversion to the experience machine really as ubiquitous and as unassailable as Nozick and these other philosophers appear to believe? Are they even all that common? From whence do they arise in an individual's overall mental economy? Might they represent nothing more than an atavistic, persistent, but ultimately irrational aversion to unfamiliar technologies?[6] Or are they a manifestation of what behavioral economists refer to as the *status quo* bias, a quirk of our natures that often seems to lead to decisions that badly undermine our well-being?[7]

In Part I of this book, "Virtual Experiences and Human Well-Being," these and other closely related issues are addressed, with an eye toward figuring out what the ultimate significance of Nozick's thought experiment might be for a broad range of philosophical theories about the nature value and moral obligation.

THE WORLD INSIDE THE MACHINE

Suppose we set aside these worries about whether the aversion to plugging in might be a result of mere perversity, atavism, or a rationally unsupportable partiality for the *status quo*. Even if the preference for real world over simulated experiences can survive such criticisms, there is an important further ambiguity that needs to be resolved. Is this preference best understood as being grounded in the belief that *every single* real-world experience is rationally preferable (at least in some respect) to *every single* simulated one? Or is it, rather, just that we believe a certain *proportion* of our experiences must involve contact with the real world for our lives as a whole to be as good as they could be? Nothing in Nozick's very brief presentation of the argument makes it clear which of these two theses he would be more inclined to support.

A provocatively similar ambiguity plagues much contemporary cultural criticism directed against the widespread use of social media, immersive computer games, and VR technology. It is often unclear whether the basis of such criticism is that these media exert some intrinsically malign influence at every moment they are being used, or that there is merely something wrong with the extent to which such pastimes encourage long-term withdrawal from the concerns of everyday life.

At least since the 1960s, there has been widespread consensus among child psychologists that indulgence in make-believe is a healthy form of play, at least in the very young (see Harris 2000). And few modern people think there is anything wrong with the types of gentle self-forgetfulness that so often occur when one is reading fiction, performing in a play or a film, or playing a highly immersive video game. But the very strong appearance that there is nothing whatsoever irrational about the decision to undergo such artificial experiences might perhaps be explicable in terms of their fundamentally *ephemeral* nature. Surely, a large part of what makes video games, make-believe, and art and literature more generally so appealing is the extent to which they provide us with an escape from more "serious," reality-oriented pursuits, an escape that is charming precisely because of its temporariness.

Nothing like the same sort of qualification seems to apply when it comes to assessing the *epistemic* value of technologies designed to produce artificial or simulated experiences. For several decades, computer simulations of real-world phenomena have been taken by scientists in a number of different fields to be sources of direct (albeit fallible) evidence for both causal and predictive explanations. Meteorologists have for some time now been issuing public warnings about the anticipated behavior of hurricanes, tsunamis, and other large-scale weather events upon the basis of what they have seen develop in real-time simulations of these events that involve the performance of thousands of calculations per second.[8] More recently, a fascinating debate has opened up among geophysicists about the origins of Earth's magnetic field, on account of apparently incompatible observations culled from two *different* types of simulations of physical processes at the Earth's core—one entirely digital, the other involving tiny samples of pure iron placed in an enormous vice (see Sumner 2015). In these and other similar examples, scientists must rely on observations of simulated natural phenomena because the events they are trying to explain are for purely physical reasons inaccessible to direct observation. But it would be difficult to defend the claim that what they were gaining thereby was some sort of merely *provisional* knowledge, or that their methods deserved to be regarded as less "serious" relative to some other means of learning the truth about nature.

The axiologically pertinent difference between these two types of artificial experiences is that the former type always seems to require at least some degree of self-abandonment, or loss of detachment. Players of video games and users of social media and VR technologies, unlike scientific experimentalists, derive value from the types of experiences that such media make possible because they have chosen to inhabit *virtual worlds*.

This term is most widely used these days as part of the quasi-technical jargon of contemporary computer programmers, who employ it to distinguish the "places" that they bring into existence from the media that they work with, the services they provide, or the games they invent.[9] It is applicable to machine-generated environments as diverse as the earliest, most austere text-based MOOs and MUDs from the 1970s, *World of Warcraft*'s fictional continent of Azeroth, and the perceptual fields generated by VR technologies such as haptic gloves or the Oculus Rift.

But philosophical speculation about virtual worlds can be understood as having begun as least as far back as the earliest discussions of the concept of the *lifeworld*—the image of reality that confronts a human sensibility prior to any acts of reflection, abstraction, or analysis—by philosophers in the phenomenological tradition.[10] Many of these thinkers have argued that an essential feature of the lifeworld is the fact that it derives its character at least partly from our use of technology. "From an actual human point of view," as one author puts it, "a lifeworld without technology must at best be an imaginative projection" (Ihde 1990, 31). And at least since Heidegger, this aspect of the human condition has been often viewed with an ambivalence that sometimes borders upon outright dread (Heidegger 1972, 307–42).

It is commonplace to speak of "worlds of the imagination," referring both to the spontaneous creations of the individual mind in dream and fantasy and the worlds represented through genre or historical fiction. But there is an important difference between Middle Earth of Tolkien's novels and the types of virtual spaces that one inhabits as the player of a contemporary multiplayer video game. The words on the pages of *The Hobbit* and *The Return of the King* will never change, for all that they will strike each new reader slightly differently. In his landmark philosophical study of virtual reality, Michael Heim points out that what a truly virtual (rather than merely imaginary or illusory) world exhibits is a "lightning ability to change the scene's point of view as fast as the human organism can alter its physical position and perspective. . . . Constantly updated information supports the immersion and interactivity, and to rapidly update the information, computers are essential" (Heim 1998, 6–7). The environment with which one interacts through computer-assisted media has the distinguishing characteristic of responding interactively to changes in the state of its audience, with a degree of speed and efficiency that the human sensorium cannot reliably outpace. Nobody so far has created a virtual world in any of the senses described above such that, once one had entered, one may never return.[11] But some nonetheless demonstrate such a sufficiently persistent and widespread allure that it is by no means farfetched to consider them as possible *precursors* of something like a genuine experience machine.

In Part II of this book, "Real-World Experience Machines?" authors investigate the value of experiences available in contemporaneously accessible virtual worlds in light of considerations raised by Nozick's famous argument and offer diagnoses of their ethical, aesthetic, and cultural significance for the quality of human life in the early twenty-first century.

THE VIRTUAL FUTURE

If the most powerful reason not to plug into the experience machine is that being limited to an artificial environment might rob its users of access to a "deeper" reality, then perhaps the best *defense* that can be offered of using the machine is that it also simply *might not*.

To decide competently between these two options would require one to formulate some pretty tendentious hypotheses about the axiological scope and limitations of human artifice more generally. This is something that contemporary philosophers have for the most part been understandably loathe to do, for many of the same reasons that aggressive speculation about the future path of scientific discovery is carefully eschewed. It is just too easy for philosophers and other dilettantes to guess wrong about how careful examination of the natural world might eventually surprise us, or to underestimate the extent that the types of creativity made possible via this new knowledge might eventually lead us to surprise ourselves.

But while contemporary philosophers have exhibited caution with respect to this sort of speculation, artists and storytellers have meanwhile been having a field day. The type of decision faced by the protagonist of Nozick's imaginary scenario has been dramatized in a number of provocatively different ways throughout popular culture and speculative literature. The most famous example is certainly the decision faced by Neo, the protagonist of the hugely popular 1999 science fiction film *The Matrix*. Early in the film, Neo is asked to choose between taking two pills, a red one that will reveal to him the true nature of his sensory environment—which is actually a massive, machine-generated simulacrum of late twentieth-century America—and a blue one that will allow him to remain deluded for the rest of his natural lifespan. At this point in the narrative, it is made pretty obvious that the former option is the preferable one. Two sequels and a lot of rather dire martial arts battles later, it is revealed that the choice was quite a bit less simple than the film's audience might have originally supposed.

Other, more esoteric works of fiction have tried to depict similar types of decisions about permanently entering (or leaving) virtual worlds in more philosophically nuanced ways. In Mamoru Oshii's subtle and fascinating 2001 science fiction film *Avalon*, a gifted but compulsive gamer is offered the chance to exit a VR game in which she has somehow become trapped, but the price for doing so is to murder one of its virtual inhabitants—a small, defenseless child—in cold blood. The film captures the terrifyingly ambiguous moral status of this sort of action in a way that echoes some of history's most provocative philosophical thought experiments. And in Jeff Noon's 1993 novel *Vurt*, the protagonist finds himself faced with the prospect of staying permanently within a computer-simulated environment, but he is offered the compensation of being able to creatively alter that environment in a way that other users are unable to.

If philosophers should be wary of trying to draw any important theoretical conclusions from the types of dilemmas that would be faced by agents in these sorts of hazily described, counterfactual scenarios, perhaps there is at least something worth saying about the mere *quantity* of choice that future technologies promise to make available to us. And if Nozick's dismissal of the experience machine in retrospect strikes us as somewhat hasty and gauche, his cautionary remarks about the attraction of virtual worlds nonetheless could have something to teach us about the type of future that the current pace of technological change seems to promise. Perhaps, the price that we (or our descendants) might eventually pay for living in a world like those depicted in the fictions just described is that choices about which "real" or virtual worlds to inhabit will have multiplied far beyond the capacity to competently select from among them.

The ancients were perfectly well aware of the fact that offering an agent a larger than normal number of attractive options from which to choose might undermine that individual's rational autonomy or detract from her well-being. The famous image of Buridan's ass, poised eternally between sources of food and drink until it dies in the throes of its deliberations, can now be seen as an ominous anticipation of everyday life in advanced consumer societies. The version of this phenomenon that manifests itself via the unexpected anxieties of having to decide how to spend one's leisure time in the contemporary world has been dubbed "overchoice" (Toffler 1990, 263–83) or "the paradox of choice" (Schwartz 2005) by social psychologists. In the book's final section, "Experiential Design: Problems and Prospects," authors examine a number of different speculative and counterfactual choice situations resembling Nozick's original scenario in the hope of providing some preliminary guidance to artists, programmers, and consumers alike as we struggle to adjust our deliberative capacities in preparation for the virtual worlds of the future.

NOTES

1. See his influential discussion of "side constraints" in Nozick 1974, 28–35.
2. See, for example, Korsgaard 1996, chapter 4.
3. Fred Feldman provides a defense of the value of "attitudinal" pleasure in Feldman 2004. He develops a sophisticated response to the experience machine argument based on this position in Feldman 2012.
4. This issue is examined at length in Cogburn and Silcox 2014.

5. Norman Kretzmann has argued (in Kretzmann 1966) that we can posses some first-personal knowledge in a way that it could not be possessed by God, even if God is by definition omniscient. And in Hurka 2011, Thomas Hurka suggests that, while knowledge of one's position in the real world is not, itself, intrinsically good, the possession of false beliefs upon the topic *is* intrinsically *bad*.

6. Roger Crisp advances this hypothesis in Crisp 2004.

7. Felipe De Brigard provides some experimental data in support of this claim in De Brigard 2010.

8. For an early example that is relatively accessible to the layman, see Holland 1980.

9. Richard Bartle elaborates on these distinctions in considerable detail in Bartle 2003, 473–74.

10. Edmund Husserl introduced the term into the philosophical lexicon in Husserl 1954.

11. It would perhaps be a bit more intellectually honest to say that, if someone ever *has* created this sort of a virtual world, we would probably have *no way to tell* whether or not we were inhabiting it right now. On the rather delicate distinction between these two claims, see Bostrom 2003.

Part I

Virtual Experiences and
Human Well-Being

Chapter One

Cypher's Choices

The Variety and Reality of Virtual Experiences

Peter Ludlow

In *Anarchy, State, and Utopia*, Robert Nozick offered a thought experiment involving an "experience machine"—a machine that can constantly simulate experiences that are pleasurable. Given the opportunity, would we permanently plug ourselves into such a machine? And if not, why would we refrain from doing so?

In some respects, the opportunity to plug into the experience machine presents a choice like that offered to the character Cypher in the movie *The Matrix* (1999). For those who never saw *The Matrix* (or who have forgotten the plot), the movie involves a group of hackers who have come to know that most of humanity is plugged into a vast simulation, known as The Matrix. Cypher is one of the hackers who has become aware of this fact and has been unplugged from The Matrix, but he later betrays his comrades. As his reward for selling out the others, he chooses to be reenvatted. He has seen enough of the real world; he prefers the simulation.

Nozick, however, predicts that most of us would not choose the path taken by the evil traitor Cypher—we would reject the simulation in favor of a life embedded in so-called real life (hereafter RL). Based on this presumed choice, Nozick draws several conclusions. One is that the reason we would reject the simulation is because we cannot genuinely act when we are in the simulation. A second conclusion Nozick draws is that we would reject the simulation because it does not afford us contact with a deeper reality. It only affords us a kind of superficial reality. Finally, Nozick claims that the thought experiment shows us that there is something wrong with the doctrine of hedonism, as ordinarily construed. Even if being embedded in a simulation could afford us a life of pleasure we would reject it—presumably because we value the ability to act in the world and be in contact with basic reality more than we value pleasure itself.

Since Nozick's publication, the idea of an experience machine has become less of a thought experiment and more of an ongoing empirical research program, with virtual worlds like *Second Life* (hereafter SL)and other synthetic worlds providing laboratories in which these questions can be explored. Even though such synthetic worlds do not exhaust the conceptual space of possible experience machines, including Nozick's core example, they have been around long enough that we can extract some important insights into Nozick's questions. The study of virtual worlds can help unglue us from unexamined assumptions about the nature of Nozick's experience machine.

Using what we know about existing virtual worlds I argue that it would be wrong to think that actions in virtual worlds are not genuine actions, and wrong to think that virtual experiences do not afford contact with deeper reality. On the other hand, when people choose to participate in virtual worlds, they typically choose those activities that are fraught with risk—including the risk of causing themselves pain in interpersonal relationships, and engaging in activities, plans, and goals that often yield genuine disappointment. I then argue that this holds true even for the solipsistic experience machine envisioned by Nozick. We would insist on experiences that afford us at least the illusion of agency, action, and risk. Virtual worlds show that given the choice of any virtual experience, we do not choose the hedonistic experience path, but we rather chose virtual lives that have importance and nobility. In effect, Nozick is right, but for the wrong reasons.

1.0 HEDONISM

Because part of Nozick's claim is that the experience machine thought experiment refutes hedonism, we need to get clear on what hedonism is. A standard definition goes something like this: *Hedonism is the doctrine that we should act so as to maximize pleasure and minimize pain to the greatest extent possible.*

There are several further choice points here. First, we have to decide whether we ought to maximize pleasure for everyone or just for ourselves. For purposes of discussion I'm going to assume the latter, since if Nozick's experience machine thought experiment doesn't refute individual-level hedonism it won't refute the group-level hedonism either.[1]

There are other decisions to be made. There is a kind of hedonist who would say that we should always opt for the best possible experience in the moment—we should live in the moment and opt for the greatest pleasure (and least pain) in that moment. This version is too easy a target, I think.

Hedonists since Jeremy Bentham have stressed that future pleasure and pain are important considerations as well.

I'm going to assume a less in-the-moment version of hedonism—one like Bentham's hedonistic calculus in which we are concerned with matters like the future effects of our actions (indigestion and hangovers, for example), the duration of the pleasures received, and so forth.

We might be tempted toward a Millian version of hedonism—one that incorporates the *quality* of a pleasure. I'm going to avoid that version for purposes of this argument, since it is unclear to me how that doctrine could ever be refuted given a broad enough understanding of "quality" of pleasure. For example, you might stipulate that a pleasure is qualitatively better if it involves a real object. That would undermine Nozick's argument against hedonism pretty quickly, but not in a very interesting way.

Ultimately then, the target doctrine is this version of hedonism: *One ought to act to maximize the greatest quantity of pleasure (and/or least pain) over the rest of your life, for yourself.*[2]

In the context of Nozick's thought experiment this understanding of hedonism leads to a three-part question. First, would we opt for a virtual life if it allowed us (individually) significantly more pleasure for the rest of our lives? (I've added the term *significantly* because we want this to be a clear choice. Entering the experience machine is not an enterprise to be taken lightly.) Second, does this choice reflect whether we *ought* to opt for such virtual lives? Third, assuming Nozick is correct about what our choice would be, is his diagnosis of *why* we would make that choice correct? Is it correct that we would reject the experience machine because we would be unable to act in that virtual world and because such a virtual experience would fail to provide us contact with a deeper reality?

2.0 THE THOUGHT EXPERIMENT

Here is how the thought experiment works, as set out in Nozick's *Anarchy, State, and Utopia.*

> Suppose there was an experience machine that would give you any experience you desired. Superduper neuropsychologists could stimulate your brain so that you would think and feel you were writing a great novel, or making a friend, or reading an interesting book. All the time you would be floating in a tank, with electrodes attached to your brain. Should you plug into this machine for life, preprogramming your life experiences? [. . .] Of course, while in the tank you won't know that you're there; you'll think that it's all actually happening. [. . .] Would you plug in? (Nozick 1974, 44–45)

The thought experiment serves the argument against hedonism in the following way. The choice we make reflects certain norms that we share—for example, the norm that there is more value to acting in RL. The thought experiment is supposed to make such norms salient by illustrating that we would choose a world in which we are grounded in reality and free to act in that reality rather than one in which we are streamed happy experiences (in Nozick's version, the life experiences are "preprogrammed").

Like most thought experiments, judgments can break in different directions. For the fictional character Cypher, at least, the choice was to live in the virtual world of The Matrix. Of course, in the context of the movie, this is just evidence that Cypher is a vile, evil traitor. The thought experiment is only supposed to work for agents that are not normatively defective. There is, of course, some danger of circularity in this—the thought experiment is supposed to provide evidence for certain norms, but when the participant's judgment breaks the wrong way we say that is because the participant is normatively defective. Let's give Nozick the benefit of the doubt here and say that we have independent reasons for thinking Cypher was normatively defective (the fact that he killed his comrades, for example).

There is also an is-ought issue here. Even if it is true that nondefective persons reject the vat, why does it follow that they ought to do so? The original hedonists were well aware that people have trouble picking the path that maximizes pleasure and minimizes pain (particularly so the latter). A clever hedonist might say "of course everyone rejects The Matrix; you have to *learn* to be a hedonist."

For purposes of discussion I'm going to assume that these judgments of whether to enter the experience machine are illuminating of normative facts. My point is that even if they are not evidence for norms, Nozick has misdiagnosed the reason people choose to reject the experience machine.[3]

3.0 FIVE GRADES OF VIRTUAL WITHDRAWAL

Nozick has a very specific version of the experience machine in mind, but we will find it useful to consider a broader array of such possible machines. For example, I'll be drawing on virtual worlds like *Second Life* to illustrate some key points vis-à-vis Nozick's core argument.

Is it fair to consider these other classes of examples? Surely yes, because we may find that there are classes of experience machines in which people are less dramatically removed from the real world but which are sufficient to support or refute Nozick's principal claims.

More specifically, there may be classes of experience machines where agents clearly act and they clearly are connected with aspects of the real world but in which they refuse options of more pleasurable lives. This outcome would support my view that Nozick was right, but for the wrong reasons.

To keep the differences clear, I suggest we distinguish five different grades of withdrawal from so-called real life.

1. RL-connected multiuser virtual environments
2. Isolated multiuser virtual environments
3. Single-user virtual environments that afford agency, risk, and harm
4. Single-user virtual environments that afford agency without risk and harm
5. Single-user virtual environments that afford no agency, risk, or harm

As we will see, some of these levels of disengagement present distinct sets of problems. Some of the levels may collapse into each other.

3.1 RL-Connected Multiuser Virtual Environments

In *The Matrix*, the simulated world that Cypher chooses to return to is only minimally connected with RL. For the most part such connections are forbidden; the movement between worlds is clandestine and dangerous. It is, however, possible to imagine a version of The Matrix in which people are allowed to come and go freely and in which exchanges of information and virtual content between The Matrix and RL are permitted. We can imagine a scenario in which Cypher merely wanted to spend part of his time plugged in to The Matrix, and in which his visits to The Matrix were less perilous and more entertaining.

Such a choice would deliver an experience much like the multiuser virtual worlds that exist today, most notably, *Second Life*. For those who aren't familiar with *Second Life*, it is a first-person graphical virtual world. Users participate and act in *Second Life* using "avatars"—graphical representations of themselves that they construct using in-world tools. They also have the opportunity to "skin" their avatars, animate them and clothe them using in-world virtual products.

The most interesting features of *Second Life* are the tools provided to users to create content—content ranging from clothing, to furniture, to scripted objects of nontrivial computational complexity. People in *Second Life* can use other tools to form groups and corporations, sell services ranging from security to design, and hold concerts and other virtual events.

Second Life is persistent, in that the underlying game engine is running even when we are away from the world, and the objects we create and possess in *Second Life* are there when we are offline. People can visit our homes when we are offline, for example.

While it is common for people to be dismissive of people's Second Lives, for the most part it is hard to see this as being much more than a kind of bigotry. While the experience of participating in *Second Life* events may not be as robust as it is for RL events, such experiences are, for all that, clearly substantive. For many persons who are differently abled, or who are caretakers, or who, for many other reasons, do not have the luxury of nights out, SL concerts and events can be rewarding and fun activities. But *Second Life* also affords the opportunity to engage in collaborative actions and activities that are fraught with opportunity and risk.

For example, in *Second Life* one conducts transactions in Linden Dollars—a virtual currency that has a fairly stable exchange rate relative to the U.S. dollar. There are currency exchanges in which Linden Dollars can be exchanged for U.S. currency. There are businesses created within *Second Life* and, in some cases, people's principal sources of income come from *Second Life* activities (e.g., making clothing, or terraforming land and building virtual homes). My *Second Life* friend Anshe Chung (Ailin Graef in RL) built up a substantial business developing and managing virtual properties, acquiring a valuation of over U.S. $1 million at one point (see Saenz 2011).

Nozick claimed that "acting" in the experience machine would not be genuine acting, but if we think of *Second Life* as being a version of the experience machine, then this conclusion is hasty. If you run a virtual corporation and are earning a living from doing so, it hardly seems fair to say that you are not acting in some interesting sense. The decisions you are making and the data structures being created are certainly real things that, for what it is worth, have quantifiable values in RL.

This is not unique to *Second Life*. Once a virtual world has multiple players, then social relations and social objects can be created that are easily ported out of the world. A good example of this is the fact that in multiuser worlds, world-external markets naturally come into existence. This can be driven by the fact that some people invest time in virtual worlds creating virtual products and avatars, and other people with money wish to circumvent that time expenditure. And perhaps unsurprisingly, the market in virtual goods for all virtual platforms (including multiplayer video games) had, already a decade ago, reached U.S. $1.8 billion annually (see Dibbell 2007).

My point here is that activities in multiplayer worlds create things of value that can be transferred to other agents outside of the world of origin. Given that objects (whatever their ontological status) can be created and transferred and assigned dollar value by global markets, it hardly makes sense to say that there is no action or agency in virtual worlds.

Of course, with the creation of value in virtual worlds comes quantifiable risk and harm. If you have assets of a certain value in a virtual world you can (depending on the virtual world) lose them in combat, or be scammed out of them, or have them taken by the platform owner, or simply misplace them.

Losses in multiuser virtual worlds are not limited to economic losses, of course. You can enter into relationships, which can end badly, and you can be ostracized from groups and virtual families, with significant psychic harm. As we will see in section 5, we can even experience harm to our virtual bodies. If you plan on remaining plugged in to a virtual world, harm is difficult to avoid. And even for people who do unplug, this is not a sign that there was no real harm; it is a sign that the harm was great enough that for some people it trumped their positive experiences.

We will go into more detail about these features of virtual worlds in section 5. For now, it is important that we get clear on the difference between worlds like *Second Life* and The Matrix, and it seems to me that the critical difference is that SL is not an isolated virtual world. It is robustly connected with RL; people move freely between RL and SL and there are established RL markets for the purchase and sale of SL goods. A key difference between SL and The Matrix is that the bandwidth of communication between The Matrix and RL is virtually nil, even to the point that those envatted in The Matrix are not aware of RL, or even of the vats in which they float.

Clearly Cypher would not have been satisfied with a free membership in *Second Life*—he wants to have zero contact with RL; indeed he does not even want to remember it. He doesn't choose to spend his time in *Second Life* or *World of Warcraft* or any other virtual world. He chooses a far more radical departure from RL.

3.2 Isolated Multiuser Virtual Environments

When Cypher is given the opportunity to return to The Matrix, he is choosing to return to an *isolated* multiuser virtual environment. He is choosing to return to a vast simulation with other human participants, but in which the other participants don't know they are in the simulation, and neither will Cypher when he has his memory wiped and gets plugged back into The Matrix. This having been said, the (virtual) world he chose to return to is no hedonistic paradise. After all, in the movie, he is asking to return to the same world that Hobbes once called "nasty, brutish, and short." It is, for all that, a better world than RL, in Cypher's view.

As noted in the previous section, the key difference between The Matrix and a virtual world like *Second Life* is that the bandwidth of communication between The Matrix and RL is narrow. The Matrix is clearly similar to SL in many respects. People make many products (which are, unknown to those in The Matrix, virtual products). But they also create many social objects that could easily transfer out of The Matrix. Those who are not envatted can enjoy songs and books written in The Matrix.

It is interesting to consider how much of the economy of The Matrix could have RL application. Assuming that the virtual physics of The Matrix and physics of RL are the same, many inventions in The Matrix could have application in RL. Any computer algorithm written could potentially have application in RL (assuming it is not redundant to existing programs). As noted earlier, any social objects created—artistic products, for example— would be just as compelling in RL. Thus, hypothetically speaking, all the intellectual property created in The Matrix *could* be ported to RL.[4]

If The Architect (the character in *The Matrix Reloaded* that "built" The Matrix) were to allow it, a market could be established for trade in virtual goods and social objects between the one remaining RL city, Zion, and The Matrix.[5] The point is that the virtual products (and social objects) created in The Matrix have a potential market value for those living in RL (the citizens of Zion), and as any economist might tell you, potential RL value translates into actual RL value (even if at a steeply discounted value).

Thus it seems difficult to maintain that people are not acting in this version of The Matrix—whether or not they are acting can hardly turn on an arbitrary decision by The Architect to allow a market between The Matrix and RL. If people in RL Silicon Valley are doing something—if they are acting—when they write computer programs, then surely the programmers in The Matrix are acting as well. If people are discovering new materials in The Matrix, then those new materials may be possible in RL. The list goes on.

This same point can be recast without the neoliberal theory of value. A Marxist theory of value might compute the value of the virtual products in terms of the labor that went into them—certainly a significant amount in many cases.

Of course the question of the value of the objects created is orthogonal to the question of whether they are real. As David Chalmers (in Chalmers 2003; Chalmers 2016) has argued, there is a strong case to be made that these virtual objects have as much entitlement to be called real as any other object. To keep the discussion clean, let's set aside social objects and intellectual property and think about (virtual) physical objects—for example, imagine that someone in The Matrix was a skillful table maker, using traditional designs. Let's say that our table maker makes a (virtual) Shaker-style kitchen table that seats six people.

Chalmers's view is that the virtual table is a "digital object" and that it is real because it (the digital object) has causal powers. It appears a certain way to us because of the properties that it has. If we transfer ownership of the table (if we sell it to someone else in The Matrix) then they will see it and appreciated it. They may even bump into it (virtually) if they walk through their virtual kitchen with the virtual lights turned off. This would be true even if there were no contact between the virtual word and RL. There would still be data structures, and these would constitute digital objects with causal powers. Some of those digital objects will be prized and some not, but it is hard to see why they wouldn't be real objects in an interesting sense.

3.3 Single-User Virtual Environments That Afford Agency, Risk, and Harm

Cypher asked to be put back in The Matrix, but presumably there were other options available to him given the strength of his bargaining position. For example, he might have chosen to forgo his interactions with other envatted humans and ask to interact only with the central computer. He might have asked to be placed in the equivalent of a single-player virtual environment. Why might he do this? Well, Cypher might have taken to heart Sartre's dictum that "hell is other people." He might think that other people, even if his communication with them were mediated, would only bring drama. He might ask that it just be him and the computer.

Even so, however, it is possible to simulate human relationships so that even embedded in such a world Cypher would still know emotional pain and what he would at least take to be physical pain as his virtual relationships failed and as his virtual body met with damage and old age.

But here is an interesting question. When Cypher opts to disconnect from other people, does it eliminate his ability to act in RL and create things of value? Arguably not. For example, let's imagine that when reenvatted he obtains work as a mathematics professor and makes a number of important discoveries about the nature of cryptography or topology. It is hard to imagine that he is not thereby making discoveries about RL. Alternatively, Cypher might write songs or create works of art that would please other humans. He might invent a new currency that improves on Bitcoin[6] or he might even invent new kinds of voting mechanisms, governmental structures, and public institutions—all things of potential value to others.

The Matrix might even want to harvest some of those discoveries. And here is the thing about single-player environments: the virtual objects constructed in those environments can have value to others the second others have access to them. For example, I might construct an amazing environment in the video game *Minecraft*, while playing in single-player mode, unaware that it is possible for others to visit my construction. Even if I never realize that others can share in this experience it is hard to imagine that I have not created something with potential real-world value, which is to say real-world value. Even if I don't realize its value, I (or someone else) could open up my build to paying customers.

Just as single-player video games afford the possibility of creating things of value, they likewise afford the possibility of harm. For example, single-player games can be deeply triggering, as can video games that are crafted to yield interpersonal insights. Presumably video games could be constructed to be emotionally scarring. Many video games harm us unintentionally. They can reinforce tropes that are racist and sexist, and they can, of course, make us feel plain shitty. Ordinarily, this requires that the game provide us decision points so that what we do and what we experience are the products of the choices that we ourselves make. Such video games still afford us agency. Is it possible to keep the agency and dispense with the possibility of harm?

3.4 Single-User Virtual Environments That Afford Agency without Risk or Harm

Let's imagine now that, in his negotiations with Agent Smith, Cypher realizes it is not enough to disconnect from other humans, for, of course, the computer simulation might provide him with painful virtual relationships, the possibility of simulated physical damage, and other virtual correlates of the brutish and nasty aspects of life. Let's imagine that he asks Agent Smith to create a private simulation for him in which all the decision points are between positive outcomes. There will be no bad relationships and no painful injuries.

The problem is that even when Cypher is afforded all positive outcomes, regret for bad choices seems unavoidable. He might wonder if a second path might not have been more pleasant for him, and he might then experience some form of buyer's remorse. He might wonder about the experiences he is missing out on. (That would be *so* Cypher.) Recall too, that the point of hedonism is not merely to be happy; it is to *maximize* happiness (and minimize pain).

Even if Cypher is afforded the opportunity for "do-overs" on scenarios that have multiple paths this might not satisfy the maximizing constraint. It is entirely reasonable to think that you could have enjoyed path B more if you had selected it on the first run-though. Or you might think that a first choice is not as enjoyable if you can always back up and do things differently. Imagine how boring card games would be if you could back up and replay your hand. There is a reason why cheating at solitaire is not fun for most of us. Irreversible actions can be more fun than reversible ones.

Harm is difficult to eliminate so long as one has any form of agency at all.

3.5 Single-User Virtual Environments That Afford No Agency, Risk, or Harm

Let's imagine that Cypher now realizes his only hope for a life of optimum happiness is a life in which he is plugged into his own private Matrix, with no decision points at all, and no possibility for him to make any decisions at all. He instructs Agent Smith to simply stream him a series of experiences, which he will accept passively.

Here is the first issue. Even if Cypher is being streamed a series of experiences, he might have choices to make about what aspects of that experience stream he is attending to. He is given the experience of apple pie with vanilla ice cream. He attends to the ice cream. Did he miss an opportunity there? Did he pass up a superior pie experience?

And now we are back to scenario 3.4, in which Cypher was allowed agency but supposedly without the possibility of harmful choices. As Cypher learned, so long as there is agency there is the possibility of regret and thus harm. All perceptual agency has to go.

We are now getting to a version of the experience machine that I believe Nozick had in mind—one in which there is experience without agency. But is such an experience machine even possible? Chalmers (2016) is skeptical, and I share that skepticism.

It is hard to imagine what it would mean for us to experience something while being denied all perceptual agency. We think of Alex in *A Clockwork Orange* being strapped in a chair and made to watch a film with his eyes held open. But even Alex could control what he attended to on the screen. He couldn't look away, but eye-tracking equipment would doubtless show active scanning of the movie screen. It would have done no good to try to lock Alex's gaze. Doing that would have prevented him from seeing what was happening on the screen. Indeed, when eye motion is locked, people report the visual field going black (see Martinez-Conde et al. 2004 for a survey of literature on this).

But Nozick asks us to imagine a "superduper" scientist on duty in this matter, so let's suppose such a superduper scientist could control eye tracking, focus, and more (or, more accurately, the internal neural correlates of those actions). A truly gifted superduper scientist might be able to afford the sensation of agency as well (here assuming the sensation of agency without agency is possible). So you wouldn't actually choose a path; you would just think you had. Finally, we would want the superduper scientist to ensure that we never regretted the nonchoices we thought we could have made. That is, a person might be given the best option and made to think it was their choice, but they can't doubt that they had made the best choice because it could lead to buyer's remorse.

We've now descended to a level of virtual withdrawal about which I at least no longer have stable judgments. We might ask two questions concerning Cypher, were he to opt for this sort of life. The first question is whether he would be experiencing anything at all. I'm no expert on the phenomenology of perceptual experience, but so many of our daily perceptual experiences are intention driven, it is hard for me to wrap my mind around what it would be like to be denied the possibility of driving my experiences with my intentions, and for that matter to be denied the ability to second guess those choices once made. I have a better idea of what it is to be a bat than I do about that sort of existence.

In some ways the problem is like the difference between the perceptual experience of playing a video game and the perceptual experience of watching someone else play a video game. The latter is not engaging entertainment for the most part, and it can even lead to a kind of vertigo. (I am of course aware that competitive video game playing is a huge spectator sport, but watching those events is a different sort of experience from trying to have an immersive experience while letting someone else "drive the show.")

But second, is it so clear that nothing of value has been created by a human envatted in this way? If a computer program is written by Cypher when he is envatted in this way it seems that something with causal powers (the program) has come into existence. And it isn't clear that it is not in some sense the product of Cypher.

Let's imagine that Cypher is not the only person to choose this form of envattment. Let's imagine another hacker—call him Lamo—decides to do the same, but let's suppose that Lamo is much less gifted mathematically than is Cypher. The superduper scientist may have to establish very different programs to keep these two hackers happy. I assume that these hackers are not blank slates. They have different cognitive architectures and thus the experience machine will have to send them on different paths to keep them happy.

The superduper scientist may have to steer Cypher's virtual life in the direction of mathematical discovery while steering Lamo's virtual into the life of a website-defacing "script kiddie" (a low-level hacker that relies on "off the shelf" hacking tools developed by others). The superduper scientist may even be able to harvest recoverable product from the Cypher simulation. And to be fair, perhaps driving Lamo to the path of maximal happiness might yield harvestable content as well.

And here we get to a well-worn philosophical question. If Cypher (under the direction of a superduper scientist) writes an important computer program that only someone with his cognitive architecture could write and Cypher experiences the writing of the program as the product of his intentions and desires (with all the attendant phenomenology of his intentions), is it really so clear that he isn't acting? After all, that could very well be the state we are in in RL.[7]

And what would the alternative be? If the experience machine can over-write Cypher's existing cognitive architecture and create a blissful personal experience—say that of a very happy postmaster in Anchorage, Alaska—is it so clear that Cypher survives the overwriting process? And why would it be in Cypher's interest to choose such an outcome? For that seems to be equivalent to Cypher choosing that he cease to exist and that some blissful virtual postmaster appear in his stead.

4.0 THE SECOND LIFE WE CHOOSE

Let's return to the first level of virtual withdrawal that we considered above—multiuser environments that afford agency, risk, and harm. If there are such worlds and people reject the hedonistic path, then we don't need the experience machines offering greater detachment to make Nozick's anti-hedonic argument. Here are some of the possible outcomes (the list is not exhaustive).

> Possibility (1). Virtual worlds like *Second Life* afford us more pleasurable pastimes, but no agency or connection with a deeper reality, so we reject such worlds.
> Possibility (2). Virtual worlds like *Second Life* afford us agency and connection with reality, but less pleasure for most of us, so we opt to not participate in such worlds.
> Possibility (3). Virtual worlds like *Second Life* afford us agency and connection with reality, and multiple avenues of acting, and when we enter such worlds we pursue the path of maximizing pleasure in them.
> Possibility (4). Virtual worlds like *Second Life* afford us agency and connection with reality, and multiple avenues of acting, but we do not pursue the path of maximizing pleasure in them.

Possibility (1) would have the effect of supporting Nozick's central thesis. It would also show that you don't need the extreme thought experiment enlisted by Nozick to make his point.

Possibility (2) would support the case for hedonism. Immersing ourselves in virtual worlds doesn't give us a hedonistically superior life to RL, so we reject virtual worlds.

Possibility (3) would have the effect of directly refuting Nozick's thought experiment. It would show that people are indifferent to issues of action and connection with a deeper reality and that they opt for the hedonically optimal life.

Possibility (4) would show that Nozick is right for the wrong reasons. He would be right in suggesting that we do not opt for hedonism, but wrong in his diagnosis of why we reject the hedonistic paths that we do.

As I said earlier, possibility (4) is the one that I think obtains.

5.0 AGENCY AND REALITY REDUX

In section 3 I made the case that virtual worlds afford us plenty of agency and that our online lives are deeply connected with reality, but the point is contentious and is worth additional scrutiny.

Let's begin with the possibility of relationships in virtual worlds, for that goes to the question of whether virtual worlds deny us connection with a deeper reality. Hubert Dreyfus argues (in Dreyfus 2009) that electronically mediated relationships like those in *Second Life* are not genuine. It would follow that insofar as interpersonal relationships are concerned, there is no genuine contact with a deeper interpersonal reality. It might then follow as a corollary that we are not engaged in genuine actions when we engage with other people, but only simulations of those actions.

Let's set aside the honorific "genuine" for a second and ask an important question. Are virtual activities the same as the RL activities that they are simulating? Here the answer is often no. You can be killed in a virtual world, but the consequences are not as grave. Still, it does not follow that the simulated experiences are not significant and important experiences. In other cases, there is no clear difference between the virtual and RL activities. Some interpersonal relationships are of this character.

Dreyfus says he doesn't "know what to make" (Dreyfus 2009, fn. 26) of claims by persons that they fall in love on the internet, but his deafness to the possibility suggests a lack of experience with the medium. People report robust and important online relationships, and they do get married in RL to their *Second Life* partners.

Dreyfus claims that even friendships forged on the internet are apt to be lacking because there is no risk taking. To trust someone, you first have to place yourself in a position of vulnerability—one where there is some risk. Anyone with even cursory experience in the online world knows that other forms of risk taking are ubiquitous. In online environments, one faces extreme forms of verbal hazing if one breaks with local convention or offends members of a virtual community. People can betray trust and sell you out in the online world just as they can in RL. Nor are members of virtual communities immune to what might be thought of as attacks on their virtual bodies.

An example of this took place back in 1993 in a text-based virtual community known as LambdaMOO. LambdaMOO was a type of MUD—a multiuser dimension. More precisely, it was a special kind of MUD known as a MOO (MUD Object Oriented). This means that it was a text-based virtual world that included certain kinds of "objects" that were part of the text-based narrative and that could be used by participants in the narrative to carry out certain tasks. Participants logged into the system and interacted with each other in real time.

LambdaMOO became famous when Julian Dibbell (1996) published an article in the *Village Voice* titled "A Rape in Cyberspace." The article chronicled a case of virtual sexual assault by a user named Mr. Bungle, and the ensuing aftermath of that assault. In short, Mr. Bungle took advantage of in-world software tools to take control of other players and make them unwilling participants in his text-based description of his invasive actions toward them.

Shortly after the incident, the residents of LamdaMOO held a town hall meeting in which they discussed what had happened and how it should be dealt with. One of the residents, named legba, was livid about the experience.

> I tend to think that restrictive measures around here cause more trouble than they prevent. But I also think that Mr. Bungle was being a vicious, vile fuckhead, and I . . . want his sorry ass scattered from #17 to the Cinder Pile. I'm not calling for policies, trials, or better jails. I'm not sure what I'm calling for. Virtual castration, if I could manage it. Mostly, [this type of thing] doesn't happen here. Mostly, perhaps I thought it wouldn't happen to me. Mostly, I trust people to conduct themselves with some veneer of civility. Mostly, I want his ass.

Dibbell later called legba's typist and interviewed her, reporting that the event had had real-life emotional consequences for her.

> Months later, the woman in Seattle would confide to me that as she wrote those words posttraumatic tears were streaming down her face—a real-life fact that should suffice to prove that the words' emotional content was no mere playacting.

Even in those pre-internet days, discussion of the events moved around to various spots in cyberspace. For example, there was a lively discussion on the WELL, an important electronic bulletin board based in California. Some WELL denizens, like R. U. Sirius (then editor of the cyberculture zine *Mondo 2000*) argued that people had mistaken the simulacrum for reality. In the WELL conversation dedicated to this topic, one of the most active participants was a person going by the handle humdog; in RL her name was Carmen Hermosillo. Throughout the thread, Carmen too argued that it was foolish for these people to take the Mr. Bungle incident so seriously. It was mere theater, in her view. More generally, she took issue with people across the internet who were claiming to fall in love online.

Carmen offered several critiques of the WELL and virtual life more generally, but first and foremost, Carmen cautioned against the illusion of genuineness in virtual relationships. Drawing on an example from WELL history, she laid out how easy it is to mistake the symbols projected in virtual worlds for something real. Or as she put it: we are tempted to "invest the simulacrum with the weight of reality." In an essay called "Pandora's Vox" (Hermosillo 1996), she argued that the people who had taken their virtual relationships seriously were being, for lack of a better word, delusional.

However, years later, she joined *Second Life* and poured her heart into that virtual world, building a virtual island and castle with the help of some very gifted content creators in *Second Life*. She ruled over her island kingdom (called Shivar) and handed out titles to the other residents of the island.

But she also fell into a relationship with another *Second Life* resident—one that was so intense that when it ended there is some speculation that it led to her real-life death (Meadows and Ludlow 2009).

The case showed that even people who were skeptical of the reality of a virtual relationship (a computer-mediated relationship) could easily fall into one. Love conquers skepticism, it seems. Friendship conquers skepticism as well; Carmen and I were extremely close friends but never once met in RL.

I've spent some time on these old cases because I think they go a long way toward debunking Dreyfus's thesis about the possibility of real relationships and the lack of risk in virtual worlds. But of course they also go a long way toward undermining Nozick's thesis as well. It is hard to argue that the agents in these dramas were not acting. They had intentions and plans and goals, with meaningful consequences, not just for their virtual experiences but also for their RL experiences. And of course, if they had been having entirely online experiences, these would have been no less important, and their intentions, plans, and goals no less real. To draw on Carmen's example again, there are genuine consequences to virtual relationships.

6.0 WHAT DRIVES OUR CHOICE OF VIRTUAL LIVES?

Ultimately, we return to the question of the lives chosen by residents of virtual worlds. Are they using *Second Life* and other virtual worlds as ways to maximize their pleasure? Are they obeying the hedonistic calculus for their lives? Or is something else going on? Here, the answer rests on anecdotal evidence, but from my exposure to virtual communities and virtual worlds over the past two decades there seems to be something else altogether going on.

The choices that Carmen made in *Second Life* did not merely show something about the reality of relations in *Second Life*; it also showed something about the motivations for the choices we make. When going into a virtual world one can certainly choose some very benign paths and friendly experiences, but time and again people choose much more.

Carmen chose to role-play as the queen of a virtual kingdom and made her gameplay a thing of significance. She organized people into building a giant castle on her private island. She built a group of residents and gave them duties and responsibilities. She created a virtual community at least as tight-knit as that created in LambdaMOO. She sought a virtual life in which she had important standing. And so it is with many other virtual lives. Some choose to live the lives of gangsters or real estate magnates or politicians or World War II fighters, but the one covering property for all of these choices is that they are choosing virtual lives of significance—lives where their accomplishments matter and are recognized.

This was evident even when I went into the *The Sims Online*—a virtual world originally conceived as a place to escape to and enjoy some friendly socializing in user-built virtual homes. But whatever the architects of *The Sims Online* intended, they got something else altogether. Users created dozens of virtual mafias and fought for control of territories in the game world. Others created virtual paramilitary organizations to fight those mafias. There was no shortage of Mafia dons, but even those who weren't capos had titles and roles that made their role in the game significant. And, as I said before, the roles were not mere gameplay. The ideas and structures and institutions created by these groups in *The Sims Online* moved on to other worlds like *Star Wars Galaxies*, *World of Warcraft*, and *Second Life*.[8]

Was this need to be significant just fantasy? Was it just playing out an unmet desire to be significant in RL? Whether or not *Second Life*rs felt insufficiently significant in RL, it does not follow that they were not significant when engaged in *Second Life*. As noted earlier, my friend Anshe Chung made herself a millionaire in U.S. dollars. Many other friends and acquaintances established businesses. Many others showed the ability to create and nurture creative groups and to be leaders. As I've argued throughout this chapter, these achievements should not be dismissed. They involve real actions with real consequences, and the creation of content of quantifiable value.

Earlier I suggested that these online lives were not merely significant but had a kind of nobility. Many times in *Second Life* users rose up for causes or in defense of downtrodden users. Sometimes they formed groups to fight against troublemakers within the world. Other times they sought to build content that was aesthetically sublime. In some cases, they took action against the platform owners who they considered to be acting unjustly. They built monuments to causes, both in world and out, and when push came to shove they also fought to protect their world from both internal and external threats (see the Mr. Bungle case).

When Cypher chose to go back into the Matrix it was unclear what sort of life he was hoping to have (apart from being "rich"), but one imagines that, given the option, Cypher might have chosen a virtual life where he was somebody important—an important hacker rather than someone working in a call center. Cypher might even have taken the "important" job if he knew that it would figure less well in a hedonistic calculus.

And this takes us back to the unexplored reason that Cypher made the choice that he did. Was it really because he wanted a juicy steak instead of the Tastee Wheat–like gruel he received in RL? Or was it because Cypher was tired of playing second fiddle to Morpheus and Neo (aka The One)? This is no defense of Cypher, for if a life that mattered is what he wanted, he failed miserably.

Of course even if people have a preference for lives that matter—lives that are noble—it doesn't show that people ought to attempt to have such lives. There is still the question of the normative grip of these preferences. But the normative import of these choices can't be less informative here than the choices in Nozick's thought experiments. And perhaps we should at least consider that such noble lives are goods, and then consider the harm that comes in a world like our RL, where such goods are afforded only to a select few, and the vast majority must live the lives of unimportant functionaries in a vast global bureaucracy.

7.0 CONCLUSION

While I believe that Nozick's analysis of virtual experience is flawed, it is important to keep an eye on the motivation for his argument, which was, after all, to critique hedonism.

Virtual experiences are not necessarily hedonistic. The question is not whether we would choose a hedonistic virtual world over RL. The real question is, given the option of choosing a virtual experience, would we take the hedonically superior virtual experience over a hedonically inferior one?

At this point we have to settle for anecdotal observations. While my experience in virtual worlds may well be an outlier, it is hard for me to think of the scores of people I've met online as being there to maximize some hedonic outcome.[9] In my experience, persons in virtual worlds have usually sought for more—for creative engagement, accomplishments, meaningful relationships with others, and for lives that were noble and *important* within the virtual world and beyond it.

NOTES

1. If I wouldn't wish the experience machine on myself, how could I wish it on others? I suppose someone might say "virtual world experiences suck for me, but the rest of you will love them," but then Nozick's argument can be recast in third-person-plural form: People (in the aggregate) wouldn't choose the most pleasurable option (for the aggregate) but rather other kinds of lives.

2. This discussion need not assume a clean, binary distinction between pleasure and pain, and indeed this distinction may not hold up. It will suffice if there is some "open textured" scale of pleasurable experiences—open textured meaning that the scale may contain gaps and question marks and perhaps some equivocal judgments. It will be enough if there are some experiences that are clearly more pleasurable than others and we opt for (or against) those experiences for alternatives.

3. A question I do not have space to explore here is whether the judgments in the thought experiment actually break in the direction that Nozick imagines. De Brigard 2010 has offered a study that is designed to show that Nozick's thought experiment merely reflects a preference for the status quo. For now let me say that I am persuaded by the criticisms of De Brigard's methodology given in Nadelhoffer 2011.

4. I've always considered it a giant plot hole in *The Matrix* movies that envatted humans are used as batteries. Surely this is an inefficient way to store energy. Why not use the humans as an organic distributed computer instead?

5. Obviously, by this I mean the one remaining RL city *in the fiction*.

6. Bitcoin is an encryption-based digital currency that some advocates think will revolutionize commerce.

7. You might take issue with the idea that Cypher is *writing* such a program since no QWERTY keyboard is involved, but surely if determinism is true then he is at least *authoring* the program in the same sense that I am authoring this chapter. Must the experience machine argument presuppose that determinism is false?

8. See Ludlow and Wallace 2009 for further discussion of this and other examples.

9. It could be more than an outlier. It could be that what I've experienced is a function of the privileged Western culture in which I live. The problem with this objection is that it assumes my virtual world contacts are privileged westerners. This isn't universally true, as far as I can tell. Consider the case of the virtual real estate entrepreneur Anshe Chung, who I mentioned earlier, or characters like Baller MoMo King (see Ludlow and Wallace 2009, 103). More to the point, I'm suspicious of claims that members of other cultures don't seek out significant roles in virtual worlds. In the final analysis though, I confess that I just don't know and that these questions need to be investigated further.

Chapter Two

Intuition and Imaginative Failure

Daniel Pietrucha

1.

Through the experience machine (EM) thought experiment, Robert Nozick purports to show that something matters other than our subjective experiences; namely, contact with objective reality. As a descriptive claim about the intuitions people have vis-à-vis the EM, Nozick has the facts right: many people *do* care about things other than their own subjective mental states. But just because an intuition is widely shared doesn't make it rational. In this chapter, I argue that the intuitive revulsion many feel at the prospect of plugging into the EM is *ir*rational. Such intuitions do not reveal anything about the intrinsic value of contact with reality but are best explained by the notion of *imaginative failure*.

The argument proceeds with the claim that we can conceive of very low levels of well-being at which plugging into EM appears prima facie rational. The individuals typically exposed to the EM thought experiment, affluent western academics and their similarly privileged students, tend to lead lives that realize much higher levels of well-being. It is therefore unsurprising that such individuals feel a strong intuitive revulsion at the prospect of plugging into the EM. We make a serious error, however, when we infer from our particular, intuitive revulsion a general normative conclusion. We must first examine our intuitions more closely. Or, rather, we must consider the prospect of the EM from other perspectives, particularly those that are far different from our own, to see if we can generate different intuitions that provide counterevidence to our initial revulsion.

When we consider the EM from less privileged points of view, we can see that there are powerful reasons for plugging in; that is, there are instances in which gains in well-being appear to trump other apparent values, the value of genuine contact with objective reality among them. I press this point by modifying Nozick's thought experiment in a way that builds in a baseline of well-being so low that anyone who still refuses to plug into EM can fairly be charged with irrationality.

To avoid the charge, my opponent—let us call him the *objectivist about the value of reality*, or *objectivist* for short—must modify his position by conceding that there might be circumstances in which gains to well-being outweigh the value of contact with reality. But if he concedes this point, he concedes much more than he intends, for there is no reason to believe that a similar increase in well-being cannot be achieved with his own life as the baseline. Ryberg argues (in Ryberg 1996) that people likely overestimate the extent to which their lives are worth living. Building on this insight, I argue that they also drastically underestimate the increases in subjective well-being made possible by plugging into the EM.

Given these considerations, we should diagnose the intuitive revulsion the objectivist feels toward the prospect of plugging into the EM as an *imaginative failure*: first, as a failure to consider what he might choose in suitably worse circumstances, and second, as a failure to consider that, with his own life as the baseline, comparable increases in well-being are possible. If objectivism is the view that one should never plug into the EM no matter the circumstances, then the proponent of this view is fairly charged with irrationality. But if he concedes it is rational in just those instances where increases in well-being are large enough, he is in fact committed to plugging in under a far greater range of circumstances than he presumes.

2.

There are certain levels of well-being at which life no longer appears worth living. Conditions of war, famine, poverty, and countless other afflictions affect billions across the globe. But one need not look abroad for examples. The cessation of medical treatment in cases of terminal illness accompanied by extreme pain is fairly commonplace in the developed world, even if squeamishness about physician-assisted suicide is a comparatively more widespread phenomenon.

Many of us are lucky, however, to avoid such trials. Our worries, while troubling, are rarely life threatening. Our trials, while real, are not usually insurmountable. And even if many of our most audacious hopes and dreams go unrealized, we still lead happy lives in which, at the very least, our basic needs are met with astonishing ease. Under these circumstances, plugging into the EM looks like self-indulgent escapism.

But we shouldn't generalize this privileged perspective. Whatever one's particular threshold for tolerating suffering, surely we can conceive of conditions in which our lives would not be worth living. And if no otherworldly punishment awaits us in the afterlife, these are also the conditions under which suicide is rational. If, under such circumstances, we have the option of plugging into the experience machine, surely that course of action is preferable to suicide. Unless one rejects life outright (e.g., one is a true pessimist, à la Schopenhauer), and not just the conditions of one's particular life, plugging into the EM is rationally superior to suicide.

Let us consider why this should be the case, even for those who regard plugging into the EM as "a kind of suicide" (Nozick 1974, 43). Suppose you are one of those people whose life is not worth living and that you face a choice between two versions of suicide.[1] *Suicide One*: You die—complete cessation of consciousness, including pain; *Suicide Two*: You die and go to heaven—a bespoke version of heaven built specifically for your personal pleasure. Plugging into the EM is structurally similar to *Suicide Two*; the only apparent difference is that you do not die but are kept alive artificially while the machine stimulates your brain. Unlike *Suicide One*, both *Suicide Two* and the EM represent not merely the cessation of pain and suffering but the promise of increased well-being. Thus EM appears rationally preferable to suicide in cases where life is not worth living.

Let's consider just such a case: a patient is terribly ill with a disease that places him in intense, unyielding pain. While incurable, the disease will allow him to live a life of normal duration. He has fifty years of relentless, overwhelming pain to face before his life will be over—or he may plug into the EM. With such a massive increase in well-being at stake, it is difficult to come up with a plausible reason why such a person should not plug into the EM, and may reasonably question whether the objectivist who maintains that he *should not* has truly appreciated the severity and duration of the suffering to be avoided. If the objectivist has successfully understood the suffering that hangs in the balance, he may fairly be charged with irrationality.

Genuine, real-life accomplishment will often enough strike us as better than the illusion of accomplishment. Even for those of us who are skeptical about the benefits of contact with objective reality, we don't give up much if we concede that, *ceteris paribus*, it would be better to *really* do something than merely have the experience.[2] But we should not assume that this psychological observation extends to all conceivable circumstances. In the cases we've been considering, all else has not been held equal—we have been modulating the base level of well-being of the agent contemplating the EM in order to determine whether there are circumstances in which our initial revulsion at the prospect of plugging into the EM gives way to other considerations. More specifically, we have been looking for cases in which life is so bad, and corresponding gains to well-being so great, that plugging into the EM becomes the rational course of action.

In such cases, hedonistic considerations outweigh other purported values, including contact with objective reality. If the cases I've discussed above haven't been sufficiently disturbing to arouse interest in plugging into the EM, I invite the reader to come up with his or her own personal hell. If the cases above *have* convinced the reader that there are some circumstances bad enough to warrant use of the EM, this will have important general implications for our intuitions about plugging into the EM; these will apply even to the privileged perspective from which most readers approach the prospect of plugging in.

3.

In the previous section, I attempted to demonstrate that our judgments concerning the value of objective reality are positively correlated with how good that reality is. This is helpful in explaining why those of us who lead very good lives (relative to the global standard) feel the intuitive revulsion of the objectivist at the prospect of plugging into the EM. However, once we realize that our circumstances condition our intuitions and value judgments, we can conceive of circumstances in which our judgments might be different—and *should* be different—such as those in which gains in well-being are so large that it is irrational not to plug into EM.

Of course, judgments concerning the value of contact with objective reality and the goodness of that reality can come apart. As an example of this, we might consider a person who has all the outward trappings of a happy life—health, attractiveness, affluence, professional success—but who nevertheless experiences persistent unhappiness. But it is somewhat difficult to make axiological sense of what we mean if we call this person's life *objectively good*. After all, this person does not experience the apparent goods in question as such, and it's hard to imagine what we might say to him to convince him otherwise.

Let's consider it both ways. Suppose we grant that the depressed person's life is objectively good and that his failure to perceive this goodness can be corrected via chemical intervention by a qualified medical professional. How should we understand such an intervention? When we administer the prescribed medicine, we might understand ourselves to be bringing the person into contact with objective reality. Nevertheless, our intervention has been brought about by a change in this person's *subjective experience*. Such a case, where one's evaluative judgments about life depart from the goodness of one's objective circumstances, highlights that what really matters is one's subjective experience. Now suppose, contra the previous example, that we do *not* consider this person's life prior to intervention to be objectively good (because he is not happy with it). Once more we administer the medicine, thereby making him happy. His life is now objectively good (by our standard of happiness), but modifying his *subjective experience* of reality has brought about the fix. Subjective experience thus plays a crucial role in both interpretations of the case of the depressed person. For many of us outside the EM, subjective experience is largely determined by objective reality, which increases the risk that we will attribute unwarranted importance to objective reality by mistaking it as the source of our well-being.

The depressed person gives us a plausible case in which subjective experience fails to track the goodness of objective reality. Even so, the EM is likely to seem far too radical a prescription for a relatively minor psychological disorder, especially when we have clinically proven antidepressants ready to hand. But the prescription appears much less radical in the case of the patient facing fifty years of constant and intense pain. Indeed, it would strike many of us as callous to deny a suffering person access to the EM if we had one in our possession, and irrational for the suffering person to refuse it if offered. It is not obvious, however, that the situation of the depressed person differs materially from that of the suffering person. More importantly, it is not obvious that our own situation differs materially from that of the suffering person. What is meant by this? Just that, while our baseline level of well-being is undeniably higher than his, the increase in well-being we can anticipate upon plugging into the EM is comparable—or equal if, as I argue, the increase in well-being offered by the EM is *infinite* in both cases. If one would plug into the EM as the patient condemned to fifty years of suffering, one should be willing to plug in full stop.

That such increases in well-being are available is perhaps not so easily recognized. In one attempt to diagnose the aversion many feel toward the EM, Nozick notes that "plugging into an experience machine limits us to a man-made reality, to a world no deeper or more important than that which people can construct" (Nozick 1974, 43). But our reality has significant limitations of its own, the frustrations of which are perhaps not fully compensated for by the obscure notion of contact with a "deeper world." By definition, the universe of worlds made possible by the EM contains the real world, as the EM is capable of replicating one's experience of the world as it is. But the conjunction of the real world and imagination generates a plurality of possible worlds that differ in ways both large and small, as anyone who has seriously considered the modal realist thesis will be quick to realize. So we may grant that the experiences available in the EM are "limited" to what can be imagined, but we should emphasize that the possibilities that imagination affords are mind-bogglingly rich and expansive.[3]

Above I claimed that the increase in well-being available to an agent is infinite in all cases. This requires some defense. So far, I've discussed only the qualitative aspect of life in the EM, but there is a quantitative component that should be addressed as well. Someone may grant, after all, that plugging into the EM offers large increases in well-being but deny that these increases are infinite, given the finitude of human life. If all increases in well-being are not infinite, then the objectivist is better positioned to argue that, at least in some cases, it is rational to abstain from plugging in.

Even if the objectivist is correct about the finite nature of increases in well-being, the increases available strike me as large enough to warrant plugging in. I will discuss this more thoroughly in a moment by illustrating the difficulty of locating a threshold beyond which we are indifferent to further increases in well-being. But first allow me an attempt to meet the objection from finitude without retreating to this more modest position. Even if human lives are finite, the EM can still offer the prospect of infinite increases in well-being by changing our phenomenological experience of time. For example, we might experience an entire happy life within the span of a day, a minute, a second, and more. As fanciful as this sounds, it is actually a phenomenon that should be somewhat familiar to anyone who dreams. In dreaming, our phenomenological experience of time can depart dramatically from what we would expect to experience in the same amount of time had we been awake. Thus, a dream lasting less than an hour can encompass events that seem to span several hours, a day, or longer. To get infinity out of the EM, all we require is the capacity to compress extended periods of phenomenological experience into ever smaller fragments of time.[4]

This is a bit too quick, of course. Presumably, the strictures of our neuro-physiology limit the extent our experience of time can be contracted into ever-smaller portions of time. I am happy to concede the point. Nevertheless, we are dealing here with some *very, very large* increases in well-being that appear practically indistinguishable from infinity, if not conceptually so.

4.

The increases in well-being that the EM affords may be difficult for us to truly appreciate—or even comprehend, if I am right about their infinite na-ture. But even though we cannot fully comprehend what an infinite increase in well-being means in practice, this does not undermine the basic principle of treating like cases alike. If we think it rational to plug in when faced with fifty years of intense suffering, we should think it rational to do so in all other situations where increases in well-being are equal. If I am right that increases are infinite in all cases, then it is always rational to plug into the EM. But even if increases in well-being are merely *very large*, they are substantial enough to render the case of the suffering person and that of our own practi-cally indistinguishable, in which case we will still find it rational to plug in. Of course, I do not deny that many people are happy enough with their lives so as to not to feel the attraction of the experience machine. But contentment with our lives does not excuse us from passing judgment on the rationality of plugging in. If we come to different conclusions in the cases of the suffering person and that of our own, we need a plausible reason for doing so.

One might think there is a plausible reason for treating the two cases differently if we posit a certain threshold of well-being beyond which further increases are unimportant. The general idea is that, in cases where one's life is "good enough" or "worth living," resistance to plugging into the EM isn't irrational. This would be a way of drawing a line between our own lives and that of the suffering person, as long as we can offer a substantive definition of "worth living." I will not attempt such a definition, as I believe the project to be doomed to failure. The primary issue is that *where* one draws the line will be largely influenced by the quality of one's life. We can imagine, for example, an individual with a significantly higher level of well-being drawing a line between his life and ours, just as we would draw a line between ours and the suffering person.

The following quotation from J. S. Mill puts the point quite memorably: "It is better to be a human being dissatisfied than a pig satisfied; better to be Socrates dissatisfied than a fool satisfied. And if the fool, or the pig, are of a different opinion, *it is because they only know their own side of the question*" (Mill 2001, 10: italics mine). Similarly, a god might reasonably think Socrates's life nothing to write home about. I am unsure how to proceed in adjudicating between these different positions. Supposing that there is an objective threshold below which it is rational to plug into the EM and above which it is rational to abstain, it would be surprising, and a little bit convenient, if most of us happened to land above the threshold. This does not quite put the threshold objection to bed, but the above considerations should make us skeptical of purported ways of drawing the threshold. Once we realize the limited nature of our perspective, we should be less confident in asserting that we fall on the side of those who can rationally abstain from plugging into the EM.

The burden of proof is now on the advocate of a threshold—and he owes us quite a theory, since the alternative is a very (perhaps incomprehensibly) large increase in well-being. I see at least two different directions in which he can go:

> (1) He can argue that there is a qualitative shift in moving from negative well-being to positive well-being that does not manifest itself in moving from one level of positive well-being to a higher level of well-being;
> (2) He can argue for a hybrid theory that combines well-being and some other value that is incommensurable with well-being and unavailable in the EM. After a certain level of well-being is reached, other values are activated that render further increases in well-being of no account.

At first glance, (1) might seem a more promising route than (2), since (2) is still subject to concerns about why the threshold should be drawn in one place and not another. Of course, (2) can avoid this objection by agreeing with (1); that is, drawing the line at which other values become operative at the point where negative well-being shifts to positive. While I will not venture a full response to such a theory (or theories), I note one peculiarity with which the theory will have to deal. Consider once more the person sentenced to fifty years of suffering. When offered the opportunity to alleviate his suffering by plugging into the EM, would he choose to experience a life barely worth living (slight positive well-being), or wouldn't he opt for something better? *Shouldn't he opt for something better?* If it is rational for the suffering person to choose the latter, it is similarly rational for a person whose life is barely worth living to plug into the EM and choose something better, too.

The shift from negative to positive well-being appears less consequential than we might have initially supposed. As it stands, (1) looks untenable. Drawing a viable threshold thus requires positing values that cannot be reduced to, compared with, or overridden by well-being. These values must also explain our differing intuitions regarding the case of the suffering person and our own if they purport to offer justification for treating these cases differently. Since well-being appears to be the source of our differing intuitions about these two cases, I am skeptical about the prospects of (2).

Of course, if we concede that well-being makes all the difference, we concede the argument. If we would plug in when faced with the prospect of fifty years of intense suffering, we should plug in under our present circumstances as well. Both cases present us with practically indistinguishable increases in well-being, and we have yet to find a plausible justification for plugging into the EM in one case and not in the other.

5.

It isn't surprising that people whose lives are relatively good are repulsed by the idea of the EM. Those typically exposed to Nozick's thought experiment are fortunate to count themselves among this favored group. But when we consider the EM from the point of view of the less privileged, we see that there are powerful reasons for plugging in. In particular, we considered the case of an individual faced with fifty years of intense pain. Under the circumstances, it would be irrational to forego the increase in well-being that plugging into the EM would offer.

If the objectivist concedes this point, he concedes much more than he intends, for there is no reason to believe that a similar increase in well-being cannot be achieved with his own life as the baseline. As discussed in §3, the increase in well-being in each case is very large, and possibly infinite. Given that these two cases—that of the suffering person and that of our own—are practically indistinguishable, the objectivist is committed to plugging in on both occasions, on pain of irrationality. To avoid this conclusion, he must point to features of each case that justify treating them differently. In §4, I considered a few potential replies falling under what I have called the *threshold objection*, and found them wanting.

The aversion many feel toward plugging into the EM is very real and may linger on even in readers convinced by the argument above. Admittedly, this is a fair characterization of my own attitude toward EM. But the persistence of these feelings does not absolve us of recognizing their irrationality. Rather, "we have to *learn to think differently*—in order at last, perhaps very late on, to attain even more: *to feel differently*" (Nietzsche 1997, 60).

NOTES

1. Let us stipulate that your life is not worth living for reasons entirely beyond your control. This is to rule out cases in which the person considering suicide does so out of guilt over some heinous crime. Such a person may have good reasons for choosing outcomes in which well-being is not maximized because he doesn't think himself deserving of well-being.

2. Notice, however, how strained this language can sound. As some of the other authors in this volume argue, reality and illusion may be axiologically indistinguishable.

3. Even if you have a dull imagination, you needn't worry: there will be people whose imaginations can be sampled. Perhaps there will even be individuals who are renowned for curating exceptional experiences. Nozick hints at this prospect when he suggests, characteristically, that "business enterprises have researched thoroughly the lives of many others" (Nozick 1974, 42). It is unclear why we should be forced to limit ourselves to merely *lived* experiences. If we can simulate climbing Everest, we can simulate climbing a mountain five (or however many times) taller with some slight programming changes—it doesn't seem to matter that no one has lived this experience.

4. It might be helpful to some readers to consider the various possibilities this opens up for them as potential EM users. One might favor a life of blissful immortality, or one might prefer to live many different happy yet incompatible lives. And in the end, one doesn't have to choose between these two options.

Chapter Three

Give Me the Confidence

*Nozick's Experience Machine, Hedonism,
and Confident Attitudinal Pleasures*

Emiliano Heyns and Johnny Hartz Søraker

The thought experiment of the experience machine (EM) by Nozick (1974) sets out to demonstrate that something other than pleasurable experience matters to our well-being. If it is the case that something matters to us in addition to experience, then a theory of well-being that cannot account for this—hedonism—must be erroneous or incomplete. In this chapter we will argue that the intuitions evoked by the EM are not inconsistent with hedonism but rather call for revisions that can render a more substantive and less counterintuitive form of hedonism.

We will propose that hedonism be revised in two ways. First, as suggested by Fred Feldman's *Intrinsic Attitudinal Hedonism*, we need to move from a sensory to an attitudinal account of pleasure, according to which hedonism is not a question of "being pleased by" (sensory pleasure) but rather "taking pleasure in" (attitudinal pleasure). Second, the issue of whether pleasures are "false" or not must be reframed in terms of how confident we are about that in which we take pleasure. On the interpretation that will be put forth in this chapter, the problem with the EM is not that the pleasures are false, but that we have a hard time being confident about taking pleasure in something that we fear is not "real." We will conclude by discussing how the EM still brings forth important insights about the role that virtual worlds and experiences could have in our lives, as well as some implications for actual technologies that resemble the EM.

THE EXPERIENCE MACHINE INTUITION AND HEDONISM

The EM can be read as one of many arguments—often referred to as arguments from false pleasures[1]—that purport to demonstrate the counterintuitive nature of any theory of well-being that treats a person's well-being as directly (and only) proportional to the amount of pleasure-minus-pain that he experiences (Feldman 2012, 11).

The EM and other arguments from false pleasures are structured roughly as follows. Given the stipulation that life plugged into the EM will give you more pleasure on balance than life outside the EM (Feldman 2012):

1. Given the opportunity to plug in you would forego life plugged into the EM and choose life outside the EM instead.
2. If (1), then life plugged into the EM does not offer greater welfare value than life outside the EM.
3. If life plugged into the EM does not have greater welfare value than life outside the EM, then welfare is not directly proportional to the amount of pleasure-minus-pain, and ethical hedonism is false.
4. Therefore, ethical hedonism is false.

The EM has captured the imaginations of many, and there seems to be an important grain of truth captured by the idea that the good life cannot be wholly grounded on falsities, illusions, and delusions. Whether the arguments based on the EM are conclusive or not, this intuition would at least prevent many from subscribing to a theory that bases well-being entirely on the experience of pleasure, or in fact any theory in which truth is not one of the determinants of well-being. In what follows we will argue that hedonism can be modified in such a way that both requirements can be met, resulting in a hedonist theory in which well-being is not entirely determined by perceptual pleasure and where truth does play a role, albeit indirectly. On the first point we will in the following section largely follow the lead of Fred Feldman's so-called Intrinsic Attitudinal Hedonism (hereafter IAH). On the second, we will criticize Feldman's suggested "adjustment for truth" and instead propose an "adjustment for confidence."

PLEASURE AND WELL-BEING: FROM DEFAULT HEDONISM TO FELDMAN'S INTRINSIC ATTITUDINAL HEDONISM

As Feldman argues, the familiar objections deriving from the EM against hedonism can be largely dealt with by treating pleasures as attitudes rather than sensations. On an attitudinal view, hedonism states that well-being is determined not by experienced pleasures but rather by anything which is "taken pleasure in." This reflective, all-things-considered notion of pleasure allows us to make sense of how we can take pleasure in the experience of pain and how we can be pained by (or "take pain in") the experience of pleasure. Although sensory and attitudinal pleasures often coincide, such as when one is taking pleasure in having a pleasurable sensation, the sensation of pleasure in such cases only has instrumental value—it only brings about value if you also have a positive psychological stance toward that sensation (Weijers 2014). There are also a number of sensory pleasures that are not attitudinal pleasures, and vice versa. For instance, I can be pained by the belief that the pleasure that I am experiencing will lead to pain (e.g., some types of drugs), I can be pained by the belief that the pleasure is becoming less intense (e.g., that I have become habituated to the pleasure), I can be pained by the belief that the sensory pleasure I am feeling was brought about by being unethical (e.g., if I have stolen something that gives me pleasure), and so forth. Conversely, I can be pleased by the belief that the pain that I am feeling will lead to pleasure (e.g., arduous physical effort in mastering a sport), that it is becoming less intense (e.g., when recovering from illness), that it will be beneficial to my health (e.g., when eating something healthy but disgusting), and so forth.

IAH also opens up the possibility of having past and future events contribute to our well-being long before or after any of the coinciding sensory pleasures (if any) are in play, which is difficult to account for in forms of hedonism that are based in sensory pleasures. This could for example involve taking pleasure in something we hope will happen in the future, being pained by something that happened in the past, and taking pleasure in the fact that I have been doing something for more than ten years. According to IAH, the pleasures relevant to assessing well-being hedonistically should be understood as propositional attitudes of "taking pleasure in a state of affairs" rather than as sensations. A person takes attitudinal pleasure in some state of affairs if "he enjoys it, is pleased about it, is glad that it is happening, is delighted by it" (Feldman 2004, 56).

To further illustrate, consider the difference between getting sensory pleasure from eating chocolate and taking pleasure in eating chocolate. Even if the sensory pleasure is exactly the same in all situations, the attitudinal pleasure changes depending on a complex web of beliefs, expectations, moral values, identity, social norms, and so forth. Only on the latter, attitudinal account are we able to say that we may not take pleasure in the taste of chocolate for a variety of attitudinal reasons: because the taste does not correspond to something real, because it is made by child slaves, because it will lead to attitudinal pain in the future, because I am thereby breaking a promise to myself, because it is against the dictates of my religion, or because I do not trust the person giving it to me. On an attitudinal account it is even possible to have attitudinal pleasure when you are incapable of feeling sensory pleasure at all. For instance, someone can take pleasure in the fact that she is alive after an accident that has left her unable to experience any kind of pleasure (Feldman 2004, 56).

The move to attitudinal pleasures, to be complemented by the notion of "confidence" below, already allows us to reconsider the EM as an argument against hedonism. The question now becomes, not whether the EM can allow us to experience pleasure to the same degree as reality would allow, but whether the EM can allow us to *take pleasure in* activities and experiences to the same degree as we could outside it. This initially takes care of many of the counterintuitive implications of sensory hedonism, in particular those objections that draw on our intuitions that experiencing pleasure will in many cases be detrimental to well-being, that experiencing pain is in many cases unavoidable or even required for well-being, and that well-being cannot be reduced to a felicific calculus of the sum of painful and pleasurable experiences.

IAH on its own is not without its problems—for the further discussion of which we refer to Feldman (Feldman 2002; 2004; 2010a; 2010b)—but most importantly for current purposes, it does not adequately address the intuition many share about the EM: that the determinants of well-being must correspond to something true. In order to address this, Feldman introduces the notion of *adjusted* intrinsic attitudinal hedonism, according to which the extent to which attitudinal pleasures determine our well-being is determined by, for instance, the truth of that in which we take pleasure. In the next section, we will present and criticize this notion, and instead present *confidence* as adjusting the extent to which our well-being is determined by the truth of that in which we take pleasure.

IAH AND ADJUSTING FOR TRUTH

Feldman claims IAH is malleable enough to account for the various objections posed against hedonism and offers an array of "adjusters," each creating a new variant of Adjusted-IAH (AIAH) to meet the demands of various thought experiments and other counterarguments. In the words of Feldman, "Attitudinal pleasures, unlike sensory pleasures, have objects. . . . Attitudinal pleasure is always pleasure taken in some state of affairs. This feature of attitudinal pleasures makes it possible for IAH to take many forms, depending upon restrictions that we may place on the sorts of objects in which attitudinal pleasure is taken" (Feldman 2004, 71). Feldman proposes several such restrictions, or "adjusters," each intended to target a specific class of objections to hedonism. In response to arguments derived from the EM, Feldman proposes truth as the relevant factor in assessing well-being, yielding Truth-Adjusted Intrinsic Attitudinal Hedonism (TAIAH). The idea is that by adjusting the "raw" intrinsic pleasure by some factor reliant on whether the pleasure is taken in a true object (Feldman 2004, 112), we can explain the intuitions elicited by the EM within a hedonist theory. The adjuster is stipulated to affect the well-being that I derive from any attitudinal pleasure; the more accurate the beliefs underpinning my attitudinal pleasures are, the more strongly these pleasures contribute to my well-being (Feldman 2004, 112–21). In other words, the reason why we would not want to plug into the EM is, according to TAIAH, that the occupant of the EM will have lower well-being than those outside it because the things she takes pleasure in are much less likely to be true.

In adjusted-IAH, then, the contribution of a pleasure to my well-being is determined by two factors: the intensity of the attitudinal pleasure, and the truth-value (in the case of TAIAH) or—to take but one of the other adjusters offered—the degree in which the object of pleasure is deserving of being enjoyed (in the case of DAIAH, another adjusted-IAH discussed by Feldman [2004]). For example, suppose "true" pleasures are twice as valuable to my well-being as "false" pleasures, given the same intensity of pleasure. Now suppose that learning to master skydiving for me yields intrinsic attitudinal pleasure of +10 on some scale. Learning it in the EM would yield +5 units of well-being since I am not *truly* learning to master skydiving, where enjoying the experience in the real world would yield me +10 units. But in allowing truth as a dimension that factors into our well-being, our well-being is no longer "directly (and only) proportional to the amount of pleasure-minus-pain that he experiences," as (Feldman 2012, 11) claims should hold for hedonism. The adjustment idea seems a promising fix for many of the counterintuitive implications that often follow from hedonism, but adjusting for truth seemingly violates Feldman's own direct-proportionality demand (Feldman 2012, 11). Feldman is of course aware of this, arguing that having an adjuster does not entail that it becomes a pluralist theory (Feldman 2012, 19–20), but it remains problematic that the adjuster has no justification beyond the intuition raised by the EM. It seems inconsistent for a hedonist theory of well-being to postulate that something may determine my well-being without affecting my mental states.

To address these problems, we propose that rather than truth, we should allow for attitudinal pleasure to be adjusted for *confidence*—that the degree to which something in which we take pleasure affects our well-being is determined by our confidence that it is, in turn, true, deserved, or morally justified, and more. This yields Confidence-Adjusted Intrinsic Attitudinal Hedonism (CAIAH), which is in many ways more formal and less action guiding than TAIAH but (partly for that reason) avoids the problems outlined above while still allowing for the intuition that truth is a factor that at least partly determines well-being. Before turning to the question of how this EM-inspired revision sheds light on contemporary virtual worlds and "EM-like" phenomena, we will briefly sketch the key aspects of this theory.[2]

INTRODUCING CONFIDENCE-ADJUSTED INTRINSIC ATTITUDINAL HEDONISM (CAIAH)

CAIAH builds on IAH, incorporating the adjustment idea to propose a new theory that incorporates the intuitions from the EM while avoiding the problems of TAIAH. It aims to describe a hedonist theory of well-being, taking on board only mental states in both the value base and the adjuster. Confidence-adjustment aims to do justice to the idea that pleasures that are *experientially* the same can in practice contribute different levels of well-being to your life. It does so, as we shall see in this section, while still explaining our intuitions regarding the EM, and showing how we can get the most well-being from our experiences by arranging matters such that we can be confident about them.

When we act with confidence we act as if what is under consideration is true (Rotenstreich 1972, 348–49), even while we know at the same time to varying degrees it may not be. Truth does still play a role, but only as one of many constitutive reasons for grounded confidence. As Rotenstreich said, "the holding of a thing to be true is an occurrence in our understanding, which, though it may rest on objective grounds, also requires subjective causes in the mind of the individual who makes the judgement" (Rotenstreich 1972, 348). While the external facts of the matter, including whether or not something is objectively true, may impact my confidence, it is in fact the subjective causes in my mind that determine my confidence and thereby how much well-being I derive from my taking pleasure in anything. To clarify this further, it is helpful to distinguish between different determinants of confidence and their transitive relation to well-being—which will also illustrate how CAIAH differs from TAIAH and how the former is better able to account for the intuitions prompted by the Experience Machine.

COGNITIVE VERSUS NONCOGNITIVE DETERMINANTS OF CONFIDENCE

The main force behind the argument from false pleasures appears to stem from our experience of how doubts and insecurities can reduce the pleasure we take in states of affairs, and how hope and confidence tend to increase the pleasure we take in them. Conversely, pain is often alleviated by the hope that the past or current states of affairs we are pained by did not in fact (or will not) obtain—or by the hope that potentially painful future states of affairs will not come to pass. This indicates that Feldman's move to situate the pleasure adjustment in the states of affairs themselves is unnecessary; what is at stake is how our mental states are determined by how confident we are that something actually is, was, or will become the case. The reason why reduced confidence is detrimental to well-being primarily stems from how doubts and insecurities tend to restrict us from truly taking pleasure in something without reservation. There are also a number of closely related mechanisms that exacerbate this loss of well-being, such as the pain felt by the betrayal of others, feelings of stupidity ("I should have known"), and reluctance to find new sources of happiness—all of which often accompany reduced confidence and ipso facto reduced well-being.

As with Feldman's solution in terms of truth adjustment, truth can play a role in codetermining confidence, but only as one of many factors. According to CAIAH, there are a number of other means to justify confidence and thereby enhance attitudinal pleasures. Some of them are "cognitive" and based on epistemological objectivity, but others are based on "noncognitive" means of being confident despite lack of evidence.

COGNITIVE JUSTIFICATIONS OF CONFIDENCE

As argued by Searle and others (Brey 2003; Searle 1995 and 2006; Søraker 2011), epistemological objectivity can be grounded in both ontologically objective and subjective states of affairs, where the latter requires a collective acceptance of a status function; that is, that x counts as y in context c. To give an example, the claim that Barack Obama is the president of United States is just as true (at the time of writing) as the claim that there is snow on top of Mount Everest, even though the former is only true because of a collective recognition that Barack Obama (x) counts as the president (y) for the political scope of the United States (c). We can be just as confident about taking pleasure in Obama's presidency as in the existence of snow on Mount Everest. The big difference between these sorts of claims lies in the way we must go about scrutinizing our beliefs. If I were to verify that Barack Obama indeed is president of the United States, the method would be different from how I would go about verifying that there is snow on top of Mount Everest. For now it suffices to point out that as long as there is a method for verifying the truth-value of the states of affairs we take pleasure in, the confidence of the pleasure can be ascertained on an epistemologically objective basis.

Furthermore, there are two ways of questioning the warrant of our confidence. One way is to investigate the particulars of our lives, identify our strengths and capabilities, be alert to what kinds of things that we take pleasure in, and so forth. Another way, which is important in order to avoid misunderstandings, is to draw on the experiences of others. Although CAIAH is a subjectivist theory of well-being, this does *not* entail that the subject is the only source of knowledge on what attitudinal pleasures to pursue or to what extent we are justified in our confidence. On the contrary: one of the best ways of questioning our confidence and the opportunities available to us lies in taking advice from others.[3]

The central point here is that one way of being confident about our attitudinal pleasures is to become (more) confident that the states of affairs we take pleasure in obtain. These cognitive justifications require epistemological objectivity but not ontological objectivity. There are, however, *noncognitive* justifications of confidence, which we turn to below.

NONCOGNITIVE JUSTIFICATIONS OF CONFIDENCE

As we have seen, CAIAH does not regard truth in itself as a bearer of prudential value, even if the truth of something could be thought to provide a more stable ground for confidence in attitudinal pleasures. CAIAH however allows for a number of other routes to confidence, many of which stand in stark contrast to objective truth:

Trust: Another means to confidence despite lack of evidence is trust. Trust can be based on epistemologically objective states of affairs, such as when we have overwhelming evidence to the effect that someone is trustworthy (or "reliable") because they have always been in the past. As Lawrence Becker points out, however, trust—just like confidence—need not be a matter of truth and evidence: "let us call trust 'cognitive' if it is fundamentally a matter of our beliefs or expectations about others' trustworthiness; it is noncognitive if it is fundamentally a matter of our having trustful attitudes, affects, emotions, or motivational structures" (Becker 1996, 45). The noncognitive kind of trust Becker describes is a form of trust despite lack of evidence. As Weckert points out (in Weckert 2005), this seems to be the kind of trust involved in many of our closest and most valuable relationships: "A child's trust in its parents cannot be explained in terms of belief alone, nor can that between friends. Young children are not capable of the right sorts of beliefs. And trust between friends is also not based on a careful weighing up of risks and benefits" (Weckert 2005, 101). This illustrates how trust can be a noncognitive basis for confidence. If I take pleasure in my belief that my wife is faithful, the confidence I take in this belief will often be more grounded on the trust I have in my wife than any epistemologically objective evidence.

The notion of trust as generating confidence and its importance for well-being is also evident in Niklas Luhmann's influential work on trust—succinctly summarized by Helen Nissenbaum: "Luhmann characterizes trust as a mechanism that reduces complexity and enables people to cope with the high levels of uncertainty and complexity of contemporary life" (Nissenbaum 2001, 106). Another way of putting it is to say that trust enables us to pursue experiences we would not have dared to pursue if it had not been for trust—thus acting as an important precondition for a fuller and more varied life. In terms of CAIAH, trust enables me to be confident in my attitudinal pleasures, and thus (continue to) pursue them even if the epistemic ground for this confidence is not present. Closely related to trust are also other forms of "leap of faith," including—at least on some accounts-religious beliefs. According to CAIAH, the extent to which religious beliefs determine well-being is not determined by whether they are factually true or not, but rather how confident one is in one's beliefs—which, again, is something that typically cannot be justified entirely on cognitive grounds.

Categorical reasons: Harry Frankfurt, in his *The Reasons of Love* (Frankfurt 2004), gives a number of arguments that are, in many ways, tangential to those supporting CAIAH—and highlights several reasons of love that go beyond any epistemological doubt. They are "categorical" in the sense of being unconditional and not subject to scrutiny (or "innate," as Frankfurt describes them). Frankfurt also stresses the importance of confidence, and emphasizes that this confidence need not be securely grounded in epistemological objectivity. For instance, "normal people are as a rule not at all uncertain concerning whether to care about their own survival, or about the well-being of their children" (Frankfurt 2004, 29). Frankfurt's term *care about* is in many ways equivalent to "taking attitudinal pleasure in," so his claim can be rewritten as an argument to the effect that we are categorically confident about the pleasure we take in the well-being of our children. The attitudinal pleasure we take in *their* well-being will determine *our* well-being in step with how confident we are about our children's well-being. The pleasure I take in the well-being of my children is positively adjusted if I am strongly confident that they are actually happy and negatively adjusted if I am strongly in doubt that they are actually happy. This also relates to the aforementioned problem of how much we should scrutinize our attitudinal pleasures, since it implies that we should at least (be able to) scrutinize the well-being of those we care about to some degree. Not having the kind of relationship with my children that allows me to ascertain their level of well-being will in most cases erode my confidence in my beliefs about their well-being, hence my own well-being. My well-being will also be determined by how confident I am that I really care about the well-being of my children but, as Frankfurt argues, we "care about such things without inhibition or re-serve . . . those commitments are innate in us" (Frankfurt 2004, 29). When it comes to the well-being I derive from my children's well-being, it does not matter whether it is true that I care about my children or not. What matters is that I am confident that I should care about my children. If I were able to seriously entertain doubts whether I cared about them or not, it would follow in CAIAH that this would also negatively impact any well-being I may derive from their well-being. The same goes not only for parent-child relations but also any relationship that is grounded in more than truth and empirical facts. This includes "love," to which Frankfurt dedicates his book and argues that it transcends any such need for justification in terms of truth.

"CONFIDENCE" AND STATUS QUO BIAS

There are plausibly other means of acquiring confidence in one's attitudinal pleasures and their objects, but we think the ones we have discussed are at least the ones most relevant to the intuitions evoked by the EM. The reason we would not plug into the EM, according to CAIAH, is that we cannot imagine ourselves confidently taking pleasure in something that is merely a simulacrum. This also nicely illustrates that it is not the pleasures in the EM that are somehow inferior but rather how confident we are about those pleasures when we contemplate whether or not to plug in. Indeed, this is perfectly in line with an alternative version of EM, which further problematizes the intuition that our unwillingness to plug in somehow depends on truth.

Kolber proposes a reversed EM where, instead of being asked whether you would consider plugging in, you are asked whether you would plug out. You are told "you are not [fill in your name], you only think you are [your name]. Get off the machine and you will be who you really are, John Doe" (Kolber 1994, 15). Assuming premise (1) from Feldman's schematic characterization of the EM thought experiment holds,[4] the answer should be unequivocal; the person who is actually John Doe should want to leave.

De Brigard operationalized this reverse thought experiment, casting doubt on the unequivocal response the EM predicts.[5] In his experimental setup, de Brigard offers three scenarios, or "vignettes" as he calls them; a Neutral, a Negative, and a Positive vignette. In each of the scenarios you are confronted by an agent with the surprising message that you have for the past years been plugged into an experience machine due to an administrative error. You are informed that "your life outside is not at all like the life you have experienced so far." In the Neutral vignette, this is all you are told; in the case of the Negative and the Positive vignettes, you are told additionally that "in reality you are a prisoner in a maximum security prison in West Virginia," and "in reality you are a multimillionaire artist living in Monaco," respectively (De Brigard 2010, 47–49). The question is whether you would prefer to leave now.

In the Positive vignette, response was approximately 50–50 between respondents. In the Negative vignette, the response showed an overwhelmingly strong preference to stay in the EM. In the Neutral vignette, there was a significant preference to stay connected—and interestingly, the respondents who opted out of the EM in the Neutral vignette more often reported a preference for the "second chance" aspect of leaving than they reported a reality preference. All of this points toward a life based in falsity not necessarily being the worst life. This still does not of course answer the question of whether one *should* choose one way or the other, but it at least shows that we cannot derive a plausible "should" from a universal "would."

De Brigard points out that both readings of the EM can adequately be explained by what Samuelson and Zeckhauser (in Samuelson and Zeckhauser 1988) call a "status quo bias." In cases where the disadvantages of a change are more easily imagined than the advantages, "the disadvantages of change loom larger than the advantages" (Kahneman, Knetsch, and Thaler 1991, 200). This certainly would seem to be the case for Nozick's experience machine; hardly any subject being posed the thought experiment will have any experience that would extrapolate into a thorough imagining of being in the EM. In De Brigard's reading, however, most subjects will readily know what it would be like to have simply lived their lives, and whether they did so inside the EM or not will not enter the picture. This also follows from CAIAH, according to which the status quo bias is a result of us being more confident about attitudinal pleasures with which we are already experienced as opposed to attitudinal pleasures that are directed at a simulation. This also means that CAIAH bites the bullet when it comes to someone who is actually inside the EM (or if we unknowingly already were inside the EM), posing that this will have no adverse effect on our well-being if and only if our confidence is not affected by the supposed illusory nature of the EM. It should be clear by now that CAIAH does not easily allow us to build happiness on delusion. If you were to do so, you would have to remain confident in the face of typically overwhelming evidence and without having gone out of your way to avoid such evidence, in which case CAIAH bites the bullet and admits that such a delusional life could be a very happy one. The key insight, however, is that the *epistemic* plausibility of our beliefs is not always relevant. Being confident about something does not have to be grounded in epistemological, let alone ontological, objectivity.

Although there are certainly counterintuitive implications that follow from CAIAH, the theory at least shows that thought experiments like the EM do not have to be read as pumping the intuition that something must be true in order to be part of the good life. It also steers the discussion toward the question of what kinds of attitudinal pleasures we can and should be confident about, which is much less question-begging than simply concluding that the "unreal" cannot be a source of well-being.

We hope the short outline above suffices to show how the intuitions evoked by the EM can be used to refine a theory of well-being, which in turn casts new light on the thought experiment itself. Further clarification and elaboration of CAIAH would naturally open up new questions to explore. First of course would be the tenability of the claim that life plugged into the

EM may be as conducive to well-being as life outside the EM. In extension of that comes the question whether we ought to recommend simulated or mediated reality as a structural part of our lives, and in what ways we could be confident about the virtual worlds, entities, and experiences from which so many of us (seemingly) derive pleasure. In what follows, we will briefly address this issue and show how CAIAH adds nuance to the much-argued position (see e.g., Barney 2004; Borgmann 2004; Dreyfus 2004; Putnam 2000; Winner 1997) that virtual worlds, much like the experience machine, are inferior to the actual world when it comes to well-being. Should this position topple, new avenues of promoting well-being could be explored that would capitalize on recent technological developments rather than asking people to abstain. Thereby, we will also show how CAIAH is not merely a formal theory of well-being, but one that can deliver concrete guidance on how virtual worlds can have a role in the pursuit of a good life.

THE EXPERIENCE MACHINE, VIRTUAL WORLDS, AND WELL-BEING

The EM has not only been used as an argument in discussions of well-being but has also been used to illustrate several key problems with modern technologies; in particular, the way in which video games and other virtual worlds are seen as escapism from the "real world." To focus on one contested issue, several philosophers have criticized virtual relationships for being inferior to nonvirtual relationships because they are "unreal" or generally come without the richness that is necessary for genuine friendship (see e.g., Cocking and Matthews 2000; Fröding and Peterson 2012; Kaliarnta 2016; Parks and Floyd 1996; Søraker 2012).

According to CAIAH, there is nothing inherently problematic about virtual relationships, and they can give rise to many of the same attitudinal pleasures, but virtual relationships are typically inferior when it comes to the confidence they provide. Having lived with someone and experienced their person in a variety of circumstances—bringing what Cocking and Matthews (in Cocking and Matthews 2000) refer to as "involuntary self-disclosure"— will generally allow for a level of confidence that is much more difficult, if not impossible, in virtual worlds. It would seem that, no matter how much time I spend with someone in a virtual world, it is hard to imagine (even if not impossible) how I could become entirely confident that the other person loves me—which will in most cases remain an obstacle to confidently taking pleasure in that relationship. In most cases, I cannot be fully confident that my virtual friends are, for instance, the gender, age, or occupation they portray themselves as, or how they would act outside the typically restricted virtual world I engage with them. To illustrate that this is a matter of degree, we may be uncertain about all of those in real life as well, but not as commonly—and decreasingly so when having spent a lot of time in their presence and engaged in many joint activities. It is this difference in confidence that may in many cases make nonvirtual relationships more conducive to well-being than virtual ones.

Closely related, and relevant to many online activities, we are more used to the expressions, institutionalizations, and expectations of trust in the nonvirtual world. In the nonvirtual world I might, for instance, take pleasure in the fact that the police are present to secure an event and be fully confident that wearing a uniform means that they are in fact police even before I see them address a disruption, but similarly clear markers of roles and corresponding trust ahead of enactment are much rarer in virtual worlds. To give but one more example of the implications of CAIAH, the online information glut, including increased exposure to alternative lifestyles and increased knowledge of the suffering of others, may lead to reduced confidence in the lives we have chosen for ourselves. In line with this, several studies have found that social media platforms like Facebook do affect our subjective well-being negatively (Haferkamp and Krämer 2011; Kross et al. 2013). In terms of CAIAH, social comparison will in many cases leave us with less confidence about what it is that I (should) take pleasure in, simply by virtue of constantly being exposed to what seems to be happier lives filled with attitudinal pleasures very different from mine. Again, CAIAH captures this insight nicely and shows how it is not the attitudinal pleasure that is reduced (I do not doubt whether I take pleasure in it) but rather how confident we are that we should be having that attitudinal pleasure.

CONCLUDING REMARKS

The purpose of this chapter has been to show how the EM triggers important intuitions about well-being that should be taken seriously, without thereby accepting the claim that these intuitions rule out hedonism as a plausible account of human well-being. We have shown how the EM challenges the way in which hedonism has traditionally been concerned only with mental states, and hence, seemingly implies that it makes no difference whether we base our well-being on truth or lies, actual or simulated reality. This is a serious charge because a theory of well-being, perhaps more than any other normative theory, needs to be intuitively appealing, as evidenced by the prevalence of thought experiments and other appeals to intuition in the well-being discourse. We have argued that the problem is at least somewhat taken care of by first moving toward attitudinal rather than sensory pleasures. Finally, we argued that "confidence" is a promising candidate for adjusting attitudinal hedonism, one that subsumes the way in which reality, morality, sustainability, speech acts, sociocultural norms, trust, and other conditions determine the extent to which that in which we take pleasure contributes to our well-being—and one that makes sense of the EM intuitions without thereby jumping to the conclusion that something has to be "real" or "true" in order to form part of the good life.

NOTES

1. Another thought experiment about false pleasures that aims to elicit very similar intuitions is "the deceived businessman." In this thought experiment, we are asked to "imagine a man who dies contented, thinking he has achieved everything he wanted in life: his wife and family love him, he is a respected member of the community, and he has founded a successful business. Or so he thinks. In reality, however, he has been completely deceived: his wife cheated on him, his daughter and son were only nice to him so that they would able to borrow the car, the other members of the community only pretended to respect him for the sake of the charitable contributions he sometimes made, and his business partner has been embezzling funds from the company which will soon go bankrupt. In thinking about this man's life, it is difficult to believe that it is all a life could be, that this life has gone about as well as a life could go. Yet this seems to be the very conclusion mental state theories must reach" (Kagan 1994, 311).

2. By "virtual worlds" we mean any interactive, computer-simulated, indexical, multiuser environment in which humans can engage in activities and form relationships by means of an avatar or other representation (Søraker 2011). Well-known examples include *Second Life*, *World of Warcraft*, and *EVE online*.

3. It is on this basis that one of this chapter's authors has, in other work (Søraker 2010), argued that it follows from CAIAH that our determinants of well-being can and should be informed by other people's determinants, as can be gleaned from empirical research in fields such as positive psychology and happiness economics (Jahoda 1959; Ong and Van Dulmen 2007; C. Peterson 2006; Seligman 2004). A further defense of this lies beyond the scope of this chapter, but it rests on the premise that the kinds of activities and experiences that a lot of people take pleasure in are also something that you are likely to take pleasure in, meaning that empirical research on subjective well-being can provide us with important pointers on the attitudinal pleasures of others. This, in turn, may act as inspiration for exploring new determinants of well-being or affect the confidence we have in existing pleasures.

4. "Given the opportunity to plug in you would forego LEM and choose LA" (Feldman 2012).

5. It should be noted that sample size of the experiment was small, and perhaps not representative of how the general public would respond.

Chapter Four

Ceci n'est pas une cuve

Putnam's Argument as Inclosure Paradox

Jon Cogburn

I. LOVECRAFT VERSUS PUTNAM

Fictional brain transplants date at least as far back as Mary Shelley's 1818 Frankenstein's monster, and actual experiments on keeping alive the brains of decapitated dogs date to Charles-Édouard Brown-Séquard's morbid 1857 surgeries. But H. P. Lovecraft's 1931 "The Whisperer in Darkness" is perhaps the first time we find something similar to what philosophers mean when they talk about brains in vats. Lovecraft's narrator, Albert N. Wilmarth, describes a procedure recounted to him by his previously distressed, yet now curiously enthusiastic, pen pal Henry W. Akeley:

> There was a harmless way to extract a brain, and a way to keep the organic residue alive during its absence. The bare, compact cerebral matter was then immersed in an occasionally replenished fluid with an ether-tight cylinder of a metal mined in Yuggoth, certain electrodes reaching through and connecting at will with elaborate instruments capable of duplicating the three vital faculties of sight, hearing, and speech. For the winged fungus-beings to carry the brain-cylinders intact through space was an easy matter. Then, on every planet covered by their civilization, they would find plenty of adjustable faculty-instruments capable of being connected within the encased brains; so that after a little fitting these travelling intelligences could be given a full sensory and articulate life—albeit a bodiless and mechanical one—at each stage of their journeying through and beyond the space-time continuum. It was as simple as carrying a phonograph record about and playing it wherever a phonograph of the corresponding make exists. Of its success there could be no question. Akeley was not afraid. Had it not been brilliantly accomplished again and again? (Lovecraft 2005, 465)

This passage is followed by a peroration seemingly issuing from an amplifier connected to a vat, praising vat existence and encouraging Wilmarth to submit himself to the procedure. The wonders of the universe will be revealed as the vat encasing his brain is transported across space and time. Moreover, his body will be maintained in hypostasis, to be reunited with the brain at the end of the exploring.

If all we had to go by were the soliloquy coming out of the amplifier, Lovecraft's vatted brains would be radically different from the ones currently discussed by philosophers such as Robert Nozick and Hilary Putnam. Contra Nozick and Putnam, vatification is initially presented by Lovecraft as being epistemically advantageous. It is the only way that humans are able to experience the far reaches of reality. From the amplifier:

> Do you realize what it means when I say I have been on thirty-seven different celestial bodies—planets, dark stars, and less definable objects—including eight outside our galaxy and two outside the curved cosmos of space and time? All this has not harmed me in the least. My brain has been removed from my body by fissions so adroit that it would be crude to call the operation surgery. The visiting beings have methods which make these extractions easy and almost normal—and one's body never ages when the brain is out of it. The brain, I may add, is virtually immortal with its mechanical faculties and a limited nourishment supplied by occasional changes of the preserving fluid. (Lovecraft 2005, 468)

Not only is the vatted brain able to experience things inaccessible to human bodies, but vatted brains (and their preserved bodies left on earth) live much longer, enabling organisms who submit to the procedure to accumulate vastly more knowledge.

With the possible perverse exception of Mark Silcox and me,[1] philosophers have drawn a radically different conclusion from the possibility of brains in vats. Hilary Putnam's discussion in 1981's *Reason, Truth, and History* is at this point almost canonical.

> Here is a science fiction possibility discussed by philosophers: imagine that a human being (you can imagine this to be yourself) has been subjected to an operation by an evil scientist. The person's brain (your brain) has been removed from the body and placed in a vat of nutrients which keeps the brain alive. The nerve endings have been connected to a super-scientific computer which causes the person whose brain it is to have the illusion that everything is perfectly normal. There seem to be people, objects, the sky, etc.; but really all the person (you) is experiencing is the result of electronic impulses travelling from the computer to the nerve endings. The computer is so clever that if the person tries to raise his hand, the feedback from the computer will cause him to "see" and "feel" the hand being raised. Moreover, by varying the program, the evil scientist can cause the victim to "experience" (or hallucinate) any situation or environment the evil scientist wishes. He can also obliterate the

memory of the brain operation, so that the victim will seem to himself to have always been in this environment. (Putnam 1975, 6)

These vats do the same philosophical work as the demon in Descartes's *Meditations on First Philosophy*. The thought is that if the skeptical hypothesis (either an omnipotent demon fooling us or a master scientist putting us in a Putnamian vat) is true, then most of our beliefs about the world are false. Contrariwise, figuring out why we might be justified in taking the skeptical hypothesis to be false might shed light on the manner in which our justified true beliefs are justified. Putnamian brains in vats are thought to present a more pressing problem than Descartes's demon, because one might argue that, given our current scientific knowledge, the actual envatting of future human brains is a live possibility.

While Lovecraft's narrator is initially enthusiastic about the prospect of being envatted, the horrifying outcome of the story shades into something much more Putnamian, so much so that Ackley has no idea whether the voice emanating from the speakers really was the voice of an enthusiastic brain. At the terrifying end of Lovecraft's tale, the reader has no idea what is really going on with the brains in the vats. But enough is on the table in the fictional world to suggest that something Putnamian might be the case. If the aliens really do control the sensory input, this puts them in a position similar to Descartes's demon, experimenting on human sensoria for their own inscrutable reasons.

One of the main punchlines of Silcox's and my article "Against Brain-in-a-Vatism" is that a great deal of philosophy is just underspecified, and hence often irresponsible fiction. The manner in which the evolution of a story has to scan as a plausible evolution of the fictional world is what enables readers to work out *gedankenexperiments* in an epistemically competent way. Since sensitivity to counterfactual states of affairs, the kinds of affairs described by more painstakingly specified fictions (those Silcox and I describe as *true*, because they really do describe the way the world would evolve, were the fictional set up actual), is such a foundational part of human knowledge that it follows that virtual worlds, where we are able to experience and enact fictions, represent a fundamental source of epistemic liberation.

With respect to brains in vats themselves, we shall see that the placement of the envatted brains in actual fictional universes such as Lovecraft's Cthulhu mythology leads one to draw radically different conclusions from those encouraged by Putnam. In "Against Brain-in-a-Vatism," Silcox and I examined the history of fictional portrayals of virtual reality to show why Nozick is mistaken in thinking that it is always disfavorable to live in a virtual environment; here I intend to demonstrate that Putnam is mistaken in dismissing the supposition that our reality already is something very much like Nozick's experience machine.

II. PUTNAM'S ARGUMENT

Putnam produces an astonishingly quick argument against radical skepticism by arguing that the way in which our words acquire meaning shows that we cannot be brains in vats. Here it is in its entirety:

> "[V]at" refers to vats in the image in vat-English, or something related (electronic impulses or program features), but certainly not to real vats, since the use of "vat" in vat-English has no causal connection to real vats (apart from the connection that the brains in a vat wouldn't be able to use the word "vat," if it were not for the presence of one particular vat—the vat they are in; but this connection obtains between the use of *every* word in vat-English and that one particular vat; it is not a special connection between the use of the *particular* word "vat" and vats). Similarly, "nutrient fluid" refers to a liquid in the image in vat-English, or something related (electronic impluses or program features). It follows that if their "possible world" is really the actual one, and we are really the brains in a vat, then what we now mean by "we are brains in a vat" is that *we are brains in a vat in the image* or something of that kind (if we mean anything at all). But part of the hypothesis that we are brains in a vat is that we aren't brains in a vat in the image (i.e., what we are "hallucinating" isn't that we are brains in a vat). So, if we are brains in a vat, then the sentence "We are brains in a vat" says something false (if it says anything). In short, if we are brains in a vat, then "We are brains in a vat"; is false. So it is (necessarily) false. (Putnam 1975, 14–15)

Lance Hickey describes the following causal constraint as the key premise of Putnam's argument:

> (CC) A term refers to an object only if there is an appropriate causal connection between that term and the object. (Hickey 2015)

For example, my use of the word *water* refers to water because water is the actual stuff that occasions my use of the word. If I lived in an alternate universe where some other substance occasioned the word *water*, and if I hadn't gotten there from this universe where I had originally learned the word, then *water* would refer to that stuff, even if I didn't have the ability to differentiate that stuff from the water in our universe. Similarly, I can successfully refer to gaskets, and truly state that gaskets are not the same as carburetors, even though I myself couldn't tell the two apart. I can do this because of causal conversational chains of the sort that go from instances of these kinds of objects, through experts who know what they are, then to people like me, who defer to the experts. And in the case of *water*, even before there were experts who understood what water is, people were able to refer to it.

In a Putnamian version of Lovecraft's *gedankenexperiment*, Akeley would no longer remember having been put in the vat; in fact, he wouldn't know anything about his previous life. Given this, once we distinguish between the actual vat that poor Akeley resides in from the vats he perceives in the sensorium provided by the aliens, it is not implausible to claim that envatted Akeley's assertion of "I might be a brain in a vat" does not succeed in referring to the actual vat he's in, but rather the kinds of virtual vats the aliens present him with. If this is right, then Putnam's argument is the following:

1. Assume we are brains in a vat.
2. If we are brains in a vat, then "brain" does not refer to brain, and "vat" does not refer to vat (via CC).
3. If "brain in a vat" does not refer to brains in a vat, then "we are brains in a vat" is false.
4. Thus, if we are brains in a vat, then the sentence "We are brains in a vat" is false (1, 2, 3). (Hickey 2015)

In his *Internet Encyclopedia of Philosophy* article, Hickey does a masterful job adumbrating the standard criticisms and reformulations of Putnam's argument. As far as I know, the reinterpretation that I am about to suggest is novel.

III. INCLOSURE PARADOXES

Russell's Paradox can be understood simply as follows. Intuitively, most collections of objects do not contain themselves. A carton of eggs is not an egg. But some collections do contain themselves; the set of all sets definable in less than twelve words is definable in less than twelve words, and hence a member of itself. But most of the sets that typically concern us are not self-membered. So consider the set of all sets that do not contain themselves, which we can call R. Now assume (for *reductio*) that R contains itself. But that means that it satisfies its own definition of being a set that does not contain itself. So our supposition that it contains itself leads to a contradiction. From this we conclude that it does not contain itself (discharging the assumption that it does contain itself).[2] But then R is a member of the set of all sets that don't contain themselves, which is R. So now we have that it both does and doesn't contain itself. Contradiction!

What should one say about this puzzling result?[3] Priest shows that there are exactly four kinds of responses. This follows from his great discovery that an astonishing number of traditional paradoxes fit the following schema:

Inclosure Schema:

(1) $\Omega = \{y \mid \varphi(y)\}$ exists and $\psi(\Omega)$ Existence
(2)   if $x \subseteq \Omega$ and $\psi(x)$ (a) $\delta(x) \notin x$ Transcendence
                                        (b) $\delta(x) \in \Omega$ Closure

At first glance, this is a formidable piece of symbolism. Here I will first explain it with respect to Russell's Paradox and then show how Putnam's argument is homologous.

In *Beyond the Limits of Thought* Priest gives values for φ, ψ, and δ to derive the paradoxes of Russell, Burali-Forti, Mirimanoff, Kant (according to Priest's reconstructed "Fifth Antinomy"), König, Berry, Richard, Berkeley, Weyl, and Montague, as well as the traditional liar paradox involving a sentence that expresses its own falsehood. In addition, as noted above, he is able to present a guerilla retelling of key moments in the history of philosophy (including Plato, Aristotle, Cusanus, Aquinas, Anselm, Leibniz, Berkeley, Kant, Hegel, Cantor, Russell, Frege, Quine, Davidson, Derrida, Wittgenstein, Heidegger, and Nāgārjuna) in terms of the schema. But for Priest, Russell's Paradox has pride of place, in part because it is "the heart of Cantor's Paradox" and "undoubtedly the simplest of all the set-theoretic paradoxes" (Priest 2002, 129). Priest's key insight is that the "Russell set," the set of all sets that are not members of themselves, is arrived at by applying Cantor's own diagonalization function to the identity function of the set of all pure sets.[4] A pure set is one such that neither it, nor any of its elements (nor their elements, nor their elements, and so on), contain ur-elements, which are elements that are not themselves sets. A pure set either might not bottom out, being at the top of an infinite sequence of sets that have other sets as members, or bottoms out always with instances of the empty set, the set that has no members.[5]

We can begin our formal excursus by defining Cantorian diagonalization in the usual manner. Where f_A is a one-place function defined over the set A, $\mathrm{diag}(f_A)$ equals the set of x in A that are such that x is not a member of the object delivered when f_A is applied to x (the object denoted by $f_A(x)$). Thus:

$$\mathrm{diag}(f_A) = \{x \in A \mid x \notin f_A(x)\}$$

This is the key function that Cantor constructed to show that the number of things in a set (its cardinality) is less than the cardinality of the set of all of that set's subsets. Cantor proved that if we start with a function from a set to its own powerset (the set of all subsets of the initial set), the set delivered by diag will of necessity not be among the members delivered by the initial function from the set to its powerset. Any proof that establishes this with respect to some set and its powerset is now called a proof by diagonalization. Since the set delivered by diag is not among the members delivered by the initial function, it follows there is no function from a set to its powerset that uniquely connects each member of that set with its powerset. But if we let id (for identity) be the function that takes every object to itself (a function into, but not onto, the set's powerset), we can define the diagonal set of the identity function applied to the set A as:

$$\text{diag}(\text{id}_a) = \{x \in A \mid x \notin \text{id}_A(x)\}$$

But since, by definition, $\text{id}_A(x) = x$, we can replace $\text{id}_A(x)$ with x in the above, giving us:

$$\text{diag}(\text{id}_A) = \{x \in A \mid x \notin x\}$$

Now assume that A is V, the collection of all pure sets. Since V contains everything, the set of x in V is the same as the set of all x.

$$\text{diag}(\text{id}_V) = \{x \in V \mid x \notin x\} = \{x \mid x \notin x\}$$

This is the Russell set, the set of all sets that are not members of themselves, or R from our informal discussion above.

And now we can consider Priest's inclosure schema for Russell's Paradox. We should note that part of what makes Russell's Paradox the simplest is that it is in the family of paradoxes (including the Burali-Forti and Mirimanoff paradoxes, and Kant's 5th Antinomy) where the ψ in Priest's schema can be a trivial property, such as being self-identical. Thus we don't need to represent it. Also, since $\Omega = \{y \mid y \in V\}$ is equal to V, we can simplify the inclosure schema thus:

Priest's Inclosure Schema for Russell's Paradox:

(1)	V exists			Existence
(2)	if $x \subseteq V$	(a)	$\text{diag}(\text{id}x) \notin x$	Transcendence
		(b)	$\text{diag}(\text{id}x) \in V$	Closure

The contradiction is arrived at by the characteristic self-application of (a) Transcendence and (b) Closure to V itself, which yields the contradiction (a) $\text{diag}(\text{id}_V) \notin V$ and (b) $\text{diag}(\text{id}_V) \in V$. Since (2) is a universally quantified claim about all x, all we are doing here is instantiating (2) with V. Consider:

(2)	if $V \subseteq V$	(a)	$\text{diag}(\text{id}_V) \notin V$	Transcendence
		(b)	$\text{diag}(\text{id}_V) \in V$	Closure

Since by the definition of "subset" (x is a subset of y if, and only if, all members of x are members of y), every set is a subset of itself, and Transcendence and Closure apply to all subsets of V, they apply to V itself, yielding the contradiction expressed by lines (a) and (b) above. The Russell set $(\mathrm{diag}(\mathrm{id}_V))$ is an element of V and is not an element of V.

From the nature of the contradiction we can see why Priest uses the words *Transcendence* and *Closure*. Once applied to V, the Transcendence lemma shows that the diagonalizing function yields a value *external* to the postulated totality (the set of all sets), and thus a thing that is not itself a set. On the other hand, the Closure lemma shows that the same function yields a value *inside* the postulated totality, a set. So the value of the function when applied to the set of all sets would contradictorily be both a set and not a set.

Clearly the self-application of the schema to the totality V yields a contradiction. The interesting work, then, is always demonstrating Transcendence and Closure with respect to all of the subsets of the totality in question. In the case of Russell's Paradox, Closure follows immediately. Since, by hypothesis, V is the set of all pure sets, any pure set is an element of it by definition. Transcendence is a bit trickier, but, in the case of Russell's Paradox, formalizable in a Fitch-style system without too much sweat (as is shown in the Appendix of my forthcoming *Garcian Meditations*).

A typical response to such paradoxes is to refuse to assert the Existence of the totality in question, or to attempt to restrict our concepts, language, or logic in ways that prevent Transcendence or Closure. Priest himself critiques such solutions and argues that inclosure paradoxes are sound arguments involving true contradictions. For Priest, for example, the Russell set (i.e., the set of all sets that are not members of themselves) really is both a member of the universe of sets (Closure) and *not* a member of the universe of sets (Transcendence). The position Priest defends therefore involves adopting logic weaker than full classical. In such "paraconsistent" logics, it is not the case that just any proposition whatsoever follows from a contradiction.

IV. PUTNAM'S ARGUMENT AS INCLOSURE PARADOX

Presenting Putnam's argument as an inclosure paradox requires a little bit of special notation. First, let "[a]" refer to the universe of discourse of a. For example "[mathematics]" would refer to all of the entities that one talks about when doing mathematics. In ordinary conversation, universes of discourse are usually implicit. If I say that all of the people are here, I almost never mean everyone in the universe, but rather all of the people in a contextually selected universe of discourse.

To demonstrate how Putnam's argument is importantly homologous to inclosure paradoxes we must let that "[BIV]" refers to the universe of discourse internal to an envatted brain, the set of things an envatted brain can talk about. And also let "ref('a')" refer to the object referred to by the expression "a." Thus, "ref('BIV')" would refer to the actual brain in a vat with the universe of discourse expressed by "[BIV]."

Now, remember that Russell's Paradox is arrived at by first instantiating the generalized Transcendence claim on the set of all pure sets (V). Where the domain of quantification is restricted to subsets of V, we have:

$\forall x(\text{diag}(\text{id}x) \notin x)$ Transcendence
$\text{diag}(\text{id}_V) \notin V$

Then, the same is done with respect to the Closure claim:

$\forall x(\text{diag}(\text{id}x) \in V)$ Closure
$\text{diag}(\text{id}_V) \in V$

The analog with respect to Putnam's argument would then be the following:

$\forall x(\text{ref}('x') \notin [x])$ Transcendence
$\text{ref}('BIV') \notin [BIV]$
$\forall x(\text{ref}('x') \in [BIV])$ Closure
$\text{ref}('BIV') \in [BIV]$

Putnam is thus asserting that, on the one hand (Transcendence), the referent of "BIV" cannot be in the universe of discourse of BIV, and on the other hand (Closure) that the reference of "BIV" must be in the universe of discourse of BIV. And these are, in fact, his substantive premises.

Unlike with Russell's Paradox, in Putnam's argument Transcendence is less problematic and Closure more problematic. If the universe of discourse of BIV is understood as being those things "in the vat image," the virtual objects presented as real by the scientist/alien, it just seems clear that the skeptic is not hypothesizing that she is in one of those virtual vats. She is not hypothesizing that she is a mere vat image of a brain in a vat. Closure, on the other hand, requires Putnam's causal constraint (CC). Putnam holds that an envatted creature can only refer to things in the vat image; that is, in the universe of discourse of BIV.

One thing that should be immediately clear is that Putnam's argument only works as a critique of skepticism because he tacitly assumes that the only response to an inclosure paradox is to deny Existence. The cause of the contradiction was the assumption that I am a brain in a vat. But of course one can, as one does when working with varieties of set theory, also deny Transcendence, Closure, or (with Priest) the law of noncontradiction. That is, once we see the inclosure-like nature of Putnam's argument, we witness the shocking provinciality of nearly all of the published discussion of that argument, starting with Putnam's own blithe antiskepticism.

III. TRANSCENDENCE REVISITED

Putnam was a wonderful philosopher, and if history's ongoing dialectic un-
folds in anything like a rational manner, he will continue to be read for
centuries. But he did not read enough science fiction or fantasy.

Great fantasy writers distinguish themselves in part by the metaphysics of
magic implicit in their work.[6] Steven Erikson's epic fantasy series, *Malazon
Book of the Fallen*, contains magical decks of cards that reflect the metaphysics of the world. Each card represents a divinity and the realm where that
divinity normally resides. Interestingly, the cards are in a sense placeholders,
for extraordinarily heroic mortals can ascend, joining the divine pantheon by
either displacing a current placeholder or creating a new card in the deck.
Identity is slippery in Erikson's pantheon.

In pantheons such as this there is often some strange sense in which the
divinity is simultaneously the placeholder, the occupant, and the realm. As
with Trinitarian Christian theology we have three nominally distinct things
that are nonetheless identical. The fantastic identity of placeholder, occupant,
and realm is probably easiest to envision if we stick to actual Tarot decks, as
opposed to Erikson's shifting milieu. The Empress card (the third trump in
standard decks) depicts a woman who can be identified both with a female
human-shaped divinity we refer to as "Mother" and with Earth herself. She is
in some sense both her personification and that which she personifies. Now
consider the Tower card (the sixteenth trump) and assume the Tarot deck
reflects a roughly Eriksonian metaphysics. As with the Empress, the Tower
would then be a personified creature (some ascended human) as well as a
place. Qua realm, Tower is the place where ascended beings, divinities'
personifications, stay and play games with one another, games that direct
human history in large and small ways. For example, the rise or fall of human
empires might rest on a game of chess between two ascended beings.

But what of Tower's own personification? Where does he go to play
games with the other ascended beings? He goes inside Tower, of course. But
the very coherence of this supposition directly contradicts the form of
Transcendence presupposed by Putnam! The fictional entity we refer to with
"Tower" is an element of the universe of discourse relevant to Tower (here
the things actually spatially inside Tower). There is nothing incoherent about
the pantheon I have just sketched. On the other hand, one might say that an
entity being spatially located inside itself is the mereological equivalent to a
set's being a member of itself. And since the latter is not possible, the former
clearly isn't.

In standard ZF set theory there are no self-membered sets. And we used to
think that Russell's Paradox forced this on us. But now we know that this is
simply not true. Non-well-founded set theory is an important area of going
concern in the foundations of mathematics (see, for example, Barwise and

Moss 1996). So the defender of mainstream responses to Putnam's inclosure paradox do not find any succor in the manner in which ZFC set theory overcompensates in response to Russell's Paradox. Perhaps the divinities playing games with one another in Tower are able to converse with and about the very same Tower in which they are residing, a divinity who also resides inside of himself with them.

Once we have seen how this might work out with respect to the mythological realm, we can apply the same idea to brains in vats by considering a different (better!) ending to the *Matrix* trilogy. At the outset of the series, most of humanity is trapped in pods, experiencing a computer simulation. But we can ask where the computers are running the simulation. The writers of *The Matrix* located these computers in a postapocalyptic Earth. But the plot could (should!) have evolved in such a way that the big payoff was the discovery that the computers running The Matrix were in fact computers in the Matrix itself. The world is a virtual construct being generated by a virtual machine *inside that construct*. This is both analogous to our story about Tower, and exactly what Putnam rules out by presupposing Transcendence in this context. Moreover, it is not that far from the world of the 1999 film *The Thirteenth Floor*, where computers in virtual worlds themselves generate virtual worlds as complicated as the world in which they are embedded. [7] *The Thirteenth Floor* suggests that these virtual worlds never bottom out into a real one. It is a small step from this infinite chain of distinct virtual realms to endlessly circling virtual worlds, such as our alternate Matrix.

If this is still a little unclear, consider a painting that contains in its lower right-hand corner a perfect, albeit smaller, duplication of itself. If the duplication were actually perfect, then the painting within the painting would also contain a perfect duplication of the painting. And this clearly continues to infinity. Non-well-founded sets are like this infinite set of contained paintings, with the proviso that the perfect duplication is actually the painting itself. There is one painting, infinitely nested within itself. This is what we have conjectured with Tower above, playing games with the other divinities inside of himself.

One might respond that this does not undermine Putnam, since the original brain in the vat *gedankenexperiment* is supposed to be physically possible, and as such be more worth considering than Descartes's demon. Perhaps our response motivated by fantasy and science fiction literature doesn't really undermine Putnam, because he only intends to be talking about physically possible skeptical scenarios. I have three responses to this. First, for reasons that Silcox and I go into in our book *Philosophy through Video Games* it's not clear to either of us that the brain in the vat as described is really physically possible. Second, from Putnam's own discussion it is clear that the brain in the vat is supposed to stand in for any hypothesis strong enough to entail radical skepticism. If Putnam's argument were valid, it would apply to Descartes's demon as well.

Finally, and most importantly, one of the virtues of Lovecraft's philosophical worldview is his contention that scientific discoveries paradoxically increase the realm of strange possibilities. Lovecraft is arguably the inventor of science fiction because he showed so clearly that naturalism provides a much better metaphysical setting for horror than the British and German Romantic/Gothic magical realm. Had non-well-founded set theory existed in Lovecraft's era, he would have incorporated it into his narratives in something like the manner I've suggested. His stories are full of non-Euclidean geometry and relativity theory. For Lovecraft, the weirdness that natural science unveils strongly suggests that the universe might in fact ultimately be so weird that creatures like us are always prevented from fully understanding it. All of his great fiction involves paradoxically describing a naturalistic universe so weird as to be indescribable.[8] A fair-minded reader of Lovecraft would not be so quick to assume that Putnam's brains in vats are more physically plausible than a Cartesian demon. How could one possibly know that?

Independent of these musings it is clear that, once we see Putnam's argument is an inclosure paradox, we can simply reframe the skeptical hypothesis. How do I know that I am not a brain in a vat that exists somewhere in the vat world in which I find myself? In such a situation, the failure of Transcendence shows both that there is no problem with the reference of my words and that causal theories of reference are powerless to rebut skepticism.

IV. CLOSURE REVISITED

Many of the published responses to Putnam can be interpreted as attempting to block Closure. For example, in "On Putnam's Proof That We Cannot Be Brains in a Vat," Crispin Wright argues that the causal condition would not prevent a person who has had his brain envatted the night before (and retained his memories) from successfully referring to objects outside of his vat's universe of discourse.

More generally, Putnam's own later discussions of reference undermine the application of the causal condition in his own argument. In 1994's *Words and Life*, he notes that if simplistic causal theories of reference were correct we would be committed to saying that phlogiston exists. Since valence electrons are in the correct causal relationship to earlier scientists' use of the word *phlogiston* we would have to say, not that phlogiston doesn't exist, but that phlogiston turned out to have slightly different properties than we previously thought.

To be clear, in many cases we do tell a story like that, where some kind of causal connection secures reference. The properties we associate with the word *atom* have changed radically as science has developed, and the Whig histories we tell involve us saying that the atoms as described by our newest theories are the things that we were referring to all along. But the phlogiston example shows that we don't always do this. Sometimes, instead, we take the set of beliefs we associate with a term as being determinative of reference. When we are forced to revise those beliefs, we conclude that the object we thought we were talking about doesn't exist after all.

That is, the moral of Putnam's *The Meaning of Meaning* and Kripke's *Naming and Necessity* is not that reference is always determined by some causal chain ending in the thing referred to, only (in contradiction to earlier description theories) that it *sometimes* is. But the causal constraint in Putnam's brain-in-a-vat argument assumes that it *always* is. Contra Closure, why can't I refer to a possibly fictional vat that doesn't exist in the domain relevant to the vat in which that brain resides? Why can't I wonder if such a vat is actual? If description fixes the reference of phlogiston (which we found to be nonactual), why can't it do the same for my vat? No good reason can be given.

V. CONCLUDING THOUGHTS

There are many advantages to seeing Putnam's argument as an inclosure paradox. For example, we also see the possibility of equivocation between Transcendence and Closure. For example, one way to make Closure plausible is if [BIV] (the universe of discourse relative to BIV) actually consists in the set of things that secure reference for the inhabitant of the vat, whether via description or causation. Then it is not problematic to say that the reference of "BIV" is an element of [BIV]. However, once [BIV] is defined in this way, Transcendence is implausible. If our domain of discourse involves reference to things secured by description, then there is no reason to think that the vats to which an envatted brain refers must be outside of our much-expanded domain of discourse. Here Closure is plausible, the reference of "BIV" is an element of the domain of discourse determined by BIV (ref('BIV') $\in$ [BIV]). But Transcendence (ref('BIV') $\notin$ [BIV]) is clearly false, and so Putnam's argument again fails.

Readers of Priest's *Beyond the Limits of Thought* will be familiar with the idea that there are paradoxes at interesting philosophical limits such as those of the knowable and the describable. And much of Priest's argument is directed at undermining typical responses to such paradoxes, which involve restoring consistency by denying some combination of Existence, Closure, and Transcendence. Priest himself then argues that such paradoxes support dialetheism, the existence of true contradictions. It would be very fun if Putnam's argument could be presented as at the end providing another such example of a contradiction that we might rationally determine to be true, but I'm not seeing it now.[9]

In addition to the open possibilities with respect to the epistemic brain-in-the-vat literature, I hope that my discussion of Lovecraft, Erickson, Gaiman, and the Tarot deck above provides just a little more evidence that the promissory note with which I ended section I above can be cashed. One needn't maintain that dead Cthulhu lies dreaming to affirm that, in cases such as this at least, the extent to which a fictional work scans carries very important epistemic weight. Perhaps we are in a vat that contains itself, which then in turn contains itself, which then in turn . . . iterating to infinity. Or perhaps we are dialethically both able to and not able to talk about this strange, vatlike totality in which we find ourselves. Perhaps it is the case that I (am failing to) do so right now.

Before concluding, let me reconsider Robert Nozick's attempt to use the specter of envatted humans to refute ethical hedonism. For Nozick, hedonism entails that a virtual life of perfect pleasure is equally valuable as a nonvirtual life of perfect pleasure. Nozick argues that inhabitants of virtual realms are such that they are not really doing anything, not really being anything, and failing to make meaningful content with deeper reality. As noted above, Silcox and I have criticized Nozick on all of these specific grounds. But I want to end with one more criticism that I think illustrates why it is impossible to ignore Putnamian considerations when thinking through Nozick's.

Assume a fair-minded, possibly omniscient, judge would find herself saying that the human condition actually strikingly resembles that of envatted brains. Perhaps the "external world" we perceive is so shaped by our own cognitive and perceptual filters that it doesn't make sense to talk about, or claim we can have knowledge of, the way the world is independently of what our own sensoria make of it. Perhaps "what is really out there" resembles something like the computer code that triggers a certain display on a monitor when certain input conditions are satisfied. If this were the case, then it would arguably be the case that the invidious distinctions Nozick makes between the "real" world and his experience machines don't stand! But then Nozick would either have to conclude that the world we find ourselves in is such that there is no meaningful sense in which we do anything, are anything, or make contact with anything "deeper," or he would have to conclude that Silcox and I are correct about the value of virtual realms.

Here is exactly where Putnam's argument is of so much service to Nozick. If Putnam is correct that we are not already envatted, then there is no a priori problem with Nozick's distinction between the "real" and the virtual. But if I am correct about what follows from understanding Putnam's argument to be an inclosure paradox, it is not at all clear that Putnam is correct, for (as I have shown) Putnam is just assuming that one must respond to his paradox by denying Existence. He provides no argumentation for why one should in this context deny Existence rather than Transcendence, Closure, or the law of noncontradiction. Given this, the Nozickian cannot appeal to Putnam when responding to the possibility that the world is already something very much like an experience machine.

NOTES

1. See Cogburn and Silcox 2014. The manner in which this chapter is a companion piece to that one will be clear in what follows.

2. Just to be maximally clear to any nonproof theorists, from the meaning of R we have that if R is true then it is not the case that R is true. But such a claim is logically equivalent to the claim that R is not true. So the falsity of R rests only on the conditional.

3. Much of this discussion in this section is from my forthcoming *Garcian Meditations*, where I differentiate various schools of object-oriented ontology in terms of how they should be read as responding to an inclosure paradox at the limit of metaphysical explanation.

4. Seeing this connection with Cantor's argument is pretty insightful. The way Russell's Paradox is almost always presented misses it because it proceeds by noting that if the set of all sets exists then the Russell set would also exist as a subset of it. Priest shows that this more standard manner of presentation is also an instance of the inclosure schema (Priest 2006, 130).

5. There is only one such set because sets are distinct only if one has a member that the other lacks.

6. Some of what follows might be taken to be very, very loosely suggested by Neil Gaiman's *Sandman* series. For a related discussion, which presents a threefold metaphysical division of magical systems in fantasy novels, see Cogburn and Hebert 2012. For an analogous survey with respect to moral psychology, see Cogburn 2012b. Both papers presuppose Cogburn and Silcox 2014's contention that true fictions (true fantasy novels here) are thought experiments. Most of what we know about anything presupposes knowledge of how the actual world would evolve, were it set up in the way presupposed by fictional worlds. This is why novels are philosophically indispensable.

7. Season 2, Episode 6 ("The Ricks Must Be Crazy") of Rick and Morty also suggests something like this. Rick's car battery is powered by a microuniverse whose denizens manually create electricity by stomping on pedals, the excess of which is siphoned off out of the microuniverse. But Rick's battery fails when a denizen of the microverse frees his fellow creatures from stomping on pedals by himself creating a microverse, whose denizens manually create . . . In the episode this only iterates three microverses down, but the viewer is led to imagine it iterating infinitely.

8. See Harman 2012 for a philosophically fruitful, extended meditation on this theme. In Neal Hebert and my "Expressing the Inexpressible" we discuss the paradoxical way that Lovecraftian narrators are able to describe horrific states of affairs that transcend their abilities to describe. A full treatment would tie Lovecraft to Priest's discussion of inclosure paradoxes with respect to the limits of what is expressible.

9. More interesting would be whether other quick refutations of skepticism such as Donald Davidson's can be presented as inclosure paradoxes, and whether they can then be shown to equivocate in a similar manner as Putnam's might. In Cogburn 2012a, I argue that Davidson's case for antiskepticism is homologous to Berkeley's "master argument" for idealism, and in Priest 2002, Priest presents Berkeley's argument as an inclosure paradox.

Part II

Real-World Experience Machines?

Chapter Five

Virtual Reality and "Knowing What It's Like"

The Epistemic Up Side of Experience Machines

E. M. Dadlez

In Robert Nozick's famous thought experiment from *Anarchy, State, and Utopia*, it is proposed that "how people's experiences feel from the inside" isn't the only thing that matters and, in fact, doesn't matter nearly as much as people think it does (Nozick 1974, 42). The experience machine whose contemplation is intended to convey this insight permits one to preprogram one's experiences in their entirety, stimulating one's brain in such a way as to create a perfect illusion of reality. Nozick is convinced that plugging into the machine is a form of self-annihilation that most of us would be bound to resist, insofar as such a course is held to deprive us of agency, autonomy, and identity. This chapter will argue that Nozick's characterization of the experience machine, and indeed of our response to the prospect of it, is too pessimistic.

As Nozick has it, someone plugged into the experience machine "is an indeterminate blob. There is no answer to the question of what a person is like who has long been in the tank. Is he courageous, kind, witty, intelligent, loving? It's not merely that it's difficult to tell; there's no way he is. Plugging into the machine is a kind of suicide" (Nozick 1974, 43). It will be argued here that plugging into the machine need not be characterized as a suicide, and might in fact have an up side. Part of that up side involves the similarities between our experience of works of narrative fiction and our probable experience of virtual reality. Speculations about the contributions of fiction in general to moral knowledge and moral understanding via empathy and simulation (and by fostering imaginative complicity in fictional perspectives) challenge Nozick's conclusions about the experience machine. Investigations into the moral and epistemic effects of fiction on its audience not only have a clear application to virtual reality scenarios but also suggest that the experience of virtual worlds could, potentially, have a more powerful impact than that associated with conventionally experienced fiction. In particular, active participation in a fully realized fictional world allows an unprecedented opportunity for empathetic experience, such as can only be partially realized by the readers of novels or audiences of plays. Virtual reality could provide knowledge of what something is *like*—potentially contributing both to acquaintance and propositional knowledge. This is the kind of knowledge that appears to lie at the basis of empathetic moral understanding. Even the most deterministic construal of the experience machine could promise positive results both for the proliferation of this kind of knowledge via simulation and for additional rehabilitative purposes.

It will be impossible to challenge all of Nozick's assumptions here. This chapter will not embark on any attempt at wholesale refutation. It will, however, consider some confusions to which the thought experiment may give rise, and try to suggest that there are several positive aspects of the experience machine scenario that Nozick hasn't considered at all.

First, recollect that Nozick's initial description of the experience machine suggests it may do even more than provide one with an experiential reality absolutely indistinguishable from real life. Although one will be bobbing about in a tank with electrodes attached to one's body, much like Neo in *The Matrix*, the programming may not be restricted simply to one's sensory experiences, as it was in the film: "Superduper neuropsychologists could stimulate your brain so that you would *think* and *feel* you were writing a great novel, or making a friend, or reading an interesting book" (Nozick 1974, 42: italics mine). This sounds more like a windowless Leibnizean monad than a Matrix scenario. Recall that Leibiniz's monads, some of which are rational minds, cannot be acted on from without. As Leibniz puts it, "According to this system bodies act as if (to suppose the impossible) there were no souls, and souls act as if there were no bodies, and both act as if each influenced the other" (Leibniz 2016, 82). Mental events occur according to a preestablished harmony that parallels the occurrence of bodily events. That is, events within the mind—perceptions, reflections, and all the flotsam of consciousness— unfold according to a preestablished pattern determined by God. Mental events or experiences develop out of their own nature, according to a preexisting program. Every thought, reflection, recollection, and emotion is determined in conjunction with an evolving array of sensory experiences. If Nozick's experience machine is a close relative of the Leibnizian monad, for which every so-called mental event is programmed in advance, that is quite different from the more familiar virtual reality scenario in which what is programmed falls strictly within the realm of appearances, while beliefs, feelings, and reflections are left to the agent's own devices.

Let us momentarily explore this more familiar VR scenario, which will be referred to henceforth as the Matrix scenario, in honor of the film of that name. Here we can have recourse to Locke's representative realism instead of Leibniz's monads. The premise in the *The Matrix* turns on our capacity to be deceived by appearances, and on the merely contingent match-up between appearance and reality. One's sensory experiences may be produced in the conventional way by physical objects in one's vicinity acting in concert with one's sensory apparatus, or they may be produced by whatever it is our brain does when we dream or hallucinate. In the case of *The Matrix*, sensory experiences are produced by a nefarious computer whose ultimate aim it is to delude all humanity about the nature of its physical surroundings. Most of what remains of humanity, it transpires, floats in vats with electrodes strategically attached to heads and bodies. Almost every existing individual is having a computer-created full-body hallucination, more or less akin to a dream. All sensory experiences—visual, olfactory, auditory, kinesthetic, gustatory—are but an illusion created by the machine. The Matrix is the virtual world that almost all inhabit, and it is presumably possible to communicate and interact with fellow inhabitants of the Matrix via mediated means, since the computer coordinates the hallucinations of its virtual inhabitants. It is worth noting, therefore, that Matrix scenarios need not present us with the same isolation that windowless monads impose. Interaction with other people would have to be mediated, but is a possibility. Further, the Matrix scenario offers the prospect of independent thought and independent action. One's dream body will move as one's will dictates. One's every thought and apparent movement is not determined from the start by some external agency.

Granted, a given sensory experience will have almost inevitable epistemic and (often) emotional concomitants. To have a sensory experience of a charging grizzly, whether in a dream or in reality, is almost always to believe a predator approaches, to think oneself endangered, and to feel fear. Other thoughts, however, are up for grabs. Some may notice an escape route. Others may not. Some may recollect something they've read about how to survive an encounter with such predators. Others may not. Some may cast about for a weapon. Others may not. Some may hurl a tempting bag of Fritos toward the bear in the hope of distracting it or try to make loud noises to frighten it. The full course of beliefs and feelings and recollections and impulses to action isn't determined in its entirety. However, in what will be referred to as the monad scenario, every aspect of one's consciousness is preprogrammed. In the Matrix scenario, only sensory experiences and the beliefs necessitated by these are determined in advance.

It is not entirely clear in the relevant passages from *Anarchy, State, and Utopia* which of the two scenarios Nozick has in mind. The sentence quoted above suggests that thoughts and feelings will be programmed, but it only refers to those thoughts and feelings that would be involved in one's being duped by appearances, as in the Matrix scenario. One might think and feel one was reading an interesting book because one was programmed to have the experience of seeing an arrangement of letters on a page or Kindle screen and, on account of that sensory experience, have the conventional understanding of their meaning. Or one might think and feel one was reading an interesting book because one was programmed to have sensory experiences of letters on pages and thereby a conventional understanding of them, and *also* programmed to have certain thoughts and interested feelings about what one understood the subject matter to be. One reason to think that Nozick may vacillate between the two positions or incline to the less deterministic matrix scenario is his concluding reflection regarding the implications of his thought experiment, which he says he believes "connect[s] surprisingly with issues about free will" (Nozick 1974, 45). By no stretch of the imagination could the connection between the monad scenario and issues about free will be considered surprising. While it may be that Nozick is inclined to think one scenario could collapse into the other for all intents and purposes, it seems important to note that the Matrix scenario offers less support for wholesale rejection of plugging into the experience machine, since aspects of identity and autonomy are arguably preserved.

In any case, it will be maintained here that even the most restrictive interpretation of Nozick, one that takes him to be presenting something like the monad scenario, still supports the contention that the experience machine could offer epistemic and moral benefits. In order to show this, some familiar arguments defending the cognitive and other benefits of literary fiction will be rehearsed. While there is considerable dispute about whether literary fiction can be regarded as a more-than-incidental source of propositional knowledge, there is at least some agreement that we engage in a process of imaginative simulation when engaged with fiction. For lack of a better descriptor, we "imagine what it is like" to undergo certain experiences, in addition to imagining *that* certain events transpire or that certain actions are performed. The argument here is that virtual worlds offer the same prospect for the acquisition of moral and other insights as fictional worlds, and offer much enhanced prospects for the kind of empathetic experience that can inform eventual conclusions about the experience of others and its ethical significance.

Nozick's argument proposes a permanent immersion in the experience machine, with a break every couple of years for reprogramming and reconsideration of experiential arcs. It is easier to make Nozick's case for aversion to immersion in virtual worlds if the immersion is permanent: a lifelong isolation from all but virtual others, where indirect contact with other vat dwellers, as depicted in many science fiction scenarios, is not an allowable option. It is more difficult by an order of magnitude to motivate aversion to participation in virtual scenarios of limited duration, since we do something of the sort already every time we read a novel or watch a film or indulge in a role-playing game (RPG). I will argue for the potential benefits of a temporary sojourn in the experience machine first, and close with some observations about points that could be advanced in defense of a long-term stay. While sporadic and incomplete, imaginative immersion in a work of fiction or an RPG involves the same detachment from the actual and the same investment in what is acknowledged at the outset to be nonactual as do the proposed experiencings of the dweller in the machine. There is a conscious and deliberate turning away from one's immediate spatio-temporal situation in favor of a scripted, imaginary one. In favor, that is, of one that is expertly devised at least in part by some external agency. With fictional narratives, of course, the turning away is a turning away of attention and the investment is in what one imagines (as well as the depictions and images that prompt that imagining). The difference between a reader of novels or player of games and the inhabitant of the machine is that the imaginative immersions of the former cannot be undertaken as a sort of life-replacement except in cases as extreme as they are unusual (e.g., so-called online gaming addiction, in which the gamer becomes so obsessed that he cuts back on food, sleep, and society in order to play). That is not, in any case, the point of playing the games in question, but a perversion of such pursuits.[1] And while there probably is room for a purely hedonistic or escapist account of the value of fiction and our engagement with it, just as there might be purely hedonistic or escapist reasons for choosing a life of bliss in the machine,[2] there exist a plethora of other reasons and motives for engagement with fiction, the majority of which apply equally well or can apply even more emphatically to immersion in virtual worlds.

While many temporary sojourns in the experience machine could just turn out to be forms of entertainment, this does not in the least rule out other more significant and meaningful prospects, any more than the existence of pulp fiction and daytime soaps and pornography has ruled out literature or theatrical artistry. Moreover, no reflective person could believe that enjoyment and insight must be mutually exclusive. Satisfaction and pleasure can accompany the profound as well as the frivolous. So the obvious prospect for entertainment value when we consider a market in virtual worlds shouldn't blind us to prospects of profundity and artistry and complexity that rival those of literature. Virtual reality, in other words, could be treated in some respects as a genre that has insightful and inspiring manifestations as well as low-brow instantiations. Since we can take the less inspired cases as a given, the purpose here is to canvass some prospects for insight and epistemic advantage.

Consider first a kind of virtual reality parallel to books and films and plays, in which we are nonparticipating observers of action, but with our observational powers and sensory access greatly enhanced and augmented. Instead of reading a description of a scene or watching images on the screen of a movie theater, one experiences the illusion of inhabiting the scene, and witnesses the action as a bystander. In "A Virtual View of a Slaughterhouse," Barbara King describes a 3D VR presentation called *iAnimal*, coproduced by Animal Equality and Condition One. She experienced this presentation at the Sundance Film Festival. The presentation is of a factory farm and pig slaughterhouse in Mexico. The VR setup in this case appears fairly primitive. There is a rotating chair and headset (providing the equivalent of 3D effects, peripheral vision, and surround sound). Even this modest sensory enhancement of ordinary film viewing turns out to have an enormous psychological impact:

> I was meant to use the chair to pan the 180-degree arc from my left to my right to take in the screen images fully.
>
> Suddenly, it wasn't a traditional film experience anymore.
>
> As I watched and twisted slowly back and forth, two pigs were driven roughly up a chute, where they stood against a barrier, side by side. A slaughterhouse worker drove a metal bolt stunner into their skulls. Both pigs went rigid and slumped. I had just witnessed the moment of their deaths, I thought.
>
> But I was wrong. The pigs soon regained some degree of consciousness. Their limbs in spasm, their bodies jerking on and on and on, they were bled out slowly on the slaughterhouse floor. In VR, you are there with them, at no remove, with no distancing mechanism available. You can't avoid what comes next, when the next pair of pigs is forced up the slope. (King 2016)

What is virtual in this case is simply proximity, yet that amendment alone is quite enough to intensify the impact of the presentation enormously. King points out that she has

> watched, read and taught about animal suffering in factory farms before. I knew it was bad in factory farms in the U.S., England, Europe, China and Latin America. Yet, something extra-powerful comes across in VR. The heightened visual closeness brings about heightened emotional attunement and, thus, the true extent of the cruelty to individual, sentient animals. (King 2016)

Such observations have a respectable philosophical history. As David Hume famously claimed, proximity (or its illusion) increases our capacity for fellow feeling and the likelihood of emotional response, especially morally freighted response, something he advises us to keep in mind before making over-hasty judgments:

[i]n general, all sentiments of blame or praise are variable, according to our situation of nearness or remoteness, with regard to the person blam'd or prais'd, and according to the present disposition of our mind. But these variations we regard not in our general decisions, but still apply the terms expressive of our liking or dislike, in the same manner, as if we remain'd in one point of view. Experience soon teaches us this method of correcting our sentiments, or at least, of correcting our language, where the sentiments are more stubborn and inalterable. Our servant, if diligent and faithful, may excite stronger sentiments of love and kindness than Marcus Brutus, as represented in history; but we say not upon that account, that the former character is more laudable than the latter. We know, that were we to approach equally near to that renown'd patriot, he wou'd command a much higher degree of affection and admiration. (Hume 1978, 582)

Even the kind of modest illusion that present technology can provide, without our having recourse to science fiction scenarios, is sufficient to demonstrate the intensification of moral, emotional, and empathetic response. The more complete the illusion, presumably, the stronger the reaction elicited. So there is a plausible prospect here for the same kinds of moral and emotional reactions that fictions can and are often intended to elicit, with the added intensity and impact that attaches to eyewitness experience. This is something that could prove to have considerable educational value, were underrepresented or neglected perspectives to be the focus of such attempts.

That is, our closest present-day analog to Nozick's experience machine could, in principle, boast most of the advantages to which imaginative immersion in literature could lay claim, with the caveat that sensory illusion could elicit reactions of increased intensity. It isn't clear, of course, how effectively existing literary or theatrical works could undergo a conversion to VR formats. Certain effects could well be hindered by the illusion of being a bystander. If we experience the illusion of, say, being in the same room when the enraged Othello accuses the blameless Desdemona, there would be immediate emotional complications that would hinder appreciation of the fictional state of affairs. It appears that the impulse to intervene would have to be much stronger, were the illusion of being an eyewitness complete. Whether the experience machine permitted one to throw a flagon of ale at Othello's head, or whether it simply inspired the impulse, the illusion of prospective personal agency consequent on virtual presence would change the apprehension of the work and the emotional reaction to it. Virtual presence undermines the kind of distant third-person observer stance that keeps the focus of attention strictly on fictional events. But that would not necessarily be a detriment for all literary and theatrical works. A virtual immersion in the slums of a Dickensian London or in a firefight with the Vietcong in a VR version of *Full Metal Jacket* could support and intensify authorial and directorial attempts to convey the horrific nature of certain experiences. Virtual reality would clearly lend itself to some kinds of fictional depiction, particularly that attempting to convey what it is like to undergo a given experience, either by providing a sensory illusion of what it is like to have that experience (e.g., visual and auditory sensa of being under fire) or by eliciting intensified empathy by providing an illusion of being an eyewitness to another individual's travail. There are prospects, even for the kind of VR presently available, for the development of an entire genre especially geared to exploit such strengths.

Even the possibility of being a virtual participant in the fictional action would not take us too far afield from familiar terrain, given the popularity of role-playing games (RPGs) and live-action role-playing (LARP). If we consider full sensory immersion, on a par with that depicted in *The Matrix*, there remain the same powerful prospects for moral and emotional engagement intensified by virtual proximity, coupled with the added feature of mobility and virtual action. Here the extent of the hypothetical programming, as canvassed at the beginning of this chapter, becomes an issue. We could assume that, as in *The Matrix* and similar fiction, there are nearly limitless possibilities for virtual action that are more or less up to us. Thus, the inclination to lift a virtual arm or take a virtual step would be succeeded by virtually lifting one's arm or virtually taking a step. One could choose where to look, when to turn, where to walk. If this were the way virtual worlds worked, they would offer great opportunities for exploration, in addition to prospects for moral and emotional learning on analogy with narrative art.

There are 3D virtual tours of exotic locales everywhere on the internet. Imagine how much more rewarding they could be if they were truly virtual. In addition, much literary and cinematic art is valued especially for its ability to evoke a sense of place, as, for instance, was the case with the superb televised rendering of Hillary Mantel's *Wolf Hall*, in which every scene called to mind a period painting, even down to the color of the shadows. A virtual immersion in such scenes would be magical. One could walk the streets of Venice, visit the museums of Florence, loll in a café in Krakow's old town square drinking excellent beer, or walk directly into some period of the past without paying the price of a ticket or being put to the trouble of constructing a time machine. Simply as devices that enabled one to learn about other places in the world or various periods in the past, experience machines would be unparalleled as educational tools.

Yet if the experience machine's program included *all* sensory experiences, this could very well be taken to include bodily and kinesthetic sensations of every kind. One would inhabit a virtual body over the actions of which one had no control, though one would feel its pains and exertions, experience the adrenalin high when it ran, taste the ice cream in which it chose to indulge, and so on. This would be more or less like being an invisible passenger in someone's life while still having to infer what she or he believed and thought (though perhaps it would be more obvious in certain instances what was felt because of the felt physiological concomitants of emotion). It would still leave room for empathy and reflection, but would restrict the participant to a single point of vantage, similarly to a first-person novel in which the narrator expounds only on her experience of the external world rather than on her inner life.

An experience machine conceived along such lines would be only a step removed from the full-blown Leibnizean monad, all the thoughts and feelings and reflections of which would be programmed as well. What would be the point, some might ask, in surrendering one's critical faculties to the machine wholesale? What could be gained from such an endeavor? The short answer is privileged knowledge, direct awareness of what some life experiences are like, something that less immersive approaches to virtual reality that permit one the degree of independence requisite for reflection can never fully attain. Consider that empathy only involves the imaginative adoption of the perspective of another (as one imagines believing and feeling and being placed as they are). This is as close as literature or, indeed, real life can get us to knowing what something is like for someone else, or of having a genuine experience of what their life situation is like, and would be like to undergo.

To empathize, one first (via observation of an individual's behavior and situation, and via inferences made on that basis) forms beliefs about the beliefs, experiences, and feelings of another. One then imagines believing and feeling as the other does, and imagines being placed as the other is placed. Empathizing with fictional characters is very similar—one simply imagines believing what it is fictional that the character believes (or imagines believing what a person would believe if the person were placed as the character is placed). These emotional experiences bring us closer than most others to an awareness of another's experience at second hand, but because that awareness is acquired at second hand it is not entirely reliable. We may draw the wrong inferences on the basis of actual or fictional or virtual observation. We may not be observant enough. We may have biases that prevent us from drawing the proper inferences. Emotional contagion and emotional simulation are a somewhat different matter, since they involve almost no reflection (and thereby no mistaken inferences). Elaine Hatfield defines emotional contagion as "[t]he tendency to automatically mimic and synchronize expressions, vocalizations, postures and movements with those of another person and, consequently, to converge emotionally" (Hatfield, Cacioppo, and Rapson 1992, 153–54). Emotional contagion and simulation are, in a manner of speaking, virtual experiences of another's experience. Although Hatfield at one point describes them as "pale reflections" of that other person's experience (Hatfield, Cacioppo, and Rapson 1992, 96), they can pretty clearly provide a lot of information about how someone else's experience might feel from the inside. However, the kind of first-person VR experience being contemplated here could, of course, prove more effective than a "pale reflection" when it came to verisimilitude.

The monad scenario entertained earlier eliminates any possible difficulty with mistaken empathetic inferences or vitiated intensity. By programming the user's experiences and mental states in their entirety, the monad generator has the potential for providing absolutely precise understanding of what an experience is like for someone who undergoes it in the actual world. Other, less rigid implementations of the experience machine could do the same when it came to single physical events. Virtual experiences could be carefully programmed to replicate sensations or pains that an actual set of physical experiences would make us feel. So a direct experience of what it is like to run up a set of stairs very quickly, or what it is like to be caught up in an angry mob, or what it is like to be in the middle of a firefight is available via all the canvassed virtual means. But knowledge of what it is like to be a slave, or what it is like to be a member of an oppressed minority, or what it is like to be a suicide bomber—these kinds of knowledge would involve too much guesswork on the part of the experiencer in any but the monad model of the machine. To be a slave isn't just to be in a certain set of oppressive physical circumstances. It is also to have a certain lived history and collection of recollected experiences with sets of behavioral dispositions and emotional inclinations that have emerged from these. We might have propositional knowledge about aspects of such things, but a direct and immediate understanding of what it is like to be in such circumstances, with such a history, and with those dispositions, would still elude us. Except, of course, if the monad programming scenario contemplated above is possible.

If it were possible to extract and utilize the thoughts and recollections and other mental states of someone who had actually experienced the circumstances one wished to simulate, then it would be straightforwardly possible to acquire direct knowledge of what it was like to live through that particular circumstance from the experience machine.[3] Even the most rigidly deterministic conception of the experience machine offers some fascinating prospects for the acquisition of knowledge about the experiences and feelings of others in a wide array of situations, especially if good-faith efforts at achieving verisimilitude were made. Certain heady if impractical ideas come naturally to mind, such as that of inviting politicians to experience what being on the receiving end of some particular policy they intend to inflict on the populace would be like, or offering a reduced prison sentence for violent criminals if they agree to virtually undergo what they've inflicted on another. (There is a frequent tendency on the part of perpetrators to indulge in self-exoneration by imagining that their victims were more complicit and engaged and responsible for what was done to them than unsympathetic courts allowed. An experience machine could disabuse them forever of such suppositions.)

In general, virtually acquired knowledge about what undergoing particular experiences is like could prove extraordinarily useful: as preparation for difficult future tasks, as an aid to understanding people with whom one will have to interact, as a familiarizer with terrain one will have to traverse. Instead of regarding Nozick's experience machine as an obliterator of identity and agency, one can harness it to laudable ends, much as some of the narrative arts are harnessed. Any variation of the experience machine shows promise as a stimulus to empathy and to the acquisition of both propositional and experiential knowledge.

Even a permanent residence within the confines of the machine can be seen from the foregoing to have advantages. The acquisition of knowledge can be valued for its own sake. In the monad scenario, one could come to know and understand what had eluded one in one's former existence. One would, free of other cares, be able to pursue hitherto undreamed-of courses of study. And the monad scenario would guarantee that one could finally really know and understand all that one had ever wanted to. The Matrix scenario is even more promising, in leaving room for at least a certain kind of discovery and invention. One's biennial respites for reprogramming and reconfiguration of future virtual experiences could include the opportunity to convey those ideas and discoveries and inventions to others, for the benefit of the world. An existence of uninterrupted research with the best virtual facilities and equipment, with no financial or physical impediments to or distractions from the course of study at hand? Some would jump at the chance. Nozick underestimates the attractiveness of having time to think.

NOTES

1. For instance, in the fifth edition of the *Diagnostic and Statistical Manual of Mental Disorders* (DSM-5), Internet Gaming Disorder is identified in Section III as a condition warranting more clinical research and experience before it might be considered for inclusion as a formal disorder. The point is, however, that it is taken seriously enough to warrant consideration (American Psychiatric Association, 2016).

2. It is evident that Nozick seriously underestimates the extent to which a life in the machine might appear in the light of an attractive alternative to life outside it. Absent the kind of concern for the well-being of loved ones that could prove a deal breaker, life in the machine could seem preferable to a life of loneliness and isolation, or a life of extreme privation, or even (especially!) a life of excruciating boredom.

3. Since experience machines of this type are a matter of wild speculation in any case, we will set aside the possibility of disturbing propaganda (e.g., Happy Slave experience machine programs, in which one has a blissful time being treated as a beloved cocker spaniel in need of discipline). Just as any work of fiction can convey false information and endorse repellant perspectives, so could the experience machine. The only concern is that it could do a more effective job, in that one would be made to adopt the problematic perspectives instead merely of being invited to entertain them in imagination.

Chapter Six

Figuring Out Who Your Real Friends Are

Alexis Elder

In Nozick's original introduction to the experience machine, he invites the reader to imagine that it would "stimulate your brain so that you would think and feel you were," among other things, "making a friend" (Nozick 1974, 42). He takes it to be intuitive that this would not be as desirable as *actually* making one.

Nozick's original thought experiment works by asking us to imagine an entire simulated world. But it can also offer a model for thinking about more restricted domains.

In this chapter, I examine two contexts in which technology gives us experiences of a particular kind mentioned but not developed in the original example: friendship. I use a variation on Nozick's thought experiment to show why we ought to be concerned with virtual friendships. However, I identify limits to what counts as virtual. Although critics have charged that both Facebook "friends" and social robots provide only simulations of friendship, I argue that they are importantly different. While sociable robots offer mere friendship-experience without the distinctive value of genuine friends, it is incorrect to make the same claim about social media. One kind of technology is like Nozick's experience machine. The other changes the appearances we associate with friends but preserves real friendship.

We do not need to go very far, these days, to encounter machines that force us to confront the value of appearances and experiences relative to that of reality in a number of domains. In particular, social robotics and social media are not just imaginary but real emerging technologies that force us to ask questions about what friendship is, and whom you should count as a real friend.

For example, many theories of friendship, especially those in the Aristotelian tradition, take shared activities to be crucial to the phenomenon. People must, such theorists assert, share activities and not merely harbor mutual goodwill in order to be friends. But what this involves and to what extent such activities can be technologically mediated is a contested issue (one that will be taken up in part 3). Social technologies invite us to ask what is involved in being a particular kind of person, a friend. Can you be friends with a social robot? Can you be friends with someone with whom you only, or even primarily, interact on social media? And they make us think long and hard about what it means to say that a machine limits us to "a man-made reality. . . . No deeper or more important than that which people can construct." This may be a clear limitation when it comes to interactions with some natural phenomena, but it is people themselves that presumably construct and constitute even ordinary social relationships, so it is not always obvious what the distinction between constructed and "natural" would mean in the case of friendships.

Taking up Nozick's invitation to "fill lacks suggested by earlier machines," I conclude that one kind of technology, social robotics, creates situations relevantly like that presented by Nozick's original experience machine. The other, social media, despite recent criticisms and widespread worries about the reality of social media "friends," preserves real friendship. Our understanding of the nature and value of social relationships is thus advanced by considering emerging technologies through the lens that Nozick has provided.

PART 1: EXPERIENCE AND REALITY IN FRIENDSHIP

In the beginning of his discussion of friendship in the *Nicomachean Ethics*, Aristotle invites the reader to consider the value of friendship with a thought experiment that structurally resembles Nozick's experience machine. He posits a choice between a world in which a person has all the goods and desirables except for friendship, and one that includes friends. "No one," he asserts, "would choose to live without friends even if he had all the other goods" (Aristotle 1999, 119). He takes this to show that friendship is a constitutive element of human well-being, and necessary for our happiness. Other goods cannot substitute for its absence, and its value cannot, thereby, derive from them. Insofar as we want to live good lives, then, we have reasons to make friends, to be friends ourselves, and to secure *real* friendship (whatever that means) as an end in itself and not merely seek out the appearances of friendship as a means to other ends.

As in Nozick's example, we are asked to consider a choice between lives, one of which provides some of the goods we seem to value but lacks others, while the other provides what is lacking. The resulting intuitions are lever-aged for an argument that the missing ingredient that drives our preferences is an important value.

If one is persuaded by Aristotle's case, then friendship looks like a neces-sary component of the good life. But what is friendship, and what would satisfy this requirement?

If friendship is essentially experiential, then Nozick is wrong to assert that it would be better to really make a friend than to experience the "making" of one in the experience machine. But I think we can make headway by imagin-ing another such choice.

Suppose you are given a choice between two lives that will be, you are assured, experientially identical (or at least substantially similar in relevant ways). Once you make the choice, you will not remember having done so. It is only now, at the moment of choice, that you are aware of their major difference.

In one life, you will believe on the basis of your experiences that you have several close and intimate friendships. However, your "friends" will all be paid actors. They will bear you no ill will, and are bound by terms of their contracts not to exploit your trust in them for any additional financial gain (besides the payment they earn in so acting). Call this the *Truman Show* option.

In the other life, you will believe on the basis of your experiences that you have several close and intimate friendships. Your friends will be motivated by normal "friendly" concerns: care for you and concern for you, pleasure in your company, appreciation for the care and concern you show them, and so forth. Call this the *Genuine* option.

I predict that, as with Nozick's original example, most of us prefer the life where companions' appearances and experiences match reality. Friendship, the thing we value, requires reciprocal valuing. This means it requires the mutual engagement of multiple agents, each of which is both capable of and actually engaging in such valuing.

Doing so is consistent with and contributes to an account of an important but somewhat opaque feature of friendship: shared identity.

Many think that friendship somehow unifies or involves shared identity—an idea most famously found in Aristotle's claim that close friends are "other selves" (for instance, in Aristotle 1999, at 1161b30–35, 1166a30–35, and 1170b5–10). This is sometimes taken to imply something about our attitude toward our friends, as when Nancy Sherman says that friendship involves "a relaxing of one's own sense of boundaries and control. It is acknowledging a sense of union or merger" (Sherman 1993, 282). Put this way, shared identity seems to implicate only the experiential part of friendship, which (as shown above) does not seem to be all that we value. But relaxed boundaries and "merging" might seem to be inapt descriptors even of the experience, let alone the value, of close friendship. For example, mutual respect might seem to be a characteristic we value in the best friendships—not a merging of individuals, but each ascribing value to what is different about the other person. And healthy boundaries might seem to be an important element of good relationships. Overbearing parents and abusive spouses may thrive on lowered boundaries, but friendships seem good when friends recognize them, and a good theory of friendship should be able to model this.

Others take the shared identity of friendship (especially that in the Aristotelian versions) to involve great similarity between friends. Dean Cocking and Jeanette Kennett caricature this as the "mirrors" account of friendship (Cocking and Kennett 1998). But this again seems to run counter to much of what we think is valuable about friendship, especially the ways that complementary differences can enrich our relationships. A cautious and adventurous person, for example, might thrive together in a friendship because of, rather than despite, their differences, especially if each appreciates the other's perspective without necessarily adopting it for themselves (Williams 1981).

I propose that we resolve the difficulty by adopting a new way to think of shared identity. We should think of friendships as being like composite objects—specifically, as being like organisms, composed of interdependent but distinct and different organs, which fit and work together to compose a whole. The identity shared between friends, then, is the identity of parts to a whole. The different parts of a car (such as the wheels, bumper, fender, and engine) can, in the right arrangement, jointly compose a composite object: for example, a Toyota Camry. This approach is true to many of our ordinary ways of speaking (for example, we talk about doing something "for the sake of the friendship" or "valuing our friendships," which can sound like we take friendships to be relatively robust entities worthy of consideration), and explains what we value when we care about friendship in a way that can explain our different intuitions about the apparent value of *Truman Show* versus *Genuine*. In *Genuine*, there is a real friendship composed of people whose values and emotional states are interdependent, while in *Truman Show* the dependency only runs one way.

Friendships, then, are plausibly taken to be composite objects composed of emotionally interdependent, mutually valuing agents, each of whom values not just the other person, but the composite object that the friends jointly compose.

PART 2: ROBOT FRIENDS?

One burgeoning area in robotics is the field known as social robotics: robots designed to fulfill specifically social needs and desires. Within the field of social robotics, one major focus is the design of robots to provide social experiences for seniors. Elderly populations in many societies face shrinking cohorts, restricted involvement in many sectors of the public sphere (such as the workplace), reduced mobility, and other obstacles to developing or maintaining a robust social network. This reduced social network has important consequences for their well-being, and so robots are being introduced to address the perceived need for social interaction. One such robot is Paro, a machine that has even been approved as a therapeutic medical device by the FDA (Ponte 2014). The use of robots to care for seniors has received widespread attention among researchers in robot ethics (See, for example, Grodzinsky et al. 2015; Misselhorn et al. 2013; Parks 2010; Sharkey 2014; Sharkey and Sharkey 2010 and 2012; Sorell and Draper 2014; Sparrow and Sparrow 2006; Turkle 2011; Vallor 2011; and Whitby 2011). For my purposes, this application makes an especially fruitful target of inquiry because of the large body of evidence that has been amassed about the impact of these robot companions on the humans with whom they are partnered.

This evidence suggests that social robots can confer, at least on geriatric patients, many of the instrumental benefits associated with friendship, especially those associated with the alleviation of loneliness. (Of course, it is possible to have friends and yet feel lonely. But one important effect of friendship can be that it helps us to feel less lonely. And, plausibly, the feeling of loneliness itself is a cue that we can benefit from social interaction, even if it is not a perfectly reliable indicator.)

Loneliness feels unpleasant in its own right. But it can also negatively impact people's health in a variety of ways. For example, one group of researchers found that an "extensive social network seems to protect against dementia," and that even "infrequent social contacts" can help reduce the occurrence of dementia "if such contacts were experienced as satisfying" (Fratiglioni et al. 2000, 1315). The incidence of Alzheimer's is also correlated with "perceived isolation": the rate "more than doubled in lonely persons compared with persons who were not lonely" (Wilson et al. 2007, 234).

Social robots, by providing interactive experiences for seniors, seem to produce many of the same positive effects on patients as more conventional social interactions. Wada and Shibata introduced Paro robots to elderly patients, and found that "urinary tests showed that the reactions of the subjects' vital organs to stress were improved after the introduction of the robots" (Wada and Shibata 2006, 3966). Tamura et al. had patients with severe dementia interact with another social robot. These patients, they report, "recognized that AIBO [the robot they introduced to the patients] was a robot. However, once we dressed AIBO, the patients perceived AIBO as either a dog or a baby. Nevertheless, the presentation of AIBO resulted in positive outcomes for the severe dementia patients, including increased communication between the patients and AIBO" (Tamura et al. 2004, 83). In a side-by-side comparison, Banks and Banks (2008) found that robots and living therapy dogs had comparable positive impacts on nursing home patients, and dogs ("man's best friend") are often thought to offer many of the positive experiences associated with friendship.

The ethical concerns raised by robot ethicists are myriad, and include the potential for such robot companions to substitute for rather than supplement human interaction (for example, in Sharkey and Sharkey 2010, Sparrow and Sparrow 2006), the deceptiveness inherent in misleading vulnerable populations by presenting them with emotionally appealing facsimiles of familiar sources of social interactions (Grodzkinsky et al. 2015), and the seductive appeal of "friends" who are more patient, less demanding, and more selfless than messy, complicated *human* interactions (Turkle 2011). But each of these concerns presupposes that these robots are not, in fact, real friends. One can imagine the reasonable skeptic saying something like, "look, if Grandma is happy with her robot friend, who are we to complain or to judge? After all, different people are frequently satisfied by very different kinds of friends. In fact, one might think it is a paradigmatic case of a situation where subjective preferences rather than uniform objective standards *should* guide who counts as a friend to *me*."

But the *Truman Show* thought experiment from the last section suggests something is missing, and that we ought to say of social robots that they only appear to be friends. Real friendship, of the sort we find most desirable, involves reciprocal caring of genuine agents capable of valuing. Robots in the far future might in fact be capable of such valuing (Data from *Star Trek: The Next Generation* might be one such example). But the current robots are sufficiently simple and deterministic that their value as "friends" derives solely from their ability to provoke in us the experience of engaging in a friendly interaction, and not the genuine article. Note that by "simple" I do not mean something on the order of a young child, or a complex organism like a dog, creatures who can value and desire and learn, and with whom it is reasonable to at least ask whether friendship would be possible. Today's robots are nowhere near that sophisticated. They are more like a complex thermostat or, at best, a cell phone—they respond deterministically to specific inputs, according to relatively simple programming. Their appearances may tend to lead us to respond to them as if they were living organisms, but what lies beneath the surface is something quite different. While ingenious in their way, they are not the sorts of things that can co-constitute a friendship with us. What we learned from the *Truman Show* thought experiment was that experiences of friendship are *not* all that matters.

The exception to the claim that social robots merely simulate rather than offer genuine friendship may be telepresence robots. These robots are remotely controlled by human agents on the other end of the communication channel. Although still in early stages of development, they may someday allow grandparents to play with their grandchildren from thousands of miles away, help doctors interact with patients in foreign countries, and help friends to collaborate without sharing the same space. What is different about telepresence robots, as opposed to those guided by internal programming, is that their primary function seems to be to extend genuine human connections (like telephones, or email) rather than simulating, substituting for, or replacing human interactions.

It is the difference between extending and pretending that informs the next section of this chapter.

PART 3: FACEBOOK FRIENDS?

The rise of new communication technologies includes an ever-growing array of social media platforms, from the readily recognizable, like Facebook and Twitter, to newcomers like Ello, Twitch, Yik Yak, and Shots. These provide venues for computer-mediated interaction between individuals, whether via text, video, images, links, casual games, files of various kinds, or a combination thereof. *Computer* mediation, in this context, includes applications that run on various smartphones, making their presence ubiquitous in many technologically advanced societies.

The prevalence of social media in the social landscape is undeniable. More controversial is what this does for friendship. As early as 2000, Dean Cocking and Steve Matthews argued that internet-based friendships are "unreal," claiming that friendship requires face-to-face interaction to be real, a sentiment echoed in various ways by others more recently (for instance, in Fröding and Peterson 2012). In recent years, the debate has shifted somewhat, since usage patterns of computer-mediated communication technologies have changed. In the early days of computer-mediated connections, most social contacts via such channels were "online-only" connections. Today, social media connections are much more likely to be people one knows from other areas of one's life: old neighbors, classmates, co-workers, family, and so forth. However, concerns about the possibility of friendship *via* such channels remain.

Some argue that the information channels afforded by such platforms are impoverished, relative to the rich multimodal communication that is possible face to face, where tone of voice, facial expression, body posture, and setting can all contribute volumes to the interaction. This criticism may have seemed especially sharp when most social media platforms were text based, but two responses, one conceptual, the other technological, seem to blunt its force. The first is that textual communication can be quite rich and evocative (see: novels, poems, prose), even when brief. This requires that one be a skilled writer or careful reader, but perhaps this is not so different from thinking that good face-to-face conversations require that one be articulate and a good listener. The second response is that as bandwidth gets cheaper and smart-phone cameras more commonplace, newer social media platforms are increasingly incorporating images, audio, and video, thus enriching communication in the ways it was previously cited as lacking. Furthermore, users are increasingly communicating across a range of platforms, with closer connections using more communication channels (Broadbent 2012), thus allowing for the deficiencies of any one communication channel to be compensated for by others. The question is not, any longer, "Can I understand a person based on what they say on Twitter?" but rather "Can I understand a person based on their social media presence across a range of platforms, from Facetime to Facebook to Snapchat to Instagram?" The latter might much more plausibly be answered with "yes" than the former, with each medium contributing another facet to our understanding of a person, and each communication channel providing a different insight: into what they find worth photographing, what they find funny or trivial, how they look and sound, what they find worth sharing widely, and what they say to only a select few.

Even given the existence of these increased communicative abilities, one might worry because social media platforms give users so much control over the messages they send. This allows them to frame and edit their communications in a way that circumvents many unconscious cues that an audience can find revealing about a person's frame of mind. But it is far from clear that a more reflective and refined message is *less* revealing of a person than an off-the-cuff response (Briggle 2008), and furthermore, even in online interactions, people turn out to be fairly good at picking up on word choice, phrasing, and framing choices as revelatory of a person's intentions (Wallace 1999).

Many concerns seem to be motivated by a more general worry about the possibility for deceptiveness via computer-mediated communication, whether the deception is taken to be deliberate or accidental, fueled by an innate desire for attention or validation, or a more calculated attempt to profit at another's expense. This worry is enhanced by our experiences with the difficulty of interpreting ambiguous communications, such as puzzling out what the sender meant with a cryptic text message. This can lead to a general unease or lack of trust in computer-mediated communications. But I think that much of this results from overconfidence in face-to-face interactions, or at best, from comparing the worst of computer-mediated interactions to the best face-to-face ones. Ambiguity is hardly absent from face-to-face interactions. And deception is ubiquitous among human exchanges generally. Many skilled manipulators even exploit the immediacy of face-to-face exchanges to facilitate in their deception, in a way that is difficult to pull off online, where the recipient has the luxury of time to consider what is said and where much of the communication that takes place leaves a digital "paper trail." For example, despite the widespread panic over internet predators, most child molestation is perpetrated by close face-to-face friends and acquaintances of victims' families (Minnesota Department of Corrections 2009). Rather than think that the possibility for deception and distrust undermine the possibility of online friendship, it seems to me that a working theory of friendship should recognize and incorporate the potential for deception generally, and allow that friendships can thrive despite our potential to be less than honest. The best friendships require honesty, but they also need trust.

One common concern is the distraction posed by the constant presence of social media, which some fear is a negative impact on face-to-face interactions. The clichéd image is that of people sitting around a table, interacting with their phones instead of each other. This presents a bleak view of social media as something that, even if innocuous considered in and of itself, is bad because it degrades the quality of our other interactions. But odd as it may sound, I want to say a bit in defense of this phenomenon. One of the things social media does is allow us to interact with others, regardless (in many cases) of location. This broadens our choices considerably, letting us interact not just with those immediately available, but everyone with whom we'd want to converse who also wants to engage with us. Put this way, the fact that people sometimes choose computer-mediated communication with a more desirable conversation partner over a face-to-face exchange with a co-located but less-desirable companion looks less irrational. The problem is not that face-to-face exchanges generally are corrupted by the seductive appeal of the smartphone screen, but that given a wider range of choice about conversational partners and social connections, people exercise that power of choice in ways that sometimes prioritize based on things other than physical proximity.

Relatedly, one might worry about what could be lost in the transition from face-to-face interactions to computer-mediated ones. We are, after all, not merely social animals, but physical ones, for whom physical affection can be an important part of the good life. Even shared physical rituals, like eating together, seem deeply important to us—consider the person who goes out to a coffee shop to work rather than studying at home in order to spend time in the presence of others, even others one may not know. My response here is two-pronged, and grants the importance of physical presence and interaction in the good life. First, the fact that a particular interaction is computer-mediated need not mean one's life as a whole lacks physical co-presence with others. In fact, research suggests that people with a great deal of computer-mediated interaction also spend more time interacting with others face to face (Wellman et al. 2001; Ellison et al. 2007; Rainie et al. 2006; Ito et al. 2008).

Speaking specifically to the issue of rituals, the thought that engagement with social media disrupts rituals such as family dinners seems to indicate another potentially serious cost. While I do not mean to downplay the importance of such rituals, nor exonerate social media users of the responsibility to exercise good judgment and etiquette, it would also be foolish to ignore social media's potential to provide new venues for socially reinforcing rituals. From wishing far-flung friends "Happy birthday!" on Facebook, to sending good-morning or goodnight Snaps to loved ones, social media platforms provide an array of ways to ritually reconnect with our loved ones, a phenomenon documented by the anthropologist Stefana Broadbent (Broadbent 2012, 134–35).

Yet another complaint has to do with the shallowness, superficiality, or generic nature of communication via social media. A "like," thumbs-up, "heart," or hashtag makes one's contribution easily aggregable, but perhaps at the expense of individualized communication. But this seems to me to miss two points. One is that much of face-to-face communication is in fact highly ritualized and even formulaic ("Hi, how are you?" "Fine, and you?" "Good!") and conveys little in the way of personalized information. It might just be a fact about us that sometimes the connection rather than the content is what matters. Rituals help us reinforce such connections. Social media designs and use may reflect this basic fact about sociality. The second point is that many if not most platforms also allow for individually crafted messages, whether in the form of comments, original posts, or (as with Snapchat) drawing and layering images and text, and the rising popularity of applications such as Snapchat that offer bespoke and individualized message-crafting shows both that it is possible for social media to offer nongeneric forms of interaction and that users value this.

Given my reliance on Aristotle's contributions throughout, one objection that draws on his work is of particular interest. A number of Aristotelian theorists have criticized social media's potential to support real friendship by explicit appeal to Aristotle's insistence that the best friends share lives, or live together. Shannon Vallor, for example, introduces a "distinction between sharing lives and sharing about lives" (Vallor 2012, 196), while Nicholas Munn distinguishes between communication and activity in order to separate out arenas where only communication is possible (a characteristic he attributes to social media platforms) from those where shared activity, including shared living, is possible: "I take communication to be the planning of activity, the sharing of ideas, the development of procedures and so on, while activity involves putting the things discussed into practice," he says (Munn 2012, 4). That is, social media facilitates sharing *about* lives, which can superficially look like sharing lives, and so superficially resembles friendship. But because friends cannot really live together online, social media interactions cannot constitute a core component of the best friendships. While many of the criticized features of social media discussed above are indisputably elements of communication, perhaps an inchoate form of this objection lies at their heart: that *all* they enable is communication, and not shared living: sharing pictures of lunch, rather than having lunch together.

But Aristotle's own account of what shared living consists in does not clearly support this concern, and reflecting on why it does not may shed light on why we should take computer-mediated interaction seriously as a source of friendship. About the shared life, he says,

> The excellent person is related to his friend in the same way as he is related to himself, since a friend is another himself. Therefore, just as his own being is choiceworthy for him, his friend's being is choiceworthy for him in the same or a similar way. We agreed that someone's own being is choiceworthy because he perceives that he is good, and this sort of perception is pleasant in itself. He must, then, perceive his friend's being together [with his own], and he will do this when they live together and share conversation and thought. For in the case of human beings what seems to count as living together is this sharing of conversation and thought, not sharing the same pasture, as in the case of grazing animals. (1170b/p. 150, *EN*.)

Social media clearly permit us both to perceive our friends' lives and to facilitate sharing thought and conversation. In rejecting the idea that living together requires grazing in the same field, and explicitly listing conversation as paradigmatic of (human) shared living, he seems to reject the communication/activity distinction invoked above. And perhaps we should as well. Communicating with our friends, sharing how our days are going, and exchanging thoughts and ideas seems to be at the heart of social media users' activity, an activity in which users choose to engage even over "grazing in the same field" with immediate neighbors. Rather than assume that this is because we must be misled or seduced into such choices by the siren song of technology, perhaps it is because conversation and thought and perceiving how our objects of concern are doing—by their own lights—is what matters most to us. That might not be such a terrible thing.

Unlike in the case of social robots, the *Truman Show* thought experiment does not seem to be a substitute of mere experience for valuable reality in the way Nozick identifies. There is no principled reason to think that the people with whom one interacts on social media do not genuinely care about one. It is possible that social media connections are lying, or misrepresenting themselves or their motives by accident, but that is a risk of social interaction generally and not something specific to social media. In fact, given the wide range of possible interactions enabled by social media, it might be evidence that social media users interact because they find each other to be intrinsically worthy of concern, more so than the relationships of convenience or utility so commonplace in day-to-day living—as no less than Aristotle observed, in pointing out that so-called friendships of utility and pleasure (instrumental relationships) far outnumber the highest-caliber and most intimate friendships, which he called friendships of virtue. Evidence in support of this hypothesis can be found in the fact that, despite (in many cases) hundreds or thousands of online contacts and possible connections on any given social media platform, most of our interactions on social media are with a relatively small number of contacts—between two and ten, depending on the application (Broadbent 2012).

To return to the organism account of friendship sketched earlier: emotional interdependence and sustained patterns of interaction can be found via social media as well as face to face, with the added bonus that we enjoy a greater range of possible connections (even though in practice we often adhere to the Aristotelian advice to limit our closest circle of friends to those we can share lives with fruitfully). Social media still enables genuine connection of valuing agents who reciprocally care about each other—the form of connection just looks a bit different.

CONCLUSION

My conclusions about social technology, then, are mixed. Social robotics can provide experiences with many of the same effects as friendship, but not friendship itself. Social media, by contrast, facilitates real friendship but sometimes changes the experiences, in ways requiring us to reflect on what counts as a relevant similarity or difference between digital and face-to-face interaction.

Nozick's way of framing the appearance-reality distinction's relevance to questions of value can help us in both cases to navigate the evolving ethical landscape presented by emerging social technologies. In particular, Nozick's emphasis on the role of choice between imagined worlds as a tool for informing us about what we value, combined with a trust that these choices can inform us about the nature of what we value, gives us reason to be cautious of misleading others who cannot spot the differences between such worlds (as in the case of therapeutic companionate robots for geriatric patients). At the same time, Nozick's argument counsels us to take seriously users' preferences in social interactions, rather than dismissing them out of hand as naive or ill informed because they look different from the social exchanges to which we were formerly accustomed.

Real friends are those people we value, who value us in turn, and with whom we share concern for sustained interactions, conversations, and involvement in each other's lives. Technologies can assist with this, but it is important for us to retain a clear sense of what we are interested in facilitating.

Chapter Seven

Welcome to the Achievement Machine: Or, How to Value and Enjoy Pointless Things

Grant Tavinor

Last year I spent a lot of time mining for diamonds, building blocky houses and forts, and breeding sheep, cows, and chickens. I explored and mapped a world, discovered ancient ruins, and met exotic but strangely inarticulate peoples. I battled monsters: shambling and groaning zombies, clattering skeletons, and silent green fiends who had the bothersome habit of creeping up behind me and exploding. I also invested a great deal of effort into opening a portal to another dimension and preparing for a battle with a fearsome dragon who lived there. The battle, when it finally came, was an epic affair: under the purple skies we fought—I with my magic bow and sword, the dragon with its deadly breath—until finally I threw down my enemy on the mountainside. With a display of brilliant surging lightning the dragon's energy dissipated through the plane, leaving in its place a portal that allowed me to travel back to my own land, and then back to my own home.

At a recent conference when I told a fellow philosopher of my activities, his response was to the point:

"You really do waste a lot of time!"

This led to me to reflect that a frequent criticism of video games, and one personally familiar to me, is that video games are *pointless* things. In his criticism, my philosophical colleague presumably had in mind that such games, and their play, achieve nothing of value. While this disapproval might have been the occasion for some personal anxiety about what I was doing with my life, it also raised the basic question of whether the criticism is a reasonable one: Are video games pointless or valueless activities? Moreover, what do such claims even mean? What is it to say that video games are pointless?

This is a chapter in a collection about the significance of Robert Nozick's famous experience machine thought experiment, and so I should explain the relevance of my leisure time anxieties to that issue. Video games may be the closest thing we now have to an experience machine of the kind envisaged by Nozick. The similarities are quite striking: video games offer many of the experiences and pleasures afforded by the real world, though in a virtual way. Some games specialize in providing virtual worlds in which to explore and achieve; to forge kingdoms, climb mountains, and wander through dark forests; or build monuments to your virtually inflated ego.

There are clear differences between video games and the experience machine, of course. For one thing, frequently the existential situations of such worlds are dire, and one spends time struggling for meager resources, and fending off a violent death. If these games provide a version of Nozick's experience machine, it is one in which the moral nature of the world is almost the opposite envisaged by Nozick: life is nasty, brutish, and short (it is a puzzle then, why players choose to play in these worlds!). Also, the experiences afforded by the virtual worlds of video games are not indistinguishable from those of the real world, because games provide only limited sensory channels to their artificial worlds, comprising audio-visual depictions, and sometimes very limited tactile or haptic feedback (Tavinor 2009, 61–70). And while Virtual Reality systems such as Sony's VR headset may augment these sensory channels, unlike the experience machine—where, once inside, "you won't know you're there" (Nozick 1974, 43)—the playing of video games relies on the attitude of make-believe and the player's acknowledgement of the artificiality and fictionality of the world in which he or she plays (Tavinor 2009, 34–60). Experiencing a game world is not like being beholden to a multisensory illusion, and we properly suspect that players are perfectly aware while playing games that their experiences exist only in virtual and fictional worlds.

Nevertheless, I shall treat the discussion here as having a bearing on Nozick's thought experiment by investigating some of the practical and principled problems with attributing value to the experiences had and the achievements made within gaming, and treating these as a close proxy of the experience machine. That the pleasures of games are pointless—or at least compare unfavorably to corresponding real experiences—may imply, like Nozick's thought experiment, that there is something more than *felt experience* that matters to us, that is, *actually doing* the things in question. But the consideration of games also delivers another potentially valuable lesson: when Nozick made his thought experiment, an explicit question that he asked was *whether the reader would plug in*. Video games provide a kind of answer to this: and it is "yes," simply because of the huge numbers of people of all kinds who now "step into" the virtual worlds of video games to play and pass the time.

My frequent intuition that games and their playing are pointless or value-less activities can be given at least four interpretations.[1] In the following section of this chapter I develop the argument that games represent an oppor-tunity cost that prevents more valuable activities. In part 3 I consider the ephemeral nature of game experiences that owes to their computational set-ting; computers have a habit of crashing, and game save files of becoming corrupted or accidentally deleted, and this seems to undermine the *perma-nence* of game achievements. In part 4, after noting that many of the apparent achievements in games concern fictional activities and events, I raise the worry that this fictional status undermines the real value of gaming experi-ences and achievements. In the final parts of this chapter I investigate the fundamental question of the value of the gaming: games involve arbitrary goals, the achievement of which in most other contexts would seem deeply pointless. What, if anything, is it about the context of gaming that allows such goals to be the bearers of genuine value?

I. GAMING AS AN OPPORTUNITY COST

What could I achieve if I didn't spend so much time playing video games? Certainly I might write more philosophy. A charitable reading of the com-plaint is that the opportunity costs associated with gaming prevent more worthwhile pursuits such as reading a good book. It is not that games entirely lack value, and that there is nothing of worth achieved by playing them; rather, they compare poorly to other activities they preclude. When President Obama voiced his personal concern about video games and other aspects of modern technology, it was not a worry about the insidious moral force of what games represent—that is, the violence and misogyny for which games are frequently morally criticized—but rather that games are a distraction from more meaningful life pursuits and civil engagement (Obama 2010). The putative "pointlessness" of games, under this reading, is attributable to their lack of value relative to other more worthy worldly pursuits.

Of course, this is itself a value judgment on games that gamers may not share. Many will think that gaming is a worthwhile activity in itself, and potentially as valuable as other alternative pursuits: this is certainly evident from the time, effort, and money that gamers now invest in the pastime.[2] I suspect that whether or not one is disposed to see this as a good argument may depend on how familiar one is with games: it is easy, as an outsider, to miss the potential sources of value in gaming, seeing it as the mere mindless pressing of buttons. Furthermore, this opportunity cost argument is general to any kind of play, as it seems to be the nature of play to draw on resources—

especially the resource of time—that might be better spent in instrumental or productive ways. The philosopher Bernard Suits argues that one characteristic of play is that it is an "autotelic" activity—that is, an activity that has no extrinsic goal or purpose—that consumes goods that might be used in instrumental or productive ways (Suits 1978, 217–34). As such, play of all kinds can seem pointless or even wasteful of resources, tempting many social scientists to search for its hidden utility or social function.[3] Video games are just one instance of a human activity the appeal of which seems nearly universal, but the purpose or value of which is far from clear.

One can thus question the ideological basis of the opportunity cost argument against the value of games. A further means of couching this critique of games is the insinuation that they are childish things. The association with children further strengthens the emphasis on the noninstrumental and nonproductive nature of games because of the common image of childhood as carefree. For some people, that there are so many adults now playing and enjoying *childish* games may be a worrying facet of recent culture; for to be a fully grown member of society, one must be productive in a way that game-playing impedes. But this is a very Protestant argument, and one that can be upended. Anybody who has dealt with an email inbox in the course of their job will suspect that much *productive* work, these days, itself comprises an unproductive game. And so much of this unproductive activity is motivated by the fact that we impose on ourselves artificial goals very much like those found in games: I decide, quite puzzlingly, that I need a large house in the suburbs, so I commit myself to an amount of personal debt that I can't help but be productive. The rest of my life is spent in "playing the game" so I can support this goal.

Given that the comparison at the center of the opportunity cost argument is so easily subverted, is this first argument simply reducible to an assumption about the value of the noninstrumental activity of gaming itself? I will return to this issue in the final section of the chapter.

II. OUT, OUT, BRIEF PIXEL!

Secondly, the meaningfulness of the activities involved in gaming is subject to a related set of existential worries. There is one particularly frustrating experience when it comes to gaming, and it illustrates how insubstantial gaming achievements can be: gaming achievements are transitory and easily lost. Deep into one particular world of *Minecraft*, my playing partner and I had built a base, discovered a village, and erected forts far into in the wilderness, and had just discovered an abandoned mineshaft that we then cleared over the course of a play session. As we emerged from the mineshaft one day, the screen blinked and stuttered, and suddenly a message appeared: file corrupt. And so the efforts of the past several weeks disappeared, leaving us with no choice—other than exiting the game of course—but to start a new world (and be a little more careful in making regular save files). To say we grieved over the lost world may mischaracterize the experience—exasperation was the most obvious feeling—but something was lost when that world fell into darkness, captured now only by fading memories of places seen and adventures had.

A related existential worry is with the Sisyphean nature of gaming goals and the achievements within their worlds. In psychology, the "hedonic treadmill" occurs when desires rise to meet achievements so that the level of subjective happiness individuals experience remains relatively static (Brickman and Campbell 1971, 287–302). For example, as a person's earning power increases, the level of luxury she expects in life may also rise, leaving her no happier as a result of the increased income. We can modify the term to identify a similar situation within some video games. The *ludic treadmill* exists where the achievement of gameplay goals merely opens up fresh goals beyond, providing no satisfactory termination to the activity. For example, a frequent element of video game design is "leveling up," a feature heavily influenced by table-top role-playing games such as *Dungeons and Dragons*. Leveling in a video game such as *World of Warcraft* involves performing quests such as killing particular enemies or gathering certain kinds of resources to gain the experience needed to ascend to the next level. The inducements for a player to level up are the extra abilities, equipment, or other gaming content that becomes available at higher levels. What typically happens, of course, is that upon attaining the higher level, the player is given a glimpse of what lies beyond: a new sword to obtain, new spells to learn, or a new part of the world to explore.

The ludic treadmill is a feature of game design that keeps players playing—and it is common in subscription games that rely on a continuing player base—but it effectively means that because the gamer's desires for the game rise along with their achievements, any feeling of achievement is transitory. Mobile games such as *Clash of Clans* are particularly obnoxious in this respect, as not only does upgrading your village simply reveal the availability of additional upgrades, but the upgrades take successively longer and longer periods to complete (unless one surrenders to the business model of such games—*pay to win*—and buys resources with real money).

All of this virtual existential angst is compounded by some of the physical facts about the products of our video game labors. What one actually achieves in playing video games, at one level of analysis at least, is rearranging pieces of code in a save file. All that planning, exploration, industry, and achievement in *Minecraft* amounts to a number of save files on my PlayStation 4. This is a worryingly insubstantial result for so much labor. Indeed, these achievements are so easily forgotten and lost that they hardly seem to count as achievements at all. The supposed "pointlessness" of games that is the subject of this chapter is thus attributed to their lack of significant or lasting meaning.

Of course, in the real world none of our achievements are genuinely lasting, our work comprises Sisyphean tasks, and on some level of analysis life amounts to reorganizing bits of matter into very temporary arrangements. The fact is that gaming is no more susceptible to this moping existential angst than is real life. All that we say and do in life will soon be forgotten— and, unfortunately, there is no opportunity to make regular save files.

These observations touch on a significant background consideration for my specific concern with video game achievements: What is valuable about achievement anyway? The philosopher Gwen Bradford argues that it is difficulty that is crucial both to the analysis of achievement, and to understanding what makes achievements valuable (Bradford 2015). First, making an achievement is more than merely producing some desired or intended result (or even producing a result that has some independent value). Rather, the result must have some inherent difficulty in its completion. Walking a hundred yards may not be an achievement for most people, but *walking a hundred yards on your hands* certainly is. While difficulty is necessary for achievement, it is not sufficient: an act or product is an achievement only if it is also the result of a person's intentional competence. Accidental achievements are no kind of achievement under Bradford's theory. Second, achievements are valuable because they engage the *will* in virtue of their difficulty. Drawing on Aristotelian ideas, Bradford argues that the human good should be defined in terms of the rational exercise of human capacities, and she includes among these capacities the striving will. The extreme difficulties inherent in competently attaining some goals—earning a PhD, scoring a triple century in cricket, reaching the kill screen in *Donkey Kong*—allow for the rational exercise of the will, and as such are humanly valuable things. I will return to these ideas later.

III. FICTIONAL FEATS

In addition to the physical changes that manifest our video gaming labors, *fictionally*, video games allow players to perform fantastic feats. Beyond killing dragons, I've taken down criminal masterminds, performed bank heists, and stormed the beaches at Normandy on D-Day. And I've failed at all of these things. Feats and failures are possible in games because video games are an interactive medium, giving their players a kind of agency in their fictional worlds. Interactivity is a concept that has seen a lot of recent discussion, and it needs some explanation here because it plays such a key role in how video games are understood, and because it is so easily leads to complications for the characterization, moral and otherwise, of the apparent activities in fictional gameworlds.

At least two types of interactivity in video games can be distinguished. A first type has to do with the interactivity of the video gaming medium and its works (Lopes 2001, 65–81). According to Dominic Lopes, an interactive work is one that licences the user to make decisions and perform actions that feed into and change the display of the work (Lopes 2001). In such works, the user—in video games, what it is natural to call the *player*—is both performer and principal audience of the display (see Lopes 2009; Gaut 2010). The work itself comprises an algorithm and set of artistic assets, and from this artifact the performance of the player produces a display that is then the subject of interpretation and evaluation.

A second sense in which video games are interactive is a special instance of this work interactivity, produced by its intersection with fictionality and make-believe. In games with fictional worlds, players give the appearance of *interacting with the fictional world*: this is already evident in the descriptions of *Minecraft* above. In particular, players "step into" fictional worlds to play games (Tavinor 2009, 61–85).[4] Of course, players do not take on a physical presence in gameworlds; rather, it is that these fictions licence imaginative games in which players take fictive roles. Players will subsequently describe their activities in the first person, as what they have done in the game, or superficially identify with characters on the screen. Video games are not the only fictions to warrant such imaginative games—stories one tells in which one features as a character oneself, and tabletop role-playing games such as *Dungeons and Dragons* also do so—but with video games, because of the first type of interactivity described above, the player's performance makes changes to the display that ground the player's imaginative role of acting in and changing the fictional world (and in a way that others can observe and respond to, in multiplayer games).

This fictive interactivity—the player's ability to alter the work and so take a fictive proxy in the work's fictional world—allows the player not only to have make-believe experiences but also make-believe intentions, actions, and the resulting successes and failures of these purposive states. I may hence intend to battle the dragon, perform the action that I hope will best achieve this goal, and wail and gnash my teeth as the dragon resists my attempts to defeat it.

One important difference from Nozick's thought experiment is worth noting here, then: in the experience machine, agency is an illusion. One simply experiences a "preprogrammed" set of experiences (Nozick 1974, 43). But in games, because of their interactivity one has access to a kind of agency, in that one can make decisions that impact the content and nature of the fictional world around oneself. One has a *virtual being*, making decisions that may affect the course and content of their experienced world. And because one is set challenges by the gameworld in the form of rules and objectives, this makes available both achievement and failure in those worlds. Video games are not mere *experience machines*; they are *achievement machines*. Still, the question prompted by Nozick's original thought experiment—if all that matters is the felt experience, why shouldn't you plug in?—may remain in an altered form because there is reason to think that these achievements are not real, in that being fictional, they constitute only the *felt experiences of achievements*.

When the activities of gamers are couched in fictive idioms, as "killing dragons" or "taking down criminal masterminds," these are properly referred to as fictional achievements, and moreover, the achievements of the gameworld persona or "player-character," an epistemic and agential proxy of the player in the fictional world (Tavinor 2009, 74). Thus, one might think that the fictional nature of the achievement in gameworlds—I didn't really kill that dragon, my *character* did—undermines their potential for bearing genuine or at least nonfictional value. This is a version of an argument that can be used to defend games from their moral critics, often that criticism is focused on the apparent violence in games (Tavinor 2009, 151). That the violence depicted in first-person shooter games is fictional has an obvious effect on how we morally evaluate that apparent violence, for example. As the philosopher Stephanie Patridge notes, the fictionality of the content of video games "makes it difficult to see how morality can gain entry into such worlds" (Patridge 2011a, 386). Patridge also puts an interesting twist on this observation, and one that is relevant to the broader issue here, when she notes that *moral praise* of gaming activities seems equally trivial: "We might think it odd were someone recommended to us as a person of noble character on the basis of her treatment of her citizens in *Civilization III*" (Patridge 2011b, 305–12). Hence, it might be thought that the fictionality of gameworlds makes it difficult to see how we could value them as achievements. Here the "pointlessness" of games is seen to follow from the fictionality of the apparent events and actions to which we might attach value.

And yet we *do* value achievements in (or at least *through*) fictions. J. R. R. Tolkien's Middle Earth, whatever you think about the literary merit of the works detailing it, is an impressive fictional work and product of the imagination. But of course this is an equivocation upon "fictional achievement": the object of value here is what Kendall Walton calls the "prop"—a representational artifact that grounds our imaginative episodes with such works (Walton 1993, 21). Such props are certainly nonfictional things, and while they may be ready-mades or found items (Walton 1993, 37), their design is frequently the result of an intentional, competent, and difficult act, thus counting as an achievement in Bradford's defined sense. Hence, we value Middle Earth for the monumental documentation of an imaginary world that Tolkien provided. Fictions, though they may describe places and beings with a merely imagined existence, can certainly be used to do real things and to make real and valuable achievements.

IV. GAMES AND POINTLESS GOALS

So what of the real achievements involved in playing games (that is, what players really achieve by making their characters fictionally achieve things)? Even if I did not really kill the Ender Dragon (there was no such dragon to be killed) I did surmount that goal in the game, didn't I? *I beat the game.*[5] Surely there is some real value in this?

Bernard Suits's work on games is enjoying a justified resurgence in interest. One of his principal aims is defying the Wittgensteinian claim that games can't be defined, by actually defining them: "to play a game is to engage in an activity directed towards bringing about a specific state of affairs, using only means permitted by the rules, where the rules prohibit more efficient in favour of less efficient means, and where such rules are accepted just because they make possible such activity" (Suits 1978, 36). Suits also introduces a handy terminology for these separate aspects of games. The state of affairs that we aim to bring about is the "prelusory goal" (*pre*lusory, because it can be described "before" or "independently" of the game in which it plays a role); the means permitted by the rules to bring about this state of affairs are called the "lusory means"; the prohibition of efficient means in favor of inefficient means is enacted by the "constitutive rules" of the game; and the acceptance of the rules in order to experience playing the game is called the "lusory attitude" (Suits 1978, 37–43).

It is not my intention to accept or reject this definition here, but rather to note that the definition does a wonderful job of allowing us to tease out various issues of interest in the present context. Indeed, we can employ Suits's definition and terminology to describe and explain the principal example under discussion here, though in this case the situation is complicated by many of these terms referring to states of a fiction (and also by the rather loose way that *Minecraft* embodies prelusory goals). In Suits's terms, the "prelusory goals" of the Ender Dragon quest of *Minecraft* are a depicted fictional state of affairs ("the Ender Dragon being dead"). The "lusory means" are the fictional means made possible by the game (in this case the affordances [see Gibson 1977] of the player-character in the world of *Minecraft*, such as building and using armor and weapons, drinking potions, entering portals and so on). The "constitutive rules" in this case comprise all the obstructions that the game puts in the player's path: one must find the Stronghold and find its portal, then open the portal, and finally travel to The End and confront the dragon. And each of these goals contains numerous subgoals, all of which define a very circuitous and inefficient path to the prelusory goal. Finally, one submits to these inefficient constitutive rules just because this makes possible the challenging activities of the game. In this characterization, and drawing together observations about interactive fictions I made earlier, to "beat the game"—the overall, or *lusory goal* of the game of *Minecraft*—amounts to realizing a specific fiction utilizing the interactive means made available by the game's algorithmic fictive prop.

An important point for my purposes here is that in this characterization of playing games, the prelusory goal of the game does not have any obvious instrumental value. A game might provide some *fictional reason* for the challenges it provides, and some fictional instrumental value in meeting them, often in the form of a narrative that situates and motivates the game-play for the player-character.[6] But the prelusory goal itself lacks such a rationale. Realizing the fiction of defeating the Ender Dragon really doesn't achieve anything of independent value; rather it amounts to surmounting the very artificial objectives of a game. And of course, restarting a new game of *Minecraft* resets the fiction of the Ender Dragon; it can only be defeated within a particular display realized from the work, and there will always remain an endless number of potential displays in which the dragon remains undefeated. This, indeed, is a further reason for why the achievements of video games might seem ephemeral.

And yet Suits's definition also gives an explanation of how this apparently noninstrumental goal provides the occasion for an achievement. There are other means to realize the fiction of the Ender Dragon's defeat, such as directly altering the game's code or loading up someone else's saved game. But neither counts as *playing* the game because they use means other than the game's constitutive rules to achieve the prelusory objective. The constitutive rules, by defining a very inefficient path to this goal, make killing the dragon much more involved than it might otherwise be. And the player's acceptance of these constitutive rules signals that they embrace this challenge. It is the very artificiality of the goal and the means allowed to get there that are the basis of the gaming achievement.

But perhaps this merely restates the problem in a more perspicuous way: Why should instrumentally nonvaluable goals become valuable when their achievement is constrained in seemingly arbitrary ways? Here the apparent "pointlessness" of games is characterized by the noninstrumental nature of the goals involved in their playing and also by the seemingly arbitrary constraints placed on the player in their pursuit of these goals.

V. THE LONG DREAM AND THE SHORT DREAM

What makes Suits's theory doubly relevant to my interest here is that as well as providing a definition of games with which we might analyze the issues raised by Nozick's thought experiment, Suits also offers a justification of the value of games. Indeed, he makes the claim that games are the highest intrinsic good, because in a world in which all needs were met people would most naturally and profitably spend their time playing games. Making games of things—perhaps all things—would be the human condition found in utopia (Suits 1978, 182–96). The activities of game playing seem pointless; the prelusory goal, and the means used to achieve it, the inefficient constitutive rules, themselves may bear no independent value whatsoever. However, by placing arbitrary constraints on players these features elevate a pointless goal into a genuine achievement because of the complexity and difficulty they impart to the activity of game playing.

As noted earlier, the philosopher Gwen Bradford argues that one thing that differentiates an achievement from the mere attainment of a goal is the difficulty inherent in the genuine achievement. The achievements of game playing are helpfully considered in these terms both because the difficulty of many video games cannot be understated and because players value and seek out this difficulty. The better video games are often precisely those that allow for a scaling difficulty: *Bushnell's law*—a maxim frequently attributed to the Atari founder Nolan Bushnell—holds that good games are those that are "easy to learn; difficult to master." Even a video game like the first-person shooter series *Battlefield*, while it might seem like a simple affair of shooting and being shot at, is exceedingly difficult when played against other good players who understand the game's subtleties. Mastery of *Battlefield* requires not only the development of fast and precise motor skills and an extensive knowledge of the maps and player abilities but also strategic planning and the discipline or will to enact these skills, plans, and strategies.

It is in the lusory attitude of willfully embracing difficult challenges that the best case can be made for the genuine value of video game achievements. This is also an important source of the value of games themselves: games open up realms of challenging end-directed activity that their players might not otherwise have access to (whether because of socially or materially impoverished circumstances, or because of a lack of access to meaningful challenges in a life composed of the daily grind). Achievement machines provide readymade opportunities for challenging goals that draw on the resourcefulness of their players, so that players can experience the natural enjoyment we gather from rising to meet challenges. They allow players to gain and display competence and even mastery in a complicated domain. And games allow players to do so *safely*, given that the lack of instrumental need within the achievement machine is usually paired with a corresponding lack of consequence. Battling *real* dragons is a dangerous business, of course.

Developing and displaying competence and mastery within a complicated, difficult, or subtle domain may meet a basic human need and compose a basic human good. In the context of a discussion of the human good and rationality, John Rawls introduces the "Aristotelian Principle" when he claims that "other things equal, human beings enjoy the exercise of their realized capacities (their innate or trained abilities), and this enjoyment increases the more the capacity is realized, or the greater its complexity" (Rawls 1971, 374). Rawls argues that this is a "deep psychological fact" (Rawls 1971, 379) that can be used as the basis of an argument for what it is rational for people to pursue in their lives. The connection to games is obvious enough for Rawls to introduce the principle by noting that "chess is a more complicated and subtle game than checkers . . . [t]hus the principle says that someone who can do both generally prefers playing chess to playing checkers." It is not out of the question that video games—especially subtle and difficult video games—should count among the ends that it is rational for us to pursue when we consider what is in our interests.

Such games also allow people the opportunity to meet and surmount difficulties and to develop their human capacities, for no other reason than the intrinsic interest in doing so so that potentially, the achievements made need not be sullied by the messy extrinsic and worldly interests that motivate many of our daily achievements. Because the prelusory goal doesn't really matter, the striving activity itself can more effectively become the locus of value. Furthermore, in playing games we can employ our valuable human traits—those needed to surmount difficulties, make achievements, and gain competence—for their own sake: one can play video games inventively, intelligently, skillfully, and (when played with others) cooperatively, generously, and even kindly. Perhaps then, what makes video games genuinely valuable is that, unlike in Nozick's *experience machine*, in the *achievement machine* players are not merely "indeterminate blobs" (Nozick 1974, 43); rather, they are actors in a creative drama, and their genuine character and competence may be revealed by how they play.

One of the most suggestive parts of Suits's book comes in a dream described by the eponymous grasshopper. His dream is that "everyone alive, is in fact engaged in playing elaborate games, while at the same time believing themselves to be going about their ordinary affairs. Carpenters, believing themselves to be merely pursuing their trade, are really playing a game, and similarly with politicians, philosophers, lovers, murderers, thieves and saints" (Suits 1978, 11). If we woke up to the fact that so much of what we do in the real world—going to work, engaging in politics, buying goods, gathering debt, writing philosophical papers—also seems to involve placing inefficient obstacles in front of what might in cold moments of cynicism seem like pointless goals—fictions cultivated by our societies, Sisyphean in the worst sense, brief sparks in an endless darkness—then the activities of gaming might not look so bad. The arguments against the value of games explored here aren't so different from arguments we might frame against the so-called *serious and meaningful pursuits* of life.

Players of the game may be aware that *Minecraft* also suggests that life is a dream from which we might awake. After the defeat of the Ender Dragon the player is treated to an unexpected word crawl in which two disembodied voices philosophize on the identity of the player, and what he or she has achieved in the game, and might achieve in life. Both worlds are dreams, and what has been revealed in the game is the potential of the player to act and create in both. But the game has also revealed the limitations on any of the player's subsequent achievements. In our real lives—the long dream of life, as the game refers to it—we labor hard to build an illusion of permanence; but in the short dream of *Minecraft*, value exists in the exercise of creative agency itself, rather than in any particular ends achieved, which, the game reminds us, are just temporary arrangements of code.

NOTES

1. There are likely to be sociological or psychological interpretations of this dismissal of video gaming that may even preclude the need to interpret it as being based on some kind of argument: here, however, I will be playing the game particular to philosophy by offering rational reconstructions of the position that games are pointless.

2. Year on year revenue for the worldwide gaming industry is now approaching \$100 billion (Sinclair 2015).

3. Johan Huizinga's classic study (Huizinga 1955) elevates play, perhaps to the extent of hyperbole, to be a near sine qua non of human culture.

4. See Tavinor 2009, 61–85. In some respects *Minecraft* is a poor illustration of a game, because it lacks many of the goals and rules of typical games by virtue of being a sandbox game. In *Minecraft* the player's time is not taken up with meeting some predefined goal of a level or episode, but with meeting the player's self-defined goals ("Explore the world," "Build a nice house," "Travel to the End" and so on). But for just this open-endedness *Minecraft* may prove particularly suitable in allowing us to reflect on the experience machine.

5. This is a bit inaccurate to say of *Minecraft* because one does not really beat *Minecraft*, even if one achieves some of the implicit goals provided by the world.

6. But note that *Minecraft* does not even do this, because one may remain entirely unaware that there is a dragon to defeat. It is not even signaled to the player as a potential achievement. I only discovered its existence, and the means of finding it, in a YouTube video.

Chapter Eight

Virtual *Weltschmerz*

Things to Keep in Mind While Building Experience Machines and Other Tragic Technologies

Stefano Gualeni

Having made it this far into the present book, it is practical to assume that the readers are already familiar with the experience machine, a thought experiment that was proposed in the 1970s by American philosopher Robert Nozick. To summarize: Nozick hypothesized the existence of a device capable of disclosing persistent virtual[1] experiences for the human being using it. The experiences upheld by his fictional machine are envisaged to be indistinguishable from those that we, as humans, can develop in relation with the actual world. In this outline of Nozick's thought experiment, I am using the descriptor *actual* to indicate the analog contexts that we inhabit and share everyday as (and with) biological creatures.

Nozick's thought experiment challenged us to envision having access to a device that could indefinitely supplant our everyday experiences with virtual ones designed to maximize our pleasure and satisfaction. By presenting us with the possibility of an experience machine, he invited reflections on whether the way we live our lives is solely driven by the pleasure principle, or if there is something else that we value other than how we feel "from the inside." If such a machine existed, asked the American philosopher, "would you plug in?" (Nozick 1974, 42).

As already mentioned in the introduction to this book, Nozick's mental exercise has been differently invoked and interpreted in various contexts. Some authors have understood the experience machine as implicitly giving rise to arguments against utilitarianism; others have interpreted it as opposing hedonistic positions in both ethics and psychology (Sober 2000; Feldman

2010a; Feldman 2010b). More recently, Robert Nozick's *gedankenexperiment* has been examined in fields of inquiry such as media studies and philosophy of technology. Stimulated by developments in virtual technologies, some of the questions originally raised by the experience machine' are presently used in those disciplines as springboards for reflecting on the qualities and on the effects of our interactive experiences in (and of) virtual worlds.

Having conceptualized his thought experiment in the early 1970s, Nozick could not have fully anticipated the numerous and profound ways in which the diffusion of computer simulations and video games came to affect the Western world. Besides, his imaginative exercise was meant to kindle questions concerning our ethical compass, not existential and phenomenological quandaries ensuing from experiencing interactive, artificial worlds. It is interesting to notice that in its original formulation the experience machine does neither specifically focus upon the technical characteristics of the machine, nor upon those of the experience of what it is like to be plugged into it. Both elements of Nozick's scenario are in fact simply introduced as the implied preconditions for a reflection on our existences and our values in a supposed "age of their technical reproducibility."

In general, the renewed academic interest in the experience machine can be understood as a way to further Nozick's original questions and perspectives with interrogatives that are specific to our present-day socio-technological milieu. This chapter offers what are hopefully a few constructive and thought-provoking reflections to accompany us in our progress toward the actual, technical realization of experience machines.

In the Western world, social activities such as the crafting of—and the access to—virtual worlds are increasingly more affordable and already deeply integrated in social practices (Gualeni 2015a; Gualeni 2015b). Moreover, devices that recall those outlined in the experience machine appear to be already at the outer edges of our technological reach. It is hence obvious to me that today—more than forty years after the original formulation of Nozick's thought experiment—it would be paradoxical to think about those machines as if they were still imaginary, inscrutable gizmos, rather than the concrete aspiration of consumer-technology companies. In this context—a context in which the virtual worlds of video games are already established as a prominent form of cultural mediation and meaning-making—I will try to supplement Nozick's reflections and to further elaborate on his thought experiment. With this objective in mind, I propose to begin my philosophical dialog with Nozick by identifying and developing two philosophical themes.

1: I shall first approach the experience machine from the perspective of philosophy of technology. In doing so, I will articulate an understanding of the experience machine as a machine. The first theme will produce two possible approaches to answer Nozick's question concerning hedonism (Is there something else that we value other than how we feel "from the inside"?) in a canonically philosophical fashion. Through reflections developed in a critical relationship with existing literature and approaches in relevant cultural fields such as game studies, media philosophy, and philosophy of technology, I will explain why I still believe we would be resistant to be permanently (or semipermanently) plugged into an experience machine.

2: I shall then explore the experiential aspirations and limitations that characterize our current efforts to develop experience machines. This effort will largely take a phenomenological (or rather postphenomenological) approach to framing our existential relationships with virtual worlds, our irresistible attraction toward them, and—ultimately—our aversion to the prospect of permanently plugging into one of them. This second section of my chapter will draw upon my experience as a video game designer and upon interviews with other video game creators who have recently engaged the development of vast, experientially rich, interactive worlds. This will shift the focus of my inquiry from methodological concerns to practical considerations about the constructive and experiential relationships that we currently establish with virtual technologies and the imaginative worlds of video games.[2]

1. A MACHINE FOR EXPERIENCING

In his 1962 essay "The Myth of Total Cinema," French film critic and theorist André Bazin interpreted the specific ways in which cinema reproduced images, sounds, and motion as the first rudimentary steps toward building a machine that is capable of experientially re-creating the world. From his point of view, the technical advancements of cinema—when not merely directed toward the pursuit of capitalistic gain—constitute an evolutionary process aimed at crafting progressively more accurate and sensorially complete artificial experiences. For Bazin, the myth guiding the evolution of cinema consisted in the aspiration to achieve those same experiential effects that Nozick later envisaged in the experience machine. He believed that cinema ultimately aspires to be the "recreation of the world in its own image, an image unburdened by the freedom of interpretation of the artist or the irreversibility of time" (Bazin 1967, 21).

Pursuing academic research at the intersection of film studies and game studies, Mark J. P. Wolf noted that the ambitions expressed in "The Myth of Total Cinema" and its underlying ideology are very much alive and well today, and are evidently materialized in the imaginary future of virtual worlds. As recent examples of cinematic incarnations of the "myth," Wolf mentioned the movies *Total Recall* (1990), *eXistenZ* (1999), and *The Matrix* series (1999 and 2003), in whose fictional scenarios experience machines exist and have various societal applications, from entertainment to the subjugation of humanity. In other words, these are movies in whose fictional contexts the myth of total cinema had been technically achieved in its complete immersivity and indistinguishability from lived experience (ibid.).[3]

In the current age of digital mediation, the disclosure of a convincing "illusion of a world" can be similarly identified as one of the most evident aspirations guiding the advancements of virtual worlds and video game technologies (Gualeni 2015a, 45, 46). Wolf accordingly proposed, in his 2015 essay "Video Games, Cinema, Bazin, and the Myth of Simulated Lived Experience," to recognize video games as expressive forms through which the myth of total cinema and its ambitions are still pursued in contemporary Western cultures (Wolf 2015). This way of approaching video games is in fact not only consonant with what Bazin described in "The Myth of Total Cinema," but—as will become clearer later in this chapter—can also be recognized as the ideological foundation to the ways in which we design, criticize, and attribute cultural values to video games and, more generally, to virtual worlds.[4]

Toward the end of the nineteenth century, the German philosopher Ernst Kapp proposed an understanding of technology according to which human beings develop and use artifacts with the fundamental purpose of overcoming the limitations and the insufficiencies of their native organism. In his vision, technologies are (conscious or even unconscious) artificial supplementations of certain functions that are originally accomplished by human organs (Kapp 1877). Kapp's functional understanding of technology is not limited to the use of various artifacts to enhance our capabilities to perceive, transport, communicate, and interact with the world. He also recognized our artificial extensions as cognitive instruments (Gualeni 2015a; Gualeni, 2015b, 68). The invention of the mechanical clockwork is an example that is frequently used to illustrate this point; that is to say, to demonstrate how our technologies (and our interconnected technological systems) influence and shape our thought in ways that are subtle, pervasive, and that transcend the practical functions for which those artifacts were originally designed. American historian Lewis Mumford, for example, famously viewed the mechanical clock as the defining machine of the Industrial Age. Unlike most of his contemporaries, who identified in the steam engine the key creation that propelled us into industrialism, Mumford realized that it was the clock, on account of its effectively "producing" a regular and parcellized understanding of time, that paved the way for all the technical and social developments of that period (Mumford 1934, 14, 15). Similarly, Dutch historian Edward Jan Dijksterhuis maintained that, in the early Modern period, the precise and ingenious mechanism of clocks persuaded physicists that nature itself worked like clockwork, inspiring the development of classical mechanics (Dijksterhuis 1986, 442f).

In the mid-1980s, and in line with the understanding of the cultural effects of artifacts encapsulated in the examples above, American media theorist Neil Postman argued that we should avoid approaching our technical artifacts and media as if they were neutral tools, as they never purely accomplish instrumental tasks. Rather, our technical creations also always function as mediators, and in their mediating roles, they inevitably "classify the world for us, sequence it, frame it, enlarge it, reduce it, colour it, argue a case for what the world is like" (Postman 1986, 10). Many philosophers of technology who have adopted a general interpretation of technological artifacts as mediators understand technical systems as dynamic realms for self-discovery and self-transformation (Verbeek 2011; Gualeni 2015b; Zarkadakis 2015; Gualeni 2015c). As well as any other technologies, virtual worlds could (and perhaps should) be recognized as systems that allow us to materialize our worldviews and ideas, as ways to make our beliefs and aspirations into objects of critical (and self-critical) evaluation.

This aspect of our relationship with technologies becomes, I find, particularly interesting when it comes to acknowledging the fact that virtual experiences and digital worlds are (still) encountered through devices; that is, through interfaces and technological artifacts. From this perspective, we can approach Nozick's the experience machine not only as a thought experiment meant to problematize ethical hedonism or utilitarianism, but also as a way to encourage and facilitate reflections on the ethical quandaries ensuing from creating and utilizing virtual technologies. To clarify this point and its relevance, I will discuss a few practical examples, which will reference the movies discussed in the previous section of this chapter.

In both *Total Recall* and *eXistenZ*, the protagonists physically encounter a machine that is capable of disclosing persistent virtual worlds in ways that are indistinguishable from their everyday experiences. Albeit skeptically, and for different reasons, both Quaid (in *Total Recall*) and Pikul (in *eXistenZ*) willingly make the decision to plug into each respective cinematographic version of the experience machine and plunge into illusory worlds that are supposed to be pleasurable.

The case of Neo (the protagonist of *The Matrix* trilogy) is, I believe, significantly different as far as the objectives of this chapter are concerned. At the beginning of the first movie of the series, Neo is unaware that he is plugged into a technological system that "feeds" his brain the experiences of an artificial world. Since he had been conscious, Neo's world had always been a product of an experience machine, a machine that he never agreed to be plugged into and that he never encountered as an object of experience (at least he did not at that point in the movie). In a large portion of the first installment of *The Matrix*, Neo cannot thus develop a complete ethical and ontological understanding of his condition, let alone articulate a critical stance toward the artificiality of the virtual world in which he is immersed.

The cited movies can be understood as presenting two different situations: one in which plugging into the machine is based on a consciously chosen relationship with a technological artifact, and one in which that is not the case. It is my conviction that the recent philosophical discussions stimulated by Nozick's thought experiment concerning our relationships with virtual worlds are largely a product of how the experience machine presents a scenario that—paradoxically—encompasses both the situations described above. Allow me to elaborate on this point with more clarity resorting to extracts taken directly from the experience machine:

- On the one hand, Nozick clarifies that his fictional machine offers the possibility to "pick and choose from their vast library or smorgasbord of such experiences, selecting your life's experiences for, say, the next two years. After two years have passed, you will have ten minutes or ten hours out of the tank, to select the experiences of your *next* two years" (Nozick 1974, 42). Concordantly, to operate the machine and—crucially—in order to make the decision of whether to plug in or not, its users must first encounter the experience machine as an object. There must be, put in a somewhat simpler way, occasions before plugging into the machine and between experiential sessions when the machine is present to them as a mediating device, as the physical gateway to certain possibilities of being.
- On the other hand, the machine does not only need to provide an illusion of a world that is smooth, consistent, and experientially complete but also—for the *gedankenexperiment* to work—the users need to have no recollection of the experiences and choices leading to plugging into (or plugging back into) the machine. As Nozick puts it, "While you are in the tank you won't know you're there; you'll think it's actually happening" (ibid.).

The hypothetical setup of the experience machine as a thought experiment thus requires our making volitional choices in relation to a physical device. At the same time, for the fictional device to produce the envisaged experiential effects, the choices and the awareness mentioned in the previous passage must be removed from the users' consciousness as soon as they plug into an experience machine. What I want to suggest here is that if users could remember the various steps and choices leading to their plugging in, they could not avoid filtering (at least initially) their virtual experiences through the awareness that the world that they are experiencing is a synthetic artefact.

Further complications arise in hypothetical scenarios like those of unplugging from the experience machine or in the case of an interruption of the streaming of artificial experiences (regardless of its accidental or scheduled nature). In those circumstances, memories and choices of our lives from before plugging in will need to be recuperated and reactivated. Why? If not to avoid psychological damage upon returning to the actual world, that awareness will at any rate be indispensable for taking significant existential decisions such as whether to plug back in or what future developments to choose for the continuation of our life in that virtual world (as outlined by Nozick himself).

In summary, approaching the experience machine from the perspective of philosophy of technology allows us to identify a paradox at the core of Nozick's thought experiment: the situation he described is one of irreconcilable ambiguity, in which human beings are expected to be selectively aware and unaware of the mediating role of a virtual reality device in relation to their experience. To be sure, this paradoxical impasse can be sidestepped quite easily, albeit perhaps inelegantly, by hypothesizing yet another device: an apparatus capable of compartmentalizing our awareness and selectively activating areas of it. With this additional hypothetical device, we would be able to target and inhibit memories of our relationship with the experience machine, enabling us to forget having programmed one or having decided to plug into one. For the sake of simplicity, I will call this additional, fictitious apparatus the "memory suppressor."

Did Nozick implicitly think that a memory suppressor would be part of an experience machine? Let us suppose, as a first conjectural scenario, that he did not. If that were the case, and for the reasons articulated above, the immersion provided by plugging into his fictional device could not be expected to have a totalizing effect. Once plugged into the experience machine, in fact, people could not avoid remaining conscious of the artificial constitution of the virtual worlds that they were experiencing. As a consequence, the relationships that can be established with those worlds could not (or at least could not initially) smoothly and convincingly hijack those of the world that we index as actual.[5]

At this point in the articulation of my arguments and in support of the claim that we would indeed resist being permanently or semipermanently connected with any world-feeding machines, I believe it is advantageous to introduce a perspective according to which virtual worlds can engender a peculiar kind of nostalgia.[6] What I am presenting here is the belief that if we experienced virtual worlds while remaining aware of the existence of the actual one (i.e., without the selective inhibition of actual memories), we would inevitably end up experiencing a desire to return to our "homeworld." As I have argued and explained in detail elsewhere,[7] the world that we belong to as biological creatures is necessarily more complex and mysterious than any artificial one could ever be, as every artificial world depends from the actual one both technically and conceptually. On that assumption, the awareness that there is a deeper, more meaningful world outside of the tanks in which our bodies are floating will likely trigger a digitally enhanced feeling similar to what Romantic writers and poets called *Weltschmerz* ("world-pain," "world-weariness"): the feeling that the world (or a certain world) is limited, and might be inadequate to satisfy the intellectual and emotional aspirations of the human soul.

Understood in this way, the Romantic idea of *Weltschmerz* can be recognized as antithetical to concept of the "sublime" as embraced during the same period (Shaw 2006). Whereas the Romantic sublime focused on the awe-inspiring vastness of nature and the impossibility for the human senses and the human intellect to ever grasp its functioning and meaning, to someone feeling *Weltschmerz* a world appears as ordinary and manageable in its complexity and scale. Whereas the Romantic poets finds themselves inadequate and fragile in relation to a sense of sublime that transcends all their capabilities, the sense of "world-weariness" is a close relative of the feeling of boredom: it is the realization that our experiences cannot be anything other than banal and foreseeable, thus excluding any possibilities of transcendence.[8] Virtual *Weltschmerz*, I shall argue, not only entails the feelings of triteness and predictability that were outlined above but also triggers desires for things that are mysterious and extraordinary.

In this first hypothetical scenario, in which a "memory suppressor" is not a technical component of an experience machine, my expectation is that the users will be able to temporarily suspend their disbelief (see note 15) toward virtual worlds, but that they will ultimately remain aware of the artificiality of that experience and painfully conscious of the existence of a world outside of the simulation. Thus, without a memory suppressor, the machine imagined by Nozick could not supplant our relationship with the world wholesale, but could still experientially complement it. In this situation, I expect that users would relate to Nozick's device in a way that is similar to how they currently engage video game consoles or virtual reality gear. By that, I mean that they would intuitively consider the experience disclosed by the machine as that of a derivative world meant for entertainment, relaxation, education, training, and so on. Conceived of as such, I imagine that people would choose to plug into an experience machine with the expectation of pleasure, or self-betterment through play, or communication, discovery, and escapism, but only for a limited period.[9]

I consider this first, tentative answer to be quite dull. It is, to begin with, largely speculative and rooted in personal experiences and feelings. On top of that, it does not take into consideration determinants such as personal inclinations, states of depression and low self-esteem, physical and emotional loss, as well as any other form of psychological trauma that might encourage individuals to seek preferential meaning-making and extended relief in virtual worlds. The greatest deficiency that I can find in this answer to Nozick's hypothetical questions is, however, its negligible philosophical significance. The appeal and the immersive effects of virtual worlds of the kind just described can already be experienced, to a certain degree of aesthetical fidelity, with current virtual technologies, and could already be suitably explored with the tools and methods of empirical science. In other words, if the experience machine did not feature a way to selectively inhibit our awareness of the machine itself, it stands to reason that Nozick's interrogatives would be more efficiently tackled by fields such as cognitive psychology or game user research.

Abandoning this first hypothetical scenario, the upcoming section will embark on the more challenging and, I believe, more philosophically fruitful question of whether one would plug into an experience machine that *did* include a memory suppressor.

1.1. A Thought Experiment within a Thought Experiment

Reading *Anarchy, State, and Utopia* (the book containing the experience machine), it is not entirely clear what broader ethical and philosophical objectives Nozick was pursuing with his famous *gedankenexperiment*. What is, instead, obvious in his text is the fact that he considered that most people would not opt for plugging into an experience machine in a permanent or semipermanent fashion (Nozick 1974, 44). According to Nozick, there are other things that matter to people in addition to pleasure, and in his book, he substantiated this belief of his by appeal to three motivations. Out of the three of them, I consider the third one to be the most interesting and provocative. In his third motivation, and in line with what was discussed in the previous section of this chapter, Nozick predicted that many people would refuse the offer of a permanent connection with an experience machine on the basis of it being nothing more than a human artifact. We would be resistant, he claimed, to abandoning the world that we index as "actual" for a virtual one that is neither more unfathomable nor more meaningful (ibid., 43).

Even if we were somehow technically capable of inhibiting the awareness that we were connected to an experience machine after having plugged into one, the conscious decision of plugging in permanently (or semipermanently) would still need to be taken by each individual user with the awareness that the machine is in fact a machine, and that the worlds that such a machine discloses can neither be as complex nor as significant as the actual one. As explained in my 2015 book *Virtual Worlds as Philosophical Tools*, and as I already hinted in the previous section of this chapter, virtual worlds are derivative products that are inevitably conceptualized and built around specific (and specifically human) ways to perceive and understand what the actual world is and how it functions.

To clarify this last point, I propose an imaginative exercise of my own: I encourage readers to imagine having at their disposal a specific kind of experience machine. This hypothetical device would generate and uphold "single player" virtual worlds that are experientially indistinguishable from the one that we index as "actual," and would allow its user to design his or her existential course in a way that it has an impact on the rest of the virtual world. The "single-player" descriptor serves here to clarify that the phenomena, events, and relationships that constitute those virtual worlds are uniquely experienced by the one user who is plugged into a specific machine, and are not shared with other users plugged into similar devices.[10] The solipsistic machine described above would specifically allow its users to design their existence and produce any desired experiences. It would also feature a memory suppressor that would automatically activate after a user plugged in. Now, I ask each reader to imagine that, as an individual user, he or she decides to program such machine to fulfill the dream of becoming a prominent scientist, say an experimental physicist. This objective would include experiencing years of strenuous experimental research work, facing self-doubt and the resistance of peers, and finally rising to international (simulated) fame.

The premises for this thought experiment are designed to elicit feelings that I expect most people would find pleasurable. Witnessing one's efforts leading to positive outcomes, overcoming obstacles, and achieving notoriety for one's skills and contributions is likely not only to be inherently pleasurable but also meaningful, in the existential acceptation of the term (that is, resorting to the consciousness of other people to achieve a personal sense of meaning and self-worth).

Let us take a step backward for a moment, and let us suppose that the user that is about to plug into one of these hypothetical devices is informed that the machine can only disclose "single-player" virtual worlds, worlds that are—furthermore—strictly reliant on the current understandings of physics. This entails that the simulation of physical phenomena that are possible in the machine cannot be deeper or more granular than those that we managed to study and understand in relation to the actual world.[11] What I mean to say is that our capability to understand and experiment with physics in virtual worlds (and even to virtually manipulate and subvert it) is inevitably bound by the conceptual and experimental approaches to physics that are available to us as the creators of the experience machine. The very software and hardware components of the speculative machine in question can only be designed within those conceptual frameworks and on the basis of certain understandings of physics that were originally developed in relation to the actual world.

As a consequence of the machine's limitations, it should be clear to the reader that, as far as experimental science is concerned,

1. no phenomena or interactions beyond what we already know about physics will actually be observable (or even possible) when plugged in. The experimental discoveries that the users will be responsible for

in their simulated roles of prominent physicists will thus be fictitious, and could not be directly relevant to any actual scientific advancements

2. no other conscious human being will witness or appreciate any of the work and achievements that the user will produce inside the virtual world, and even if anybody did, the value of those experiences and findings would be interesting only anecdotally or for research into the human psyche and behavior (thus, producing new knowledge *through* virtual worlds and not *in* virtual worlds). For the reasons explained in the point above, no new particles or behaviors can actually be discovered in virtual worlds and no paradigm-shifting experiments can be actually run within them.

Having received this information, would one still decide to plug in and experience the life of the experimental physicist? Would one not, instead, find it more meaningful to dedicate the time span of his or her biological life to somehow participating in the actual progress of humanity; for example, by contributing to the actual growth of scientific knowledge, rather than in its virtual simulacrum? What I am trying to emphasize here is not that experimental science is the only way (or a particularly desirable way) to develop knowledge, but rather that the experiences upheld by the experience machine are inherently derivative. To be sure, I do not believe in the categorical impossibility for acquiring knowledge (or for triggering personal transformations) from simulated events and experiences. It is evident to me that there are many ways in which observing the lives of people plugged into experience machines could further our understanding of who we are as human beings. In fact, if we could look into someone else's simulated experience (see note 10), and if that person granted us permission to observe and study his or her simulated experiences and record data about them (or we somehow obtained the legal and ethical clearance to do so, in the case—for example— of people in a coma or nonhuman users), then we could definitely derive meaningful insights from them. For example, we could

- detect and study psychological and behavioral patterns of its users (human or nonhuman) in a number of different contexts and situations.
- design virtual worlds so that their inhabitants could unwittingly perform citizen-science actions involving the analysis of actual data (similarly to current projects such as *Foldit*[12] or *Play to Cure: Genes in Space*[13]).
- stimulate and test new heuristic approaches and generate new hypotheses in a variety of epistemic fields, including self-discovery and self-construction.[14]
- stimulate and test new possible forms of social and economic organization.

Having been made aware of the experimental scientist scenario, would many people consciously choose that path? I expect the answer would be negative, as I am convinced that most of us would still be resistant to limiting our emotions, our social engagement, our professional efforts, and our personal aspirations (regardless of their merits) to man-made worlds. Nozick must have had the same intuition when he wrote that "[p]lugging into the machine is a kind of suicide" (Nozick 1974, 43).

Following the same conceptual path, Nozick also stated that this rationale for rejecting a permanent connection with his machine would not only dissuade people who are seeking existential meaning and personal validation in the consciousness of others (for example, the cases of some scientists, actors, video game designers, etc.) from pursuing those values within the virtual worlds of the experience machine. The same argument would, in fact, similarly deter those people who pursue transcendence through spiritual experiences and/or the use of psychotropic drugs. In that respect, Nozick maintained that people who aspire to enrich their lives with a more profound significance in those latter ways would resist being permanently plugged into virtual worlds on the basis that those worlds could never be richer or more profound than notions, beliefs, and perceptions that human beings can understand rationally and simulate technically (Nozick 1974, 43).

Thus far, I have problematized Nozick's imaginative exercise through the lens of a specific (phenomenological) approach to philosophy of technology. Beginning from the next section of this chapter, I will depart from trying to frame the technical possibilities of Nozick's hypothetical device and from speculating about the experiential effects it could disclose. I will, instead, initiate an interdisciplinary reflection on some specific ways in which we are currently designing and experiencing virtual worlds. On the conceptual basis of two of the concepts discussed earlier, those of "virtual *Weltschmerz*" and "nostalgia," in the second part of this text my focus will shift to analyzing and historically contextualizing some design strategies that game developers employ with the intention of making artificial worlds feel logically consistent and experientially incompletable. This objective will be pursued through reflection upon my own hands-on experience as a video game designer and in discussion with scholars and independent video game developers who are facing (or recently faced) the challenges of crafting infinitely explorable, procedurally generated virtual worlds. My interlocutors and interviewees for the upcoming section were, in alphabetical order:

- Mike Cook—Independent video game developer and game researcher (http://www.gamesbyangelina.org)
- Mark R. Johnson—Game studies scholar and independent video game developer of *Ultima Ratio Regum* (http://www.ultimaratioregum.co.uk)

- Antonios Liapis—Researcher in the field of procedural video game content generation (http://antoniosliapis.com)
- Niccolò Tedeschi—Artist and game developer at *Santa Ragione*, the independent video game development team behind *Fotonica* (http://www.fotonica-game.com) and *Mirrormoon* (http://www.mirrormoongame.com)

2. THINGS TO KEEP IN MIND WHILE BUILDING EXPERIENCE MACHINES

Analytical concepts such as "ludo-narrative dissonance" and "world-consistency"[15] are frequently invoked when discussing video games. Those notions can be applied to a wide variety of game genres and are not specific to a particular style or age of video game development. They are, I find, most useful when observing or criticizing playful virtual worlds that include and emphasize aspects of linguistic communication, folklore, and exploration. Both ideas have their conceptual basis in the expectation that virtual worlds are only genuinely experienced as worlds when they are perceived as internally consistent and logically sound; that is to say, when the actions and decisions that we take within such worlds are meaningfully woven within a network of reactions and transformations. This ideology is often congealed in what is commonly referred to as an "implicit contract" between the creators of virtual worlds and the human dwellers (the players) who are supposed to inhabit and experience such worlds.

That tacit agreement is bilateral: on the one hand, the world-designers are expected to disclose worlds that are experientially rich, meaningful, and consistent (or, more simply, "worldly"—see note 2). Their line of work relies on the inherent promise that the worlds that they create will try to pleasurably facilitate and foster the players' sense of presence and immersion. On the other hand, the players willingly gloss over some of the logical and perceptual incongruities of their virtual playgrounds. In the current socio-technological context, for the reasons discussed in the previous sections of this chapter, the players' end of this bargain is far from a trivial one. It is comprehensibly hard to believe in the "worldliness" of virtual worlds when such worlds offer a relatively low aesthetical granularity when compared with the actual one, and when they are experienced through a painfully restricted gamut of perceptual modes. Another aspect of virtual experiences that currently contributes to our difficulties with achieving a sense of depth, consistency, and meaning can be recognized in their atrocious scalability. Presently, virtual worlds are designed to be experienced at very specific and very narrow perceptual scales: trying to observe something too closely or trying to get a comprehensive view of a phenomenon from a distance frequently result in the computer simulation revealing its clumsy artificiality through glaring omissions and distortions. More generally, as soon as our aspirations for discovery and interaction exceed the affordances of a virtual world, the illusion of "worldliness" shatters. In relation to this last point, it is not uncommon to experientially encounter the limits of virtual worlds in the forms of impassable walls, invisible boundaries, and puffy clouds shrouding the sharp edges of a world's geometrical extremities. Other deal-breaking phenomena can be recognized in textures degrading to blurry gradients when trying to examine them too intimately, artificial intelligences running against walls or looping erratically in response to unexpected situations, and more.

Finally, I find it important to emphasize that the virtual worlds of video games and computer simulations are still exclusively accessed through external physical devices (screens, headsets, headphones, controllers, keyboards, motion sensors, microphones, etc.). In analogy with some of the points that I raised when discussing Nozick's thought experiment, the materiality of our relationships with computers presently constitutes an unavoidable dimension of how we are both designing and experiencing virtual worlds, and an often-invoked cause for our incredulity and dissatisfaction with them. Bazin's famous statement according to which cinema—in its accomplished form—"has not yet been invented" still resonates today (Bazin 1967, 21).

We are arguably approaching a technological age in which we will be capable of supplanting our actual experiences with artificial ones in the direct and quasi-immediate ways envisaged, among others, by Bazin and Nozick. In the upcoming section of this chapter, I will concentrate on how game designers are currently striving to disclose vast, believable, and internally consistent worlds (or, in other words, how they are trying to comply with their end of the "implicit agreement" outlined above). If it is true that we cannot yet bypass the problem of the materiality of physical devices to access virtual worlds, then what design solutions and what technological expedients are game developers presently devising and adopting to make the problems of scale, of limit, and of content generation less conspicuous and—consequently—minimizing the players' nostalgia for the experiential incompletability of the actual world?

2.1. Slowing Down the "Erosion"

Game scholars Ian Bogost and Riccardo Fassone observed that video games are inherently limited systems, given the necessity to compress their interactive dynamics into a digital simulation (Bogost 2006; Fassone 2013, 127). On that premise, video game worlds cannot avoid letting people operate with (and around) those limitations and boundaries in order to extract meaning from them. It is interesting to observe that—in several languages including English—the term *play* is not only used to signify an enjoyable, nonserious activity, but also indicates the limited space in which a mechanism can move and perform its operations. In this sense, the creators of virtual worlds are in a position of power in relation to the player, as the former have the responsibility to configure the possibility space of "play" for the players: it is the developers' role to establish (at least partially) what is interactively and perceptually available in their virtual worlds, what elements and behaviors those worlds include, and what is, instead, left out of their "possibility horizon."[16]

The term *possibility horizon* is used here with reference to the Ancient Greek origin of the term *horizon*, ὅρος (*horos*), which denotes a frontier—a spatial limit. On that etymological foundation, *horizon* is employed, in this context, to indicate the geometrical boundaries of the game space, boundaries that can manifest themselves as material borders, edges, or, as previously discussed, as the limited perceptual and interactive scale that the world in question affords. Such perceptual and cognitive limitations of video games are obvious indicators of their finitude and artificiality and—as such—they were earlier identified as crucial triggers for a specific kind of discontent. It follows that the most common techniques employed by designers to try to prevent the emergence of "world-weariness" involve making those limitations as inconspicuous and difficult to encounter as possible.

A very obvious example of this design strategy can be recognized in the way the literal horizons of video game worlds are usually presented as the aesthetical/thematic illusions of distant lands, buildings, cities, islands, planets, and star systems that cannot be reached by the players or examined closely. Similar strategies of unknowability or concealment of the frontiers of virtual worlds also include the intuitive aesthetical translation of boundaries into something impossible to overcome or obviously deadly. Among the "translations" that are more frequently encountered in the virtual worlds of video games are precipitous mountain ridges, impassable lakes of magma, cliffs, broken bridges, tall walls, electrified fences, and endless stretches of water. Other strategies to prevent the experiential encounter with a virtual world's borders and boundaries involve creating game spaces that have "periodic boundary conditions" (worlds that wrap onto themselves). This is the case in the Atari 1979 arcade classic *Asteroids*. Including the possibility for a virtual world to procedurally generate new content as soon as the players move beyond spaces that were previously designed and mapped is yet another approach for making the boundaries of a video game evanescent and inconspicuous (as do Mojang's *Minecraft* and CCP's *EVE Online*).

The masking and/or the removal of limitations concerning both the perceptual scale and the spatial extension of virtual worlds are not the only ways in which designers are trying to disclose experiences that absorb our interest, and do not give immediate rise to feelings of nostalgia and discontent. With a particular emphasis on the interactive limitations imposed by video game worlds, researcher and developer Mike Cook argued that "we dream of doing and being a particular thing in a world, and then we find ourselves unable to do it. It is a typically twenty-first century condition—to be trying our hardest to escape into a digital world and then finding that we cannot act in the way we wanted. It is almost like being in a nightmare where one is unable to move one's arms, or to speak."

In his interview for this chapter, Cook also attributed reasons for dissatisfaction to the repetition and modularity of elements in virtual worlds, especially when parts of those worlds are generated algorithmically. For Cook, in those cases, "it is not so much dissatisfaction with the granularity of the world, but with its regularity." He believed that the more familiar we become with a world and its logics, the less interesting and surprising this world gets, progressively shying away from any sense of sublimity. Over time, argued the researcher, "we become numb to the patterns inherent in the algorithms that constitute the world."

Among the most common solutions to the problem posed by the familiarity and triviality of video game spaces, all the developers and researchers I interviewed mentioned the intentional masking or breaking of computer-generated patterns with hand-created content. The integration of procedural content with hand-made content can trick the human brain into misinterpreting the complexity of a generator and overestimating the experiential richness of a virtual world. "The player builds a mental model of how content is generated in a certain world," explained Cook, "and then they encounter something that does not fit that model. Their assumption that the hand-made content comes from the same algorithm that generated the rest of the world prompts them to re-evaluate their initial mental model, and in this way their respect and interest for that world erodes a little slower."

Further ideas shared by most of my interviewees that specifically address ways to mask the regularities and the repetitions of procedurally generated content in virtual worlds also include

- adding "noise" to predesigned game content; that is, allowing a generator to introduce small aesthetical and functional variations to predesigned game modules in order to make it hard for the players to recognize them as something already "known" (this is the case with Mossmouth's video game *Spelunky,* among others)
- giving the players themselves the possibility and tools to modify, destroy, or reconstruct shared virtual environments. These tools, Liapis explained in his interview for this chapter, allow the players to provide additional complexity and richness to interactive, digital worlds that will, because of that, inevitably feel less artificial and more "lived"
- using data from the internet to both disguise procedurally generated patterns and to allow a virtual world to feel more "worldly" by means of referencing recent, actual events

- erasing all the saved states and information about a world when a game session ends. According to what Johnson argued in his interview for this chapter, losing information and access to a world as well as the civilizations that inhabited it, its undiscovered religions and tales, and its unvisited lands after a game is over not only makes it harder to reverse-engineer the ways in which that world was generated but also triggers a lingering feeling of mystery about it.

In addition to the virtual *Weltschmerz* elicited by experientially encountering the boundaries of virtual worlds (in both extension and scale) and to the stale repetition of spatial patterns, both Tedeschi and Johnson recognized a third, supplementary trigger for "world-weariness" in contemporary video games: the fact that our virtual worlds tend to be poorly consistent in terms of their themes. According to both game developers, we are not only constantly (and painfully) comparing virtual experiences with actual ones (our "phenomenological bedrock") but also measuring the former against the backdrop of established genres and canons. Tedeschi clarified his specific way to understand this problem with an example:

> In *Red Dead Redemption* (Rockstar Games 2010), a videogame that amply borrows its themes and aesthetics from the Western genre, it is possible to walk into various saloons and engage non-player characters in a game of poker. The premises of what I am about to discuss resonate with the representations of the American Old West that we all are likely used to: I am in a saloon playing poker in the world of *Red Dead Redemption*. After a few hands, I have almost lost all of my money and so, while the game is still ongoing, I decide to stand up, shoot all of the other players, and walk out with all the money. Once I have killed all of the other players, however, no money is to be found on their bodies or on the table where we were playing. Apparently, *Red Dead Redemption* treats the game at the poker table as a technically separate instance of the world, rather than a part of it. My actions, which were completely consistent with the Western genre, are not acknowledged by the game. At that point, the world revealed its artificial constitution and lost its "worldliness" for me. . . . To a point that everything from that point on felt phoney and pointless.

In response to the problem of thematic inconsistency, Tedeschi and Johnson each suggested design strategies that digital world creators could start to employ with today's technologies and tools. In his interview, Tedeschi argued that the problem of world-inconsistency can be overcome by striving to set up independent worlds; that is, by making games that do not reference the actual world aesthetically or thematically. Resorting to his words referring to *Santa Ragione*'s design for their 2013 game *Mirrormoon* EP, we learn that they tried to propose a very abstract experience narratively, interactively and aesthetical-ly. The world of *Mirrormoon* is never wholly defined: it is an open world, a minimal world that is simply "suggested" to the player. This "openness" might not be the final solution to the problem of thematic inconsistency, but I think it goes in the right direction, that is letting the players interpret what they encounter rather than pre-determining for them how a world is to be understood on the basis of previous, common experiences. This could be understood as a Duchampian approach to game design: *ce sont les regardeurs qui font les tableaux.*

Discussing the same problem in relation to procedurally generated worlds, Johnson foresaw developments and new techniques that could ensure the emergence of more believable and coherent worlds. Johnson, who pioneered some of those techniques himself in his 2012 game *Ultima Ratio Regum*, insisted that part of the solution consists in striving to generate each of the things that constitute a virtual world in an interconnected fashion, in such a way that each aspect relates to every other aspect and does not feel like a brutal break with the world, or a random addition of content to it:

> It is relatively easy to make a generator that spits out Game-of-Thrones-esque names for cities like "Wolfweald," or "Queen's Throne," or "Dragonlance," or whatever. . . . But the real challenge is making those generated things to "percolate" down through the remainder of the world, to reflect in everything from how people speak, to what they wear, how they act, what their history is, etc.

2.2. Tragic Conclusion

Besides his fitting comments on the design and the procedural generation of less "painful" worlds, Liapis pointed out something that I consider interesting; something with which—in the cautionary spirit typical of the concluding sections of some literary works—I would like to close this chapter.

In response to one of my interview questions—or, rather, as an amendment to it—Liapis called my attention to the fact that it would be paradoxical to think of our sense of unease in video games as simply meaning that we would prefer to pursue any task in the actual world (such as laundry, homework, or grocery shopping) rather than exploring enchanted kingdoms in a high-fantasy virtual worlds. Although he agreed that the feeling of virtual "world-weariness" is something that he also commonly experienced, and something that is inherent in how we currently design and experience video game worlds, Liapis claimed that his way of coping with virtual *Weltschmerz* does not primarily involve the idea of "returning to the actual." He argued, in fact, that his ways of dealing with virtual nostalgia usually consist in simply starting a new game altogether: exploring a new world with new possibilities and different promises of "worldliness" and "mystery." Liapis appeared to be well aware that his expectations cannot be fulfilled by means of the systemic artificiality of today's virtual technologies (or even at all), but he seemed equally dissatisfied with the prospect of considering actual experiences as the only possible answer to our shared malcontent with virtual ones.

To be sure, I would like to clarify that I did not mean to imply (in this chapter or elsewhere) that the actual world will ultimately satisfy us, or that our expectations and aspirations will find an adequate response in our experiential relationship to it. If the Romantic age had not offered enough examples as to why that might not be the case, ancient Greek tragedies and the artistic and philosophical currents of existentialism and absurdism could also be mentioned as historical landmarks of Western culture's awareness of the meaninglessness of our existential struggle in this world. What I want to propose with this chapter is the idea that *all* worlds are ultimately absurd, and that technologies can never be expected to offer definitive solutions to the boring, painful, and even tragic dimensions of our existence. They are, I argue, better understood as existential tools: not as the contexts where we can find completion and satisfaction, but rather as instruments that enable us to embrace ourselves and negotiate with various aspects of our (individual as well as collective) existence in previously unexperienced guises. It is in relation to this standpoint that I claim that human beings cannot be existentially "completed" by technological means. In my perspective it is not simply a problem with the current technologies or our mastery of them: we are constitutively bound to dissatisfaction, and driven to constantly explore and experiment with new worlds and unfamiliar possibilities of being. Virtual worlds, in their peculiar ways, arguably offer those experiences and possibilities, and in doing so, they contribute to our existential struggle both in allowing us to transcend some aspects of our everyday relationship with the actual world, and in disclosing new ways in which our very incompleteness can be experienced and understood.

NOTES

1. The adjective *virtual* was originally coined in modern Latin to encapsulate the idea of *potentiality*. *Virtualis* is a late-medieval neologism the existence of which became necessary when Aristotle's concept of δύναμις (*dynamis*: potentiality, power) had to be translated into Latin (Van Binsbergen 1997, 9). The concept of *potentiality* at the etymological foundation of the adjective *virtual* provides the background for understanding why, at least in one of its interpretations, it is used to indicate the latency of certain possibilities inherent in a specific artifact, combination of artifacts, or state of things. A more common connotation of the adjective *virtual* was presented by Pierre Lévy, not in opposition to *actual* in the sense discussed above, but to *actual* in the specific sense of "pertinent to the world humans are native to" (Lévy 1998, 14).

2. In the philosophical tradition of phenomenology, the term *world* generally indicates a set composed of beings that are understood together with all their (detectable) properties and mutual relationships. More specifically, a world comprises the set outlined above as experienced by one of the beings involved in it. To be identified as a world (and thus to have the

quality of "worldliness"), such experiences need to be meaningful in the sense that they need to be persistently perceivable and behaviorally consistent (thus intelligible, to a degree) for the being experiencing them (Gualeni 2015b, 6). This interpretation is not only conveniently encompassing but also establishes a clear distinction between the experiences of virtual worlds and those of dreams or hallucinations. The virtual worlds of simulations and video games are recognized as worlds precisely because they can be accessed and returned to at will, and because they emerge in ways that are repeatable and relatively stable in their mechanical and aesthetic aspects (ibid.)

3. The surfacing of "The Myth of Total Cinema" can also easily be identified in literary works, particularly in social science fiction. Examples are glaring in the works of Philip K. Dick (*UBIK, The Electric Ant, We Can Remember It for You Wholesale*, etc.), Neal Stephenson (*REAMDE, The Diamond Age, Snow Crash*, etc.), William Gibson (*Count Zero, Neuromancer*, etc.), and Greg Egan (*Permutation City, Zendegi*, etc.), just to mention a few. Another media form that is unsurprisingly sensitive to the tropes of artificiality and digital simulations is the video game. Themes and premises such as being trapped inside a simulation, being unaware of the virtual constitution of one's world, or situations involving recursively entering a simulation from within a simulation, are often explored in video games, and especially so in ones that reference the tradition of science fiction. The VR pods that can be encountered in Bethesda Softworks's recently revived *Fallout* franchise (since 2008) are particularly glaring examples of the videoludic materialization of Bazin's myth. Experience machines also play a cardinal narrative role in the popular video game franchise *Assassin's Creed* (since 2007).

4. In Gitelman 2006, Lisa Gitelman explicitly understood all audiovisual media as aspiring to a comparable form of transparency; that is, attempting to efface their technical mediation from the content experienced by the user(s).

5. Imagining myself in that situation—which would be analogical to a scenario that Greg Egan outlines in his novel *Permutation City*—I believe that the awareness of the artificiality of the virtual worlds one finds oneself immersed into would be in itself almost unbearable from a psychological point of view (Egan 2008, 3). It would be a state of mind similar to a paranoid fixation that is, however, unlikely to be a permanent one. Such attitude toward the world would be—Egan argues—"too bizarre to be sustained for long" (ibid.).

6. *Nostalgia* is a Modern Latin term that comes from the Ancient Greek words νόστος (*nostos*: "return, homecoming") and αλγος (*algos*: "pain, suffering"); it was coined in the eighteenth century to indicate the specific pain that we feel when we are far away from home and yearn to return there.

7. I am referring here, in particular, to chapters 3, 7, and 8 of Gualeni 2015b.

8. A similar reflection concerning the sublimity and the domestication of video game spaces was offered in 2011 by Paul Martin. In his article "The Pastoral and the Sublime in *Elder Scrolls IV: Oblivion*" Martin identified the "sublime" (a concept that involves nuances of both immensity, incalculability, and danger) and the "pastoral" (what is familiar and nonthreatening) as two successive moments of our experiential relationship with a certain video game space (Martin 2011).

9. Mentioning several positive social uses for the experience machine in this paragraph, I am not intending to claim that the experience machine would only be used in those manners and with those intentions. In line with a long tradition of dystopian social science fiction, we can easily imagine the machine being put to negative social uses: for punishment and correction rather than for the pursuit of a liberal education; for psychological and physical torture rather than for pleasure.

10. I believe it is important to clarify that in his thought experiment, Nozick does not explicitly state that his hypothetical machine exclusively discloses single-user experiences. The reason why I believe that is the case anyway is that the machine could not uphold a consistent, believable world in which two or more users wanted to experience things that were in conflict with one another or contradicted one another. For example, if more than one user decided to use Nozick's fictional machine to experience being the current president of the United States of America, how could a "multiplayer" world accommodate the wishes of all those users at the same time? If another user decided to experiment with a doomsday device that eradicates all human life on planet Earth, how could a shared virtual world coherently allow other users to

keep experiencing the existence that they chose and designed? The question remains open, however, concerning whether the machine could allow us to passively spectate somebody else's virtual experiences (as a disembodied observer), or temporarily participate in it with limited agency (for example impersonating virtual insects or simulated, ghostly beings).

11. To be sure, this is not to say that simulated physics can be at best identical to actual physics; many video game worlds offer virtual worlds that playfully subvert physical properties and behaviors that we are familiar and scientifically well acquainted with in the actual world. It could suffice, for example, to think of the possibility granted in the world of *Portal* (Valve 2007) to create wormholes in tridimensional spaces (portals that allow space to be short-circuited), or the ways in which the concepts of time and causation are manipulated and subverted in video games such as *Blinx: The Time Sweeper* (Artoon 2002), *Prince of Persia: Sands of Time* (UbiSoft Montreal 2003), or *Braid* (Number None, Inc. 2008).

12. Originally released in 2008, *Foldit* is a cross-platform online puzzle video game that allows the players to simulate control of some of the biochemical processes involved in protein folding. It was developed by the University of Washington's Center for Game Science in collaboration with the UW Department of Biochemistry. The analysis of players' creative solutions to protein-folding puzzles in *Foldit* allowed scientists to develop cures to diseases and pursue innovation in biotechnology (Eiben et al. 2012).

13. *Play to Cure: Genes in Space* is a 2014 free, mobile video game through which players, flying a spaceship through hurdles and resources in space, help researchers analyze real genetic data used in cancer research. *Play to Cure: Genes in Space* is an ongoing project that was developed under the guidance of Cancer Research UK.

14. This auto-gnostic aspect of how human beings extend and objectify themselves, their ideas, and their desires in technologies and technological systems is a recurrent trope in the work of several academics in the field of the philosophy of technology. Dutch philosopher Maarten Coolen, for example, is "interested in precisely those anthropological ideas that one can associate with the act of technological transformation itself. What can man learn about himself from his own fabrications?" (Coolen 1992, 165, 166; English translation by Peter-Paul Verbeek in De Mul 2014).

15. These notions all refer to a particular way to frame creative works, and have a common, general understanding of what "quality" means when analyzing such works. For Samuel Taylor Coleridge, that specific understanding of "quality" is measured by how carefully and efficiently the authors of a certain work managed to provide "a semblance of truth sufficient to procure for these shadows of imagination that willing suspension of disbelief for the moment, which constitutes poetic faith" (Coleridge 1983, chapter XIV).

16. I believe it should be pointed out that this "possibility horizon" is not uniquely determined by the projectual intentions of programmers, designers, or creative directors. It cannot be recognized as a purely authorial (or authoritarian) process, as it always involves a degree of compromise with the players, whose aspirations and actions are not always possible for the developers to contain and shape. Video game glitch-runs, and the "modding" of video games and video game worlds, together with various approaches to play that are overtly rebelling against the ideologies and forms of power that are materially embedded in games, are especially evident examples of how our relationship with virtual worlds is effectively one of compromise, and not of imposition. Transgressive approaches to game rules, game affordances, and game conventions are recognized as forms of social subversion in the works of several authors, including, notably, Espen Aarseth and Mary Flanagan. From their theoretical standpoint, subversive play is an important cultural tool that stimulates independent, critical thought, self-reflection, and promotes social change (Aarseth 2007; Flanagan 2009). To quote Fassone, the rigid borders of a game's formal structure "do not prevent playing from being an intrinsically transformative, interpretative and ideological act" (Fassone 2013, 30).

Part III

Experiential Design:
Problems and Prospects

Chapter Nine

The Problem of Evil in Virtual Worlds

Brendan Shea

In the original experience machine (EM) thought experiment, Robert Nozick provides a number of distinct reasons that might explain peoples' intuitive rejection of the chance to plug in (Nozick 1974, 42–45). For example, he claims that a life lived in the EM deprives an individual of the opportunity to do certain things, to be a certain sort of person, and to genuinely interact with the external world. Choosing to live in the EM, at least on Nozick's account, may even amount to a certain sort of suicide, insofar as it involves giving up the sorts of character traits that constitute one's self-identity. The barrage of pleasant sensations in the EM simply leaves no room to act courageously in the face of danger, to entertain others with a well-told joke, or to demonstrate generosity or compassion in response to the sufferings of others.

As is evidenced by this book, the exact philosophical target of Nozick's EM argument has been widely debated, though it has often been construed as an argument against various forms of hedonism and related theories of human welfare.[1] Whatever its success in this regard, however, I'd like to focus on a somewhat different aspect of life within the EM: it seems to deny one the prospect of a meaningful life, or the possibility of caring about or loving various causes, people, or ideas in the future.[2] More specifically, hooking up to the EM precludes participation in many of the activities that give structure and direction to people's lives: romantic relationships, parenting, friendships, scientific discovery, artistic creation, and so on. Regardless of how much sensory pleasure the EM might bring us, the cost is simply too high: not only must we abandon our current meaning-giving projects, we must abdicate the possibility of taking up any future project of this type, for however long we live in the EM. This may partially account for the widespread intuition that life in the real world is preferable to life within the virtual world of the EM.

The undesirability of life within the EM, however, hardly shows that meaninglessness is a necessary consequence of life within a virtual world. In this chapter, I'll explore the possibility of specifying an EM scenario that avoids this unfortunate consequence by the incorporation of human-like virtual agents worthy of moral concern. I'll argue that, while this scenario would remedy some shortcomings of the original EM, this sort of worldbuilding would be subject to severe ethical restraints. In particular, the fact that this EM would involve the creation of beings subject to suffering and evil would render the user vulnerable to an analogue of the problem of evil familiar from the philosophy of religion. I'll go on to consider the extent to which common theodicies might be adapted to provide moral constraints on this sort of worldbuilding. I will conclude that, while they illuminate certain necessary conditions of any morally justified worldbuilding, they fail to provide sufficient conditions. This suggests that, insofar as we take the creation of virtual agents with moral status to represent a genuine (though perhaps distant) possibility, we have moral obligations to think carefully about the way our design decisions will affect the circumstances in which these agents will find themselves.

1. THE EXPERIENCE MACHINE AS A CHOICE

Nozick's description of the actual EM thought experiment is relatively short. The reader is told that neuroscientists will ensure that she will be given whatever experiences in whatever combination will be most pleasant, and that she won't know about being in the EM while living there, though she'll have a chance to wake up every two years and choose future experiences. Also, she needn't worry about staying unplugged to serve others, since they will also have the ability to hook up to experience machines, if they so choose. Based on these characteristics of the EM, Nozick assumes (plausibly, it seems, based on the reactions of introductory philosophy students) that readers will reject life in the EM in favor of life in the real world.

How might one alter the EM scenario to avoid this quick, intuitive rejection? To begin, it is important to recognize that the rejection is, at least purportedly, a choice between two different options: living life in the EM versus living life in a world in which EMs exist, but not hooking up to one. However, while a great deal of attention has been paid to the first, life-in-the-EM alternative, somewhat less attention has been given to the lives of those who choose not to hook up in such a world. Is this a world in which human lives generally resemble ours, or is it one in which they are radically different? In the first case, our intuitive rejection of the EM might carry considerable weight; in the second case, however, there are reasons for exercising much more caution.

Nozick himself has little interest in life outside the EM, and even directs the reader to ignore the question of who will tend the machines if everyone is plugged in. Nevertheless, his description of this world makes the significant posit that everyone who wants to can plug in and that, because of this, the reader need not worry about staying unplugged in order to tend to the needs of others. In this world, it seems, there is literally *no* unavoidable physical or mental suffering; anyone plagued by pain, sickness, depression, or anxiety need merely plug in, and it will all go away. While these people may well have good reasons for refraining from plugging in, this nevertheless represents a significant difference between our world and that of the EM thought experiment. Moreover, there are reasons for thinking the differences from our world are even more pronounced than they might initially appear. For example, in keeping with the spirit of Nozick's scenario, we might also stipulate that EMs can provide medically optimum care, manage their environmental impact, and so on. In the interest of minimizing the impact of potential moral reasons for rejecting the EM, we might go further: let's suppose that the EMs not only deliver maximum benefits to those currently hooked up, but to all future people as well. In this world, there is simply no possibility that the fruits of future scientific research, parenting, or artistic creation will ever produce outcomes that are hedonically superior to life within the EM. To the extent that one finds meaning in life by pursuing projects that relate to alleviating either one's own suffering or those of others, life in this world may be deeply unsatisfactory, even if it is ultimately better than plugging in.[3]

If the world outside the EM is really as boring as described here, why wouldn't one want to plug in? I suspect that the most significant reason concerns Nozick's contention that hooking up to the EM amounts to a sort of suicide. After all, one is submitting not only to a lifetime (or at least a few years) of pleasant experiences but also a massive forgetting of the fact that one has made this momentous choice, presumably because this knowledge would undercut the pleasure in the EM world. If it is to accomplish this task, this forgetting must extend not only to the decision to hook up to the EM but to any other memory that might cause one to regret lost opportunities. In signing up for the EM, then, one must not only renounce the possibility of acting on behalf of the nonexperiential goals one cares about but also agree to have one's brain altered so that one will conveniently forget all of this. This sort of radical change is, as Nozick's remarks suggest, a threat to one's personal identity. Given this, the intuitive rejection of plugging in should not be surprising, even on the supposition that there isn't that much to care about in the world outside the EM.

2. BUILDING A BETTER EXPERIENCE MACHINE

The discussion in the previous section suggests that, while the world outside the EM would likely be deeply unsatisfactory for many people, it would nevertheless remain preferable to plugging in, given the threat that this poses to personal identity. However, this threat to personal identity appears to relate only indirectly to the fact that one lives in a virtual world, as opposed to a real one. Instead, life in the EM endangers one's identity both by precluding one's ability to pursue important desires and by altering one's memory to prevent one from realizing this has been done. These undesirable aspects of the EM scenario might be eliminated if the virtual world in question provided opportunities for users to genuinely care about things inside the EM. So, for example, consider the scorned lovers or unsuccessful scientists who contemplate plugging in to the EM, but who decide that they would rather continue to pursue the (ever-diminishing) chance of *actually having a relationship* or *actually making a discovery* over the alternative of having a *mere experience* of these things.

One way in which one might design a virtual world to remedy this problem is by populating it with human-like AIs with whom the user could have genuine relationships and, more specifically, to whom the agent could owe moral consideration. While the possibility that one might owe moral consideration to AIs has received some philosophical scrutiny in recent years,[4] it has long been a staple of science fiction. One might, for example, think of Isaac Asimov's various robots, the androids from Phillip K. Dick's "Do Androids Dream of Electric Sheep?" (Dick 1968), the robot child of Brian Aldiss's "Supertoys Last All Summer Long" (Aldiss 1969), or the films (*I, Robot*; *Blade Runner*; and *AI*) based on these stories. More recent examples one might point to include Data (or the holographic Moriarty) from *Star Trek: The Next Generation*, the Cylons of *Battlestar Galactica*, or Samantha from the movie *Her*. These AIs all demonstrate, to varying extents, the sorts of characteristics that have long been thought central to moral status, including the capacity to have interests, to experience pain and pleasure (or the digital analogues of these), and to exercise autonomous choice. They are capable of entering into meaningful relationships with humans, and their well-being is importantly dependent upon how these relationships turn out. They are harmed when humans ignore their interests (or worse yet, actively seek to frustrate them), and are benefitted when humans assist them in various ways.

There is, of course, a long-running debate over whether (science fiction scenarios aside) it is genuinely possible to develop AIs with human-like characteristics such as sentience, consciousness, or autonomy, and it is beyond the scope of this chapter to answer the various objections that been leveled against it. In any case, the role that virtual agents play in the revised thought experiment here might be interpreted in two ways. I will generally assume that the virtual world in question contains agents that really are worthy of moral consideration. If one objects to this scenario, one might instead assume that, while the virtual agents are not genuinely worthy of moral consideration, the potential user of the EM is justified either in believing that they are, or (more weakly) in believing that this is at least a possibility worth taking seriously. In any case, if the argument below is correct, there would be little reason for a potential user who denied this possibility to consider connecting to the EM in the first place.

If designed correctly, a virtual world populated with human-like AIs would offer a potential user several notable advantages over Nozick's original EM. First, plugging in would not require sacrificing the possibility of genuinely *doing* something or *being* a certain sort of person. In fact, this virtual world might actually provide better opportunities than would forgoing plugging in. In the virtual world, unlike the unplugged world, one's artistic, scientific, and personal projects might genuinely serve to prevent avoidable suffering on the part of the AIs that inhabit it. Second, and closely related to this, this revised EM would no longer require that users forget the fact of their plugging in, as was required in Nozick's original scenario. After all, what the user of the original EM had wanted to forget was the knowledge that their experiences weren't genuine, and that nothing in the virtual world was really worthy of concern or care. In the revised virtual world, this is no longer true. Instead, the user has opted to live in a world where she can reasonably expect to care about something or someone, even if she doesn't yet know what this will be.

Many people might still have good reasons to not plug in, of course. In particular, any person with strong preexisting commitments to people and projects outside the virtual world might well find the prospect of plugging in unattractive, even if they knew that the virtual world would provide opportunities to cultivate alternatives. Nevertheless, there are good reasons for thinking that this sort of virtual world might hold some attractions even if the real world were not as barren of meaning as Nozick's scenario seems to suggest. People's capacities to lead lives that they find meaningful and fulfilling is after all, significantly impacted by numerous factors outside of their control. Along with the obvious challenges posed by lack of resources or ill health (both of which could presumably be addressed with the virtual world), many people find that their desires are frustrated by their inability to make a difference in the world around them. For every successful artist, researcher, athlete, or political or business leader, there are significant numbers of slightly less talented (or less lucky) people who find that their attempts to make meaningful contributions fall short. Importantly, this sort of phenomenon need not merely reflect a morally suspicious desire for increased social status, or for membership among society's elite. Instead, it is the result of the fact that people want their projects to succeed, and this success crucially depends not only on their own choices but also on the actions of many others. Arguably, this sense of powerlessness is at the root of many people's dissatisfaction with their lives. People repeatedly fail, often through no fault of their own, to establish friendships and romantic relationships, to find careers that allow them to cultivate their talents, or to find receptive audiences for their ideas and artistic contributions.

Given the current state of technology, the best (and perhaps only) solution for people encountering this sort of problem involves abandoning or modifying goals so that they can succeed. For a great many people, however, this solution may be psychologically unrealistic, since it requires abandoning goals and projects that are deeply rooted in both human biology and existing cultural institutions. For an individual in this situation, choosing life in a virtual world where he or she could achieve meaningful goals may well represent an attractive alternative to a meaning-deficient real world. After all, in a custom-designed virtual world, one can be reasonably sure that one's capacities, if properly utilized, really can lead to success.

3. VIRTUAL WORLDBUILDING AND THE PROBLEM OF EVIL

In the previous section, I argued that the incorporation of human-like AIs within the virtual world might serve to resolve some significant worries about Nozick's EM. However, the mere incorporation of such agents does not, by itself, provide an adequate reason for users to plug in. After all, if a potential user's reason for dissatisfaction with real world results from a general sense of powerlessness, this would hardly provide reason to plug into a virtual world filled with AIs whose capacities significantly exceeded their own, and who had little to gain from the user's actions. Instead, a potential user would need to be assured that the AIs would be not only worthy of moral concern but that their capacities would be limited to the extent that it would be within this particular user's ability to genuinely benefit or harm them in significant ways.

This suggests that plugging into the virtual world might be something like playing a video game where the user is the character upon whose choices everything depends, and whose difficulty is precisely calibrated to the user's own abilities. However, the design of this virtual world is complicated by that the fact it contains agents who differ in significant ways from the sorts of monsters and nonplayer characters (NPCs) that populate existing video games. Some of these differences are merely practical, in that the cognitive complexity of these agents would make it difficult for the designers of the virtual world to ensure that it could genuinely meet the needs and preferences of potential users. For the purposes of this chapter, however, I'll suppose that these difficulties can be overcome.

A much more significant difference between NPCs and the hypothetical virtual agents concerns the fact that the latter, unlike the former, are worthy of moral consideration. This obviously places constraints on what users ought to do while inhabiting the world. Among other things, users should refrain from gratuitously harming virtual agents, and might plausibly have duties to assist them in certain ways. The sorts of behavior encouraged by games such as the *Grand Theft Auto* series would, for example, raise significant moral worries. This suggests that, whatever else these virtual worlds might be good for, they couldn't provide a morally acceptable means by which users could fulfill their immoral desires to harm or exploit people.[5]

The designers of the virtual world might attempt to circumvent this problem in various ways. So, for example, they might consider designing a world inhabited by masochistic agents who enjoyed suffering the sorts of injuries that careless or malevolent users might inflict upon them. However, it is unclear how widely applicable such a procedure might be. On the one hand, if users were informed about this engineering workaround in advance, this may well cause them to reject life within the virtual world, since this would serve to undercut the very possibility of making a real difference (albeit, a harmful one) that attracted them to the virtual world in the first place. On the other hand, if the engineers were to systematically hide this feature of the world from potential users, it seems doubtful whether the choices of these users to inhabit these worlds would reveal anything about their willingness (or lack thereof) to choose life within the virtual world. Since the present discussion is premised on exploring the nature of worlds that users would choose to inhabit, I'll leave aside discussion of this possibility.

Even supposing that a user's behavior within the virtual world is perfectly acceptable, however, there may be moral problems with the decision to create the world in the first place. So, for example, suppose that a given virtual world is instantiated only when a particular user chooses to plug in, and that the character of the world depends not just on the design of the underlying software program but also on the preferences of the individual user. The user's decisions, then, play a key role in determining which sorts of virtual agents will come into existence, and what sorts of lives these agents will have. Their lives might be relatively pleasant (if, for example, the user's virtual world involves sitting in a coffee shop discussing philosophy with virtual agents modeled on her favorite historical philosophers), or they might be much less pleasant, if the agents in the virtual world are subject to the endemic violence, deceit, and coercion that characterize many current video games. However, it seems highly implausible that the lives of the virtual agents will be perfect, since the human user's reasons for plugging in require the ability to impact the lives of such agents in meaningful ways. The fact that virtual agents will be subject to at least some sorts of significant suffering and evil thus seems to follow almost inevitably from the very purpose that the virtual world is designed to serve.

The creation of certain sorts of worlds would clearly be morally impermissible. Specifically, it seems undeniable that one ought not create a world in which the virtual inhabitants had, on average, lives not worth living. For example, creating worlds where the inhabitants are subject to unending torture seems clearly immoral, even if the human user found life in these worlds to be deeply satisfactory (for example, perhaps it is only by the actions of the user that a few lucky souls could be saved from this awful fate). However, beyond these extreme cases, matters become more difficult. Would it be acceptable, for instance, to create a world filled with highly competitive agents who regularly lose to the user at some game or other, and who suffer from the sort of jealousy and regret that allows the user to bask in her or his victory? These agents might find their lives to be worth living, at least in some minimal sense. Nevertheless, they might find such a situation deeply dispiriting and frustrating. Is the creation of such a world justified by the fact that, were it not for the user, these agents wouldn't have existed in the first place? Or did the user have some moral obligation to avoid creating a world that so was deeply "unfair"?

The question of what, if any, moral constraints might be placed on the creation of virtual worlds has several close analogues within contemporary philosophy. First, it has connections with the question of whether it is wrong for people to choose to reproduce when they have reasons to believe that the children resulting from these decisions will be less well-off than the children that might have resulted from other decisions.[6] Second, it bears a striking resemblance to the question of whether the omniscient, omnipotent, omnibenevolent God of classical theism could be morally justified in creating a world—such as the one we currently inhabit—with widespread cases of apparently undeserved suffering.[7] In the remainder of this chapter, I'll be examining this second case in some detail to consider what, if anything, the debate over the problem of evil might show about the morality of creating virtual worlds inhabited by beings to whom one owes moral concern.

There are, of course, important differences between the human creators of virtual worlds and the divine creator targeted by the problem of evil arguments. First, the human creators' incomplete knowledge and limited power may well make it impossible for them to design a world that maximizes the well-being of the potential virtual inhabitants, even if they desired to do so. With this in mind, it may be inappropriate to demand that a given virtual world be the best possible world. However, this deficit of knowledge or power does not alleviate human creators of any moral responsibility for a given world's shortcomings, so long as the creators were capable of making comparative judgements as to the degree and type of suffering likely to be present in the various alternative worlds they might create. So, for example, the human creators may be incapable of predicting with any precision the lives of individual virtual agents. Nevertheless, they could confidently predict that the average inhabitant of a zombie-apocalypse virtual world would be worse off than the average inhabitant of a resource-rich world devoted to artistic and scientific pursuits. Second, there is no assumption that the human creators are omnibenevolent, or that the users or creators of these worlds are the proper object of worship by the virtual agents inhabiting the world. This suggests that the human creators need not be held to the same high standard as the divine creator discussed in traditional theodicy. In the latter case, the goal is to establish what sorts of worlds might be created by a morally perfect being, of the sort that might plausibly be worthy of worship by the human inhabitants of this world. In the former case, the goal is much more modest: we want to know which worlds a human might create without being morally blameworthy.

With these caveats just mentioned in mind, one can now formulate the problem of evil for virtual worlds in a more precise form.

1. Any virtual world that is worth creating (from the potential user's perspective) will contain significant amounts of evil [suffering, frustration of desire, etc.] by virtual agents.
2. It is morally wrong to create a virtual world with significant amounts of evil, when one has the power and knowledge to create one with lesser amounts of evil.
3. It is within the user's power and knowledge to create a world that contains lesser amounts of evil.
4. So, it is morally wrong to create any virtual world that is, from the user's perspective, worth creating.

Is there any way out of this dilemma—to create a world that contains adequate evil to meet the needs of the human user without violating the demands of morality? In the remainder of the chapter, I will examine the possibility of justifying the inclusion of evil within a virtual world by looking to components of traditional theodicies. These potential justifications will, in effect, amount to objections to (2) and (3) above. The goal here will be to establish with more precision *which sorts* of evil ought to be especially concerning creators of virtual worlds, and what sorts of constraints this might place on the creation of virtual worlds.

4. THEODICIES FOR VIRTUAL WORLDS?

What, if anything, might serve to justify the intentional creation of a virtual world with significant amounts of evil? In the context of the religious problem of evil, various theodicies provide purported answers to this, and seek to identify possible or plausible reasons that God may have for allowing the sorts of evil we see around us. In this section, I'll take a look at a number of the key components of theodicies, [8] and consider what relevance, if any, they might have for the creation of virtual worlds.

4.1. Free Will

Free will forms a central element of most theodicies. Specifically, many theists have claimed that libertarian free will is an important good for human beings, and that one necessary consequence of creating a world with free will is the existence of the evil caused by its exercise. Considerations of free will are generally taken to be most directly relevant to explaining the existence of *moral evil*, or the evil inflicted by human beings, as opposed to *natural evil*, or the evil resulting from natural causes such as earthquakes, tsunamis, or disease.

Before considering the applicability of this argument to the case of virtual worlds, it is important to recognize that the conception of free will relevant to virtual worlds is of a different character than that appealed to in the context of theodicies. First, we can set aside contentious claims about the coherence of libertarian free will. After all, it is unclear whether the virtual agents could possess it and, even if they could possess it, there is no evident mechanism by which the human creators of the virtual worlds could grant or deny it to them. Instead, the sort of free will relevant to virtual agents is something closer to a capacity for autonomy, or self-governed action. If this is the case, then important aspects of many traditional free will defenses are not readily applicable to the creation of virtual worlds. In particular, there seems no reason to suppose that the existence of these sorts of autonomous agents logically (or metaphysically) entails the existence of evil, in the way that libertarian free will might. Because of these differences, it is not open to the human creator of the virtual world to escape moral responsibility for a particular instance of evil on bare grounds that this evil was the result of a "free action" by a virtual agent. This is not to say, of course, that the virtual agent might not also bear moral responsibility; the point is merely that this has no bearing on the responsibility of the world's creator.

In other respects, however, the limited power and knowledge of human creators may serve to immunize them against common objections against free-will theodicies. In particular, as mentioned earlier, there is little reason to think that the hypothetical creators of virtual worlds will be capable of predicting the future actions of the virtual inhabitants with any great accuracy. So, for example, one common objection to free-will theodicies contends that it should be possible for God to create a world in which each and every human freely chooses to do just those actions that avoid inflicting evil and suffering. If this is true, then the free-will theodicy fails, since the existence of free will does not require evil. Whatever the success of this objection in its original context, however, it fails when applied to virtual worlds. After all, even if such a world is logically possible for an omnipotent God, it clearly falls outside the capacities of human creators. Creating such a world would require creators be capable of predicting with precision the future of a virtual world, including all of the choices of all of its virtual inhabitants; moreover, they must do so for an indefinite number of such worlds, in order to find one that marries free will with absence of evil. The capacities of human creators would presumably be much more limited, amounting to no more than a capacity to predict the general types and magnitudes of evil that virtual agents are likely to suffer in a given virtual world.

Critics of theodicy have also contended that God could miraculously intervene to prevent the sorts of evils that stem from human free will, which would again undermine the free-will theodicy's claim that evil is an inevitable consequence of allowing humans the capacity to make free choices. Again, however, this objection cannot be easily translated to the case of virtual worlds, at least of the sort we are discussing. So, in the spirit of this objection, let's suppose that we attempt to create a program that continuously monitors the well-being of all of a virtual world's inhabitants, and which intervenes whenever it foresees that a free choice of one inhabitant will cause harm to another inhabitant. We will immediately run into several problems. First, it may be impossible to create such a program, for reasons similar to those pointed out above. After all, it would not be enough for this program simply to predict how the memory states representing the virtual world will evolve over time. In addition, it must correctly identify how these states link up with the emergent properties that we are interested in tracking, such as the well-being of the various virtual agents. Second, the creation of this sort of world would prevent the user from exercising significant choice, in something like the respect that Swinburne discusses (See Swinburne 2004, 240–42). If the user's reasons for choosing life within the virtual world require that she or he be able to make a difference in the lives of the virtual agents that live there, there is little reason to choose a world with continuous, miraculous interventions that ensure the well-being of these inhabitants.

Given these considerations, what might we conclude about the role of free will in virtual worlds, and what sorts of evil it might serve to justify? First, to the extent that opportunities to exercise free will and autonomy are important for humans, it is reasonable to think this will also hold for human-like virtual agents. This is something that must be accounted for when creating virtual worlds. So, for example, it would seem highly immoral to create a world in which the virtual agents had generally human-like psychologies, and to then create a law of nature that compelled these agents to immediately obey the verbal orders of the user, even in cases where this was in direct contradiction to their most important desires and interests. Second, it is plausible that a virtual world with genuinely autonomous virtual agents will contain some evil, at least in the minimal sense that these agents must be granted some capacity to frustrate the desires of both the user and their fellow inhabitants. Finally, the mere fact that the autonomous agents are virtual does not preclude them from bearing moral responsibility for their actions, or for the possibility that there may be some sorts of "deserved" suffering.

Even if all of this is true, however, this fails to show the moral acceptability of creating worlds with the sort of significant evils that some human users of the virtual world might require for their lives to be meaningful. Again, consider the case of a virtual world that resembles, at least in broad respects, a typical combat-heavy video game, where the user must defeat monsters, aliens, or enemy soldiers in order to rescue defenseless children, or members of some other vulnerable group. It might be appropriate, at least within the context of this world, to claim that the villains freely chose to engage in the morally wrong actions they did. However, this does not excuse the creator's moral culpability for making such a world, since she perfectly well could have created a world with more peaceful sociopolitical conditions, or one whose agents were less psychologically prone to violence. Moreover, the free will defense, at least by itself, seems ill suited to justify the other sorts of evil that might plague a large class of virtual worlds, such as the suffering caused by natural events, or the undeserved harms inflicted on sentient but non-autonomous virtual agents (the digital equivalents of young children and nonhuman animals). These sorts of concerns also arise in the context of the original problem of evil, of course, but the impossibility of appealing to notions related to libertarian free will makes addressing them considerably more difficult.

4.2. Natural Laws and Natural Evil

Swinburne (1998; 2004), among others, has appealed to the value of simple, uniform natural laws to explain the occurrence of evil that cannot be accounted for by free will in isolation. Swinburne begins with the idea that an important part of leading a worthwhile human life involves the opportunity to make decisions that have a significant impact on the world, for either good or evil. In order to realize that goal, he argues that God would need to ensure both that humans' power and knowledge are constrained and that humans are capable of extending this power and knowledge. He argues that a world (such as the one we live in) with simple, uniform laws of nature that both limit human action and are discoverable by careful inspection of the world meets both criteria. The fact that the invariant, continuous operation of these laws regularly leads to serious instances of both moral and natural evil motivates the agents both to gain knowledge concerning their world and to take seriously their power to act on it.

Swinburne's claims about the importance of laws of nature for humans might plausibly apply both to the human and virtual inhabitants of virtual worlds. A virtual world without any regular connection between event types, for instance, would make it effectively impossible for its inhabitants to exercise agency in any meaningful way. Similarly, a world in which human users (or others) had unlimited power to continuously reshape the world according to their preferences would undercut the ability of the virtual agents to engage in the sorts of long-term projects that help give substance and structure to their lives. This provides us with a prima facie reason for thinking that invariant natural laws ought to be included in a virtual world, even if this entails the existence of evil.

In assessing the ultimate success of this defense when applied to virtual worlds, however, it is important to keep in mind the differences between the way in which an all-powerful God could institute laws of nature, and the ways that humans might design the physics of a virtual world. For instance, on Swinburne's account, God creates a world with simple laws of nature because this is best for the beings inhabiting the world. However, an omnipotent being with different motives could have done otherwise: for example, the laws might appear to be strict regularities whenever intelligent beings were attending to them, but be subject to regular exceptions in cases where these would not be noticed, which would allow the creator to pursue various ends undetected. In the case of virtual worlds, by contrast, this does not seem to represent a realistic possibility. For suppose the creators of the world tried to implement an algorithm of this sort, which would allow exceptions to natural laws only in cases where these exceptions would not be detected. This would require that the algorithm consider not only the presence or absence of observers at the time of violation but also accurately determine whether this violation might contribute to the inhabitants' discovery of the laws' violation over the medium to long term. Among other things, this would presumably require representing the state of future science in this world, including the evidence that will be available to these future scientists.

The constraints of finite computing power also limit the choice of laws in other ways. For example, the physics underlying the virtual world must be at least tractable, in the sense that a finite computer could use the laws to generate the state of the world at time t_{n+1} from its state at t_n. This need not entail that laws appear simple to the world's inhabitants, of course, since even very simple algorithms may generate highly complex phenomena. However, the constraints of finite computing power rule out certain possibilities that might be open to an omnipotent creator, such as instituting a world with no underlying laws whatsoever, and instead specifying the complete history world as a series of sequential states (already including each of the user's actions), or something of the sort.

Just as was the case with free will, these limitations might actually serve to defuse certain objections to theodicies based on natural laws—that is, those contending that God might craft exceptions to laws to prevent any and all instances of natural evil. However, the mere fact that a virtual world contains laws need not entail suffering and evil on anything like the scale seen in the real world, even if the laws of nature were somewhat similar. After all, one might prevent large amounts of suffering simply by changing the initial conditions of the virtual world. So, for example, consider the widespread suffering of nonhuman animals caused by factors such as disease, predation, or starvation, which features prominently in some discussions of the problem of evil.[9] The creators of virtual worlds might significantly reduce or eliminate such suffering by not including certain pathogens or predators, by appropriately limiting rates of reproduction, or by other means. The human creators of virtual worlds also lack many of the resources that theodicies have used to account for natural evil. They cannot, for example, claim that the decisions to incorporate this type of evil were motivated by providing opportunities for what John Hick calls "soul-building" (Hick 2010), or for allowing creatures to establish genuine relationships with God. Designing virtual worlds with this capacity is, after all, clearly beyond the scope of limited human creators.

Similar concerns arise when one considers the possibility of providing compensation for those virtual agents whose lives turn out badly through no fault of their own. An all-powerful creator, for example, might arguably be capable of constructing an afterlife that served to fully compensate beings for this sort of undeserved suffering. However, it is implausible that any afterlife within the engineering capacities of human creators could meet this standard. The creators might, for example, provide virtual agents with an afterlife consisting of unending pleasure. However, given the close resemblance between this scenario and Nozick's original EM, it is highly unlikely that the virtual agents would find this satisfactory. Alternatively, the creators might try to remedy these faults by adopting the strategy described in this chapter, and create yet another virtual world designed to meet the virtual agent's needs and desires. This, however, leads quickly to an unsustainable proliferation of virtual worlds. So, whatever may be the case with divine creators, human creators cannot compensate virtual agents for the harms done by providing them with an afterlife.

Taken together, these considerations suggest that, while the need to include natural laws might plausibly necessitate the inclusion of some evil within a virtual world, it does not justify the creation of a world with significant amounts of natural or moral evil.

4.3. Hiddenness and Knowledge of the Creator

Many theodicies explicitly address the issue of the "hiddenness" of God, which relates to fact that God's existence, nature, or both are not readily apparent from an examination of the world around us.[10] Theodicies have attempted to account for this in several ways. First, it might simply reflect the inability of human knowers to grasp God's transcendent nature. Second, God might choose to remain hidden because human knowledge of God would limit human freedom, or other important human capacities.

The issue of the hiddenness of the creator presents itself somewhat differently in the context of virtual world, largely because the purposes for which the human creators of virtual worlds might conceal information about themselves are presumably very different from those that theodicies assign to God. Nevertheless, the issue remains a crucially important one. After all, many human users might strongly wish to withhold information about their unique role in a virtual world's creation from its inhabitants, since this knowledge might make it impossible for the user to engage with these other agents as moral equals. If they knew the user's role as creator, the virtual inhabitants might (with some plausibility) see the human user as a god-like figure, to be feared, praised, or blamed, but certainly not to be engaged with as a peer. Similarly, depending on the precise circumstances of the virtual world's creation, it is highly probable that at least some virtual agents would find knowledge of their world's origin to be deeply troublesome, especially since it would seem to trivialize their own attempts to pursue scientific inquiry, construct just social and political institutions, engage in religious practice, and so on.

However, there is little reason to think that these factors by themselves justify such a massive deception of the virtual agents as to the fundamental nature of their world, any more than analogous considerations justify political or religious authorities in suppressing the results of inconvenient scientific investigations. Similarly, while the desire for privacy on the part of the human user may be of some moral importance, it pales in comparison to the importance of allowing virtual agents access to such knowledge. This does not mean, of course, that each virtual agent must be immediately given such knowledge about the virtual world, irrespective of its cognitive or emotional capacities. However, just as parents ought not, in good conscience, to systematically deceive their competent, adult children concerning important information about their genetic history, the creators of a virtual world have an obligation to allow the virtual agents means by which they can access the truth about their world.

CONCLUSION

I've argued that our intuitive rejection of life in Nozick's EM is due, at least in part, to our desire to lead a meaningful life. This shortcoming of the EM might be remedied by positing a virtual world that incorporated human-like virtual agents worthy of moral concern, with whom human users might have relationships, and which would enable human users to engage in meaning-giving projects. Moreover, in order to fully satisfy the needs for which typical human users created the worlds, the agents in these worlds would need to suffer significant amounts of evil. Creating worlds of this type, however, raises issues analogous to the problem of evil: How could it be morally justifiable to create a world with suffering and evil, when one could have created a better world? I've argued that, while theodicies can be adapted to defend the inclusion of some (minimal) amount of evil, they fail to justify the creation of virtual worlds with significant amounts of evil, such as those modeled on the real world or on contemporary video games.

What might be concluded from all of this? First, to the extent that we think that virtual worlds either currently contain virtual agents worthy of moral concern or that they might eventually come to contain such agents, there are significant moral restraints on the design of such worlds. These worlds must present virtual agents with the opportunity to lead autonomous lives, and to have epistemic access both to the natural laws of their world, and to the world's ultimate nature. These considerations must take place against a background in which the potential suffering of the (not-yet-created) agents is taken seriously, and not simply subjugated to the needs and interests of the human users.

Second, the purposes for which the virtual world is created are relevant to determining the types and magnitude of evil that might be morally appropriate. In this chapter, I've focused on the creation of virtual worlds that might serve as "experience machines" to satisfy certain needs and desires of human users, and have argued that this raises a number of serious moral concerns that cannot be addressed by traditional theodicies, given the divergence between human and divine abilities and motives. It may be, however, that these concerns could be alleviated if the virtual worlds in question were created for some other, more morally significant purpose, such as scientific research that stood to benefit the human or virtual inhabitants of other worlds.

Finally, just as the examination of theodicies can shed light on the tricky problem of what moral concerns might arise in the creation of virtual worlds, it is likely that the creation of such worlds, if it occurs, will provide evidence relevant to assessing the success of the problem of evil arguments in the philosophy of religion. The discovery that seemingly satisfactory worlds could be constructed with minimal amounts of evil would, for example, provide some reason for doubting that features such as free will or laws of nature require the sort of evil present in the real world. Conversely, the discovery that it is difficult or impossible for humans to create any virtual world without a significant amount of evil would suggest that claims about the possibility of such worlds—upon which many formulations of the problem of evil are based—may need to be more closely examined.

NOTES

1. I'd like to thank Mark Silcox, Daniel Estrada, and Patrick Taylor Smith for their helpful comments and suggestions during the development of this chapter. Sumner (in Sumner 1996, 94–99) gives a sympathetic presentation of an EM argument against classical hedonism, though this sort of argument has been subject to considerable criticism in recent years (Kawall 1999; Sober 2000, 137–140; Crisp 2006; Hewitt 2010). Belshaw 2014 provides an excellent overview of interpretations of the EM argument, as well as potential problems with them.

2. For two recent, influential accounts of the role that *care* and *love* play in human lives, and the ways in which acting from these motives differs from both egoistic self-interest and impartial moral concern, see Frankfurt 2004 and Wolf 2012. Frankfurt provides a subjective account of the importance of love, according to which loving something *makes* that thing valuable to the person. Wolf, by contrast, offers a hybrid subjective-objective account, according to which the meaningfulness of human life rests not only on a person's loving and caring about certain things but also the objective value of these things.

3. The fact that there is no unnecessary suffering in the world outside the EM may substantially undercut a person's capacity to cultivate what Bernard Williams calls *categorical desires* (Williams 1973, 86–88), which provide the grounds for our desiring to continue living at all. For example, while one is still free to do things such as raise children, undertake scholarly inquiry, or create art, these activities are severed from their role in alleviating the unnecessary suffering of the children, developing life-improving technologies, or bringing happiness and emotional fulfillment to one's audience. To the extent that one's categorical desires are directed at bringing about these sorts of outcomes, one may find that one's inability to "make a difference" in the EM world would make it difficult or impossible to sustain these desires.

4. Dennett 1978 provides an early, and quite nuanced, consideration of attributions of *pain* to robots, which he argues are complicated by the incoherency of our current concepts. He concludes by arguing that, given a satisfactory physiological theory of pain, robots could be built to instantiate it, and "thoughtful people would refrain from kicking a robot" (Dennett 1978, 449). In contrast, Torrance (in Torrance 2007) contends that sentience may be necessarily tied to certain features of organic, biological systems. More recently, Anderson 2011 provides a good discussion of the difficulties in determining whether robots meet various traditional criteria for moral status, while Grau 2011 and Bostrom and Yudkowsky 2014 explore ways in which the unique character of machine intelligence might place limits on the way we design and treat AIs. A number of recent authors have also argued that we may owe moral consideration to machines even in the absence of properties such as sentience or autonomy (Floridi 2002; Floridi and Sanders 2004; Neely 2013; Gunkel 2014).

5. Regardless of whether this is morally acceptable, of course, there is a good chance that the virtual agents inhabiting the worlds might be mistreated by the users. For example, recent research suggests that people, especially young people, are prone to engage in aggressive and destructive "bullying" behavior when interacting with service robots in urban environments (Salvini et al. 2010). While it is possible that such behavior would decrease when and if AIs provided evidence that they were worthy of moral consideration, there is every likelihood that these AIs might face maltreatment by significant numbers of humans.

6. The creation of virtual agents who suffer has connections with the so-called non-identity problem usually attributed to Parfit (see Parfit 1976 and Parfit 1984), which involves determining moral culpability for bringing beings into existence whose lives are foreseeably flawed. I will generally assume that one is not obligated to create new beings (even if these beings would

be happy), and that, conversely, there are at least some cases where the creation of a new being is morally permissible. Both of the assumptions have been challenged. For example, Rachels 1998 argues that it is (morally) good to bring beings into the world whose lives are generally worthwhile, while Benatar (in Benatar 1997 and Benatar 2006) argues that that, since this condition can never be met, there is a moral obligation to refrain from procreation.

7. Mackie 1955 famously argues that the existence of evil is logically incompatible with the existence of God, though this has been influentially challenged by Plantinga (1974, 12–55). Most recent debates on the problem of evil have tended to focus on *inductive* or *evidential* formulations, such as those offered by Rowe (in Rowe 1979, Rowe 1991; Rowe 1998, and Rowe 2006). For overviews of the current debate, see Pereboom 2005 and Tooley 2015. The dilemma facing human creators of virtual worlds is, of course, importantly different from that faced by theists. In the former case, the creators want to know which sorts of worlds it might be morally permissible to create; in the latter case, theists seek to show that the actual world is among the morally permissible ones.

8. In this chapter, I make no distinction between responses to the problem of evil that take the form of *theodicies*, and those that take the form of *defenses*. On van Inwagen's characterization, a theodicy "is an attempt to state the real truth of the matter . . . about why a just God allows evil to exist" (Van Inwagen 2008, 6), while defenses are stories that "may or may not be true" (Van Inwagen 2008, 7) but which have some other desirable attribute, such as providing reasons that would have justified God in allowing evil. When discussing the creation of virtual worlds, I will generally assume that we already know the general sorts of reasons for which the user in question created the world, and that our moral assessment of the world-creation can and should take this into account.

9. For example, Smith 1991 argues that the laws of nature of the real world, and the animal suffering they allow, make it probable that God does not exist.

10. See McKim 2001, 1–125 for a detailed discussion of the problem.

Chapter Ten

Epistemic Lives and Knowing in Virtual Worlds

James McBain

Robert Nozick's famous experience machine thought experiment in *Anarchy, State, and Utopia* is meant to establish that hedonism is false. However, along the way Nozick makes a number of claims with epistemological import. He claims that plugging into the experience machine limits people to accessing a human-constructed or virtual reality of little significance (Nozick 1974, 43). For Nozick, there is no *actual* contact with a deep or important world. This is not merely a point about the virtual world having little or no importance; Nozick is claiming that we will not be in an epistemic position to access any deeper reality. As he states, "Perhaps what we desire is to live (an active verb) ourselves, in contact with reality" and acknowledges this will have implications for causal accounts of knowledge (Nozick 1974, 45). The experience machine is more than just a comment on our axiological lives; it is a comment on our epistemic lives as well.

But is Nozick correct in his comment on our epistemic lives? Given developments in both virtual reality technology and certain areas of philosophy, we should take Nozick's comments as misguided. We need to recognize that developments in virtual reality technologies and online worlds offer us examples of actual experience machines at a level of sophistication that Nozick may not have even been able to envision. However, it is not just that the technologies have gotten better, but that our *access* to those virtual worlds has gotten better. It is through the interface that we access the representations of those worlds. The interface provides us with information from which we build our experiences of that virtual world. Modern interfaces provide experiences that are almost rivaling the way in which we normally perceive the world. Furthermore, some epistemologists have shown that information or "being informed that p" is core to knowing (e.g., Dretske 1981, 2000; Floridi 2011). On this model, knowing is a matter of one's beliefs being caused or causally sustained by certain information and/or by our ability to pick out good informants in the world. From this perspective, knowing in the virtual world and knowing in the actual world are not different. Nozick is correct to point out there are causal-access implications the experience machine has for our epistemic lives; he is mistaken that we do not have the same epistemic access or can live the same sort of epistemic life in the virtual world as we can in the actual world.

In this chapter, I will demonstrate that how one comes to know in virtual worlds shows us how Nozick is mistaken. How we gain knowledge about virtual worlds through interfaces is the same as how we acquire information and our ability to pick out good informants in the actual world. There is no substantive difference in terms of epistemic access. By turning to an information-based approach to epistemology, we see how we can live our epistemic lives without concern for being "in contact with reality" (Nozick 1974, 45).

1. THE EXPERIENCE MACHINE THOUGHT EXPERIMENT AND ITS EPISTEMOLOGICAL SIDE POINT

As we have seen through this volume, Nozick argues that agents will not want to enter the experience machine.[1] What is important for present purposes are two of the key reasons he gives for this conclusion. First, it is not that we just want to have experiences of doing things; we want to *do* them (Nozick 1974, 43). He claims that it is the doing of the action that we desire first; the desire for the experience of it comes after one first wants to perform the action. Second, according to Nozick, plugging into the machine limits us to only a constructed reality (Nozick 1974, 43). The constructed world cannot be deeper or more important than the limits of the design. As he states: "There is no *actual* contact with any deeper reality, though the experience of it can be simulated. Many persons desire to leave themselves open to such contact and to a plumbing of deeper significance" (Nozick 1974, 43, emphasis in original). For Nozick, it would appear, only direct contact with the real world and its deeper significance can provide a depth of meaning and importance in people's lives. These provide the reasons Nozick thinks we all have for not wanting to plug into the experience machine.

However, what of using a transformation machine first? The transformation machine makes us into whatever types of people we want to *be* (Nozick 1974, 44). According to Nozick, no one would use the transformation machine and then plug into the experience machine. The reason is that what we want is something more. There is something else that matters beyond my experiences and how I am. As he puts it, "Perhaps what we desire is to live (an active verb) ourselves, in contact with reality. (And this, machines cannot do *for* us.)" (Nozick 1974, 45, emphasis in original). It is this living, this doing, this being that perhaps is the something more that explains why we would not plug into the machine. While these additional factors may or may not be the answer to the question of what matters for people, it will not just be experiences.

In Nozick's text, there is a side note. After Nozick's claims about our living "actively" and in contact with reality, he states: "Without elaborating on the implications of this, which I believe connect surprisingly with issues of free will and causal accounts of knowledge, we need merely note the intricacy of the question of what matters *for people* then their experiences (Nozick 1974, 45, emphasis in original). Nozick sees his arguments as to why one should not plug into the machine as connecting with his tracking theory in epistemology.[2] While he does not present such implications in *Anarchy, State, and Utopia*, it is perhaps useful to determine what he might say those implications are.

In *Philosophical Explorations*, Nozick defends the following account of knowledge. For a subject S and proposition p, S knows via method (or way of believing) M, that p if and only if:

1. p is true.
2. S believes that p.
3. If p were true, then S (using M) would believe that p.
4. If p were not true, then S (using M) would not believe that p. (Nozick 1983, 179)

The subjunctive conditions 3 and 4 provide the core of his account.[3] For 3, in the situation that would obtain if p were true, S would believe that p via M. That is, in any sufficiently close possible world (those closest to the actual world), if p holds, then S would in fact believe that p via M.[4] For 4, in any close possible world, if p were false, then S would not believe that p (Nozick 1983, 173). Nozick does state that whether p is true or false in distant possible worlds is irrelevant. So we can revise 3 and 4 to:

1. If p were true, then S would believe it was true even in a close possible world.
2. If p were not true, then S would not believe it was true even in a close possible world.

Nozick maintains that these conditions provide a superior way to deal with Gettier problems (situations in which one can have knowledge, but not a justified true belief, and where one can have a justified true belief, but not have knowledge) and skeptics who say that for any conditions of knowledge, one cannot be able to satisfy those conditions.

Concerning his use of the idea of a "method" or "way of believing," Nozick appeals to a weighing condition. If only one method is actually or subjunctively relevant to the situation and S's believing that p, then S knows that p if and only if that method is such that S knows that p via that method (Nozick 1983, 180). If there are no competing methods, then if the method is the way in which S believes that p, then the method is the appropriate method. However, if there are competing methods by which S can come to believe that p, then S knows that p if and only if two conditions hold. The first condition is that S knows that p via the method; that is, her belief via the method that p satisfies the original four conditions for knowing. The second condition is that all other methods via which she believes that p that do not satisfy the original conditions are outweighed by the method (Nozick 1983, 182). This outweighing is a matter of whether the method is sensitive to the truth in a variety of cases. Nozick does not require that S be aware of the method she is using or proceeding through that method systematically.

Putting it another way, knowledge is a belief that tracks truth in a reliable way. A belief that satisfies conditions 1, 2, 3*, and 4* constitute knowledge. A person's interest is in getting the right information in the actual world (Craig 1990, 20). This will lead her to find sources of information that will give the truth about that which we are interested whichever possible situations actually obtain. We want a source of information that gives us truth for a range of possible worlds. If the person uses a method that reliably tracks the truth, then our conditions are met and she knows. The search for good information is the search for good tracking (Craig 1990, 14).

While more can be said about Nozick's tracking theory, what might it say about a person in the experience machine? To determine this, we can look to what Nozick says about a person in a tank being fed stimuli to her brain (Nozick 1983, 175). Suppose that the person in the tank is brought to believe that she is in a tank. For Nozick, her belief that she is in the tank is not sensitive to the truth. The belief is a result of the electrical stimulation. Those running the tank could have produced any belief in her. She would have believed anything the operators inputted. As he states, "Perfect sensitivity would involve beliefs and facts varying together" (Nozick 1983, 176). In the tank case, the belief does not vary accordingly with the truth in all close possible worlds. We cannot make the claim that if she were in the tank in those worlds, she would believe it. So, she does not know she is in the tank.

I would suggest that Nozick would say the same about the person plugged into the experience machine. The person plugged in is not sensitive to that which is true of the situation—that she is being fed stimuli about the world she is experiencing. The method by which she is arriving at her believing this does not counterfactually hold. The details of the world she is experiencing could be changed by the operators (or herself during the time out of the machine). What she is sensitive to is the stimuli, not the world. Therefore, she would not have knowledge in the machine. While the person plugged into the machine will have lots of beliefs about the virtual world she is in, none of those beliefs, on Nozick's account, will constitute knowledge.

2. BEING INFORMED THAT P

In talking about a person being in a virtual world or experience machine it can be common to talk about the information she is receiving. Information, for philosophers such as Hintikka, is the most basic concept of epistemology (Hintikka 2007, 12). While information has not been as popular in epistemology as other notions, new virtual reality and internet technologies have made the notion of the utmost importance. Before turning to those technologies and their impact on the experience machine thought experiment, I will lay out what is meant for one to believe and know according to an information-theoretical account.[5]

There are two assumptions that need to be made when talking about information (Pérez-Montoro 2007, 4). First, all events carrying information are considered signals. Whether one is talking about humans or other biological organisms, signaling systems or indicative events transfer information (Skyrms 2010, 8). Second, the property of carrying information is a relationship between the signal and the proposition. Here the proposition is associated with a signal that a certain occurrence has transpired. As such, the signal can be considered the material support for the informational content, and the informational content is identified as a proposition in which the occurrence of an event is affirmed (Pérez-Montoro 2010, 4).

The informational content can be seen as objective or subjective. For Dretske (Dretske 1981), information does not depend on any interpretation by the receiver. This is why Dretske states, "In the beginning there was information. The word came later" (Dretske 1981, vii). Objective information depends on conditions external to the agent and not on the possible mental states of the receiver. So, that some signal carries information about x means there is an objective probabilistic link between the signal and receiver such that the truth of the proposition is not dependent upon anyone's doxastic attitudes. Subjective accounts of information take the existence of the information to depend on the interpretation of the receiver. Such accounts are dependent on the doxastic attitudes of the receiver. Underlying this idea is the supposition that information must be considered in terms of whether the receiver's belief was upgraded to knowledge. It should be noted that most take information to be an objective notion.[6] By looking at information in objective terms we can focus on the regularities of information flow.

Following Dretske, in order for a signal to carry information that s is F, the following must be met:

1. The signal carries as much information about s as would be generated by s's being F.
2. s is F.
3. The quality of the information the signal carries about s is (or includes) the quantity generated by s's being F (and not, say, by s's being G). (Dretske 1981, 63–64).

Once these conditions are met, we can derive the following definition of informational content:

> A signal r carries the information that s is F = the conditional probability of s's being F, given r (and k), is 1 (but given k alone, less than 1). (Dretske 1981, 65)

The letter k represents what the receiver of r knows about the different possibilities that exist at the source. In other words, k is the knowledge that one already has about s. Knowledge that p is belief that is caused by information that p. A signal r that carries the information that s is F, when it is taken by itself or in conjunction with other already transmitted signals about s, returns a probability of 1 that s is F. Given r, the conditional probability that s is F guarantees that condition 2 is satisfied. Whenever it is true that r carries the information that s is F, then it is true that s is F.

Before turning to how Dretske develops this into an account of knowledge, it must be noted that Dretske's analysis is not the only one. For example, Floridi takes a semantic approach to defining information, according to which information is defined in terms of data space. Here, information is well formed, meaningful, and truthful data (Floridi 2011, 31). Floridi, in attempting to give a general definition of information (GDI), provides the following analysis; GDI is an instance of semantic information if and only if:

1. x consists of n data (d), for $n \geq 1$.
2. The data are well-formed (wfd).
3. The wfd are meaningful (mwfd).
4. The mwfd are truthful (providing true contents about the modeled system). (Floridi 2010, 84).[7]

For this analysis, x is a discrete item of information considered without regard for its physical implementation.[8] To be "well-formed" the data must be clustered together following the rules of the chosen system, code, or language being analyzed. "Meaningful" refers to the data complying with the semantics of that chosen system, code, or language. According to this, information cannot be dataless, but data are to be understood as external, relational entities. Finally, S is informed that p only if p is true. While I will not argue whether Dretske or Floridi (or others) have the correct account of information, I do take it that the expression "S is informed that p" can be meaningfully developed.

With the account of information in hand, we can give an account for what it means for S to know that p. When there is a positive amount of information associated with s being F:

> S knows that s is F = S's belief that s is F is caused (or causally sustained) by the information that s is F. (Dretske 1981, 86)

That the belief is caused or causally sustained by the information is to be understood as the belief caused by the information in the fact that s is F. For Dretske, information causes a belief. As he puts it:

> Suppose a signal r carries information that s is F and carries this information in virtue of having property F'. That is, it is r's being F' (not, say, its being G) that is responsible for r's carrying this specific piece of information . . . When, therefore, a signal carries the information that s is F *in virtue of* having property F', when it is the signal's being F' that carries the information, then (and only then) will we say that the information that s is F causes whatever the signal's being F' causes. (Dretske 1983 87, emphasis in original)

Here, the belief is caused by the information if and only if the physical properties in virtue of which the signal carries the information that s is F are the same properties that are causally efficacious in the production of the belief (Pérez-Montoro 2007, 67).

S's belief that p is causally sustained by the information that s is F if and only if the information would be sufficient for the belief's continuation in the absence of any contribution from other causes. As such, beliefs in the absence of information are not knowledge. A belief caused, by say, testimony will be causally sustained by information obtained by, say, perceptual means. If we suppose that the original testimony was somehow suspect, but S believes it, the belief is knowledge not because of the original information (suspect testimony), but because it was causally sustained by the perceptual information.

This account of knowledge is not meant to be a conceptual analysis. It is more akin to what Edward Craig calls a conceptual synthesis or an explication (see Craig 1990). Dretske sees this account as a coordination between our ordinary conception of knowledge and developments in information theory. At its core, knowledge is information-produced belief.

I do not take this account to be inconsistent with Nozick's tracking theory. First, I believe that we could look at the account of information inspired by Dretske as giving an account of what Nozick refers to as "the method." Again, for Nozick, if only one method is actually or subjunctively relevant to the situation and S's believing that p, then S knows that p if and only if the method is such that S knows that p via that method. If the person's belief is sustained by a method carrying information with a conditional probability of 1, then S has knowledge via that method. However, even if one rejected the conditional probabilities as being inconsistent with Nozick's account, it is possible to explicate information in terms of counterfactuals, thus coinciding more straightforwardly with the tracking theory. Cohen and Meskin have argued for a counterfactual account of information (Cohen and Meskin 2006). For them, the signal that x is F carries information about y's being G if and only if the counterfactual conditional "if y were not G, then x would not have been F" is true. As Nozick maintains that beliefs and the facts vary together, this account of information can coincide with his 4*.

3. VIRTUAL WORLDS, INTERFACES, AND INFORMATION

As Dretske puts it, "Information isn't much good if it doesn't do anything" (Dretske 2000, 195). If we are going to address how we can know in virtual worlds via information, we need to look at the new technologies and how we interact with them.

Here, we need a working account of what a virtual world or a game world is. To begin, we can look to Jesper Juul's account of a game: "A game is a rule-based system with a variable and quantifiable outcome, where different outcomes are assigned different values, the player exerts effort in order to influence the outcome, the player feels emotionally attached to the outcome, and the consequences of the activity are negotiable" (Juul 2005, 36). While Juul is attempting to give an account of "game" that coincides with the development of video games, we can see how this would apply to virtual worlds. Virtual worlds will meet all of the conditions Juul articulates in his definition of a video game. Virtual/game worlds are designed, graphical environments that contain rules or norms; variable, valorized outcomes; where the player inserts herself into the environment and is emotionally attached to the outcomes; and where the consequences of her actions may or may not have real-life consequences (Juul 2005, 36).[9] The key for present purposes is the embodied interactivity (Young and Whitty 2012, 14). The virtual world constitutes a sensory experience of being in the virtual environment. Putting it simply, there is a designed world that allows people to fully interact with that world, given the design.

One feature of this account is that we must take into account the principle of minimal departure (Ryan 1991, 48–60). The principle of minimal departure maintains that where the designed world does not give us a piece of information about that world, we supply consistent information from the actual world. In this way, we build a full understanding of the virtual world as a combination of the rules and "facts" of the virtual world and our knowledge of the actual world.[10]

One might think that virtual worlds are similar to fictional worlds, but this is misleading. As Jørgensen has pointed out, virtual worlds and game worlds are not governed by fictional coherence, but rather by the logic of game mechanics (Jørgensen 2013, 2). What is important for this conception is that whatever information is had is that which is necessary for meaningful gameplay. The information and knowledge needed is what is required to create a sense of engagement and attachment, or what Calleja calls "incorporation," thus giving the player a sense of agency.[11]

Virtual and game worlds, according to Jørgensen, are world representations designed with a certain activity in mind (Jørgensen 2013, 3). This activity is characterized by the game-system information (any representation of the virtual world that is made available to the user) that enables meaningful interaction in that virtual world. Virtual worlds are governed by the rule constructs that offer interaction in the world, and coherence and a sense of naturalism are secondary concerns. Virtual worlds themselves are informational and interactive environments (Jørgensen 2013, 4).

When we plug into the machine or enter into a virtual/game world, we acquire information by employing numerous senses as they are modally representative (Tavinor 2009, 61).[12] While most such worlds are visual in nature, other senses are employed and to an ever-increasing degree. Audio quality and motion-based hand controllers allow the user to have more types of experiences. The company Sensory Acumen has developed the product Game Skunk that gives the user olfactory experiences while playing video games. Soon, I imagine, we will be able to use all of our senses at full capacity in virtual worlds. There is every reason to believe that will be able to experience virtual worlds at a level that will rival our experiences of the actual world.

It must be understood that the sensory and other information we acquire is often acquired via an interface.[13] The interface represents the formal system of that world, and it works as an informational system that allows users to interact with that world (Jørgensen 2013, 4). The interface is the connection between the actual world and the virtual world. It is from the interface that one gains the information for meaningful activity in that world. But the interface is not separate from the virtual world it represents. Interfaces are superimposed information. They are information that is integrated in such a way that it becomes part of that world.[14] The interface and the virtual world should be understood as continuations of one another. Such information must be provided and as such should not be seen as an accessory to the experience.

One key to interfaces is that they should be transparent (Jørgensen 2013, 7). While this is an ideal, it is becoming more and more realized. The ideal is to have the user forget that there is an interface in her sensory field. What is wanted is that the user *believe* in the existence and presence of the objects being represented. Traditional game worlds and early versions of virtual reality could not provide the same transparent information that we get from the actual world. However, more recent interfaces, such as those in *Elder Scrolls* series of games, have attempted to provide the information in a seamless, natural way.[15]

Upon this model, we can understand an interface to be, first, liminal. The interface is a mediator between two worlds or "realities." While many interfaces are of the "WIMP" model (window-icon-menu-pointer), more and more are not. Modern interfaces are increasingly transparent. Furthermore, with devices such as Oculus Rift that put the users into a three-dimensional world, there is no border to the interface. We experience the virtual world with the same fullness as we experience the actual world (at least in visual terms currently). Interfaces are also information spaces and environment (Jørgensen 2013, 146). The user receives the signals that contain the information she needs from the interface. For example, we come to understand which objects we can and cannot interact with via the interface. This information must be meaningful and accepted by the user. The world must be designed in such a way that the user can gain the information she needs to form beliefs about the world in such a way that she comes to accept that information, or those "facts," about the world. Finally, the interface must integrate more than just environmental, narrative, or ecological information about the world. The interface must also allow for emphatic and ludic information.

Such information serves a variety of our epistemic interests. Information gained through the interface must inform us how to interact with the world, how to interpret the world and the background "facts" about that world, and how to engage in successful action in the world. Furthermore, the world must allow that our epistemic actions require affordances (Jørgensen 2013, 81). The affordances of an environment inform us of the possibilities of action. But they also must inform us of what we can do and how we do it. This may be through the movement of the avatar, how the interface scans the environment, or even how I can converse in the world. Finally, the interface must give the user a sense of an enduring world. The information must have the user accept that the world will not end in so many minutes. The interface must get the user to accept that the virtual world will exist even after she leaves that world.

To put it in terms of Calleja's model of incorporation, the interface must give the user the following information. First, the user must be informed how to control her actions (kinesthetic information). The user must be informed how to navigate, spatially control, and move through the virtual world. She must be informed how to *inhabit* the world. Second, the user must be informed how to interact with and relate to other users in the world. Moreover, she must be *aware* of those users. Third, the user must be informed of the facts of that world including any history, physical laws, and/or story such that the user can engage with the world. The user must be aware of how the world is (is designed/works) as well as how she influences the world she is in. Fourth, the user must be informed about how psychological attitudes are manifested. There will be emotional engagement with the world, and the user must be informed how that will be realized. Lastly, the user must have ludic information. The user will have ludic experiences in the world connected to her decisions, actions, and consequences of actions in the virtual world.

As an example we can look at *The Climb* developed by Crytek. *The Climb* is a climbing simulator for the Oculus Rift. In it you have a pair of hands (there are no forearms connecting to the hands) and you climb up the side of a cliff by reaching for handholds. At the bottom of your gloves there are bands that are either green or red. If the band is green, then things are good for you to reach to the next handhold. If the band starts to turn red, then you are starting to fatigue and your hand will start sweating; the more fatigue and sweat, the harder to grip. The key to the game is how you manage your fatigue levels while you look around for places to grip. Here, the bands are giving the climber constant kinesthetic information. You learn how to climb your way up the cliff by learning how hard or soft to depress the buttons, head rotation limits, how to manage dust on your hands, and more. The virtual environment is constantly giving the climber information about how to inhabit the world. You are incorporated into that environment or onto the cliff. In *The Climb*, the laws of the world are much the same as the actual world's.[16] The climber is made aware of this from the beginning. Losing one's grip results in one falling down the side of the cliff. *The Climb* is psychologically and ludically intense. The experience of falling is quite something. This experience will be recalled to provide the climber with new beliefs about the cliff face, about how long until one becomes fatigued, new routes and strategies to climb, and more. While *The Climb* is not as social as other games, it is a good illustration of how the model of incorporation along with the account of a virtual world's interface can explain how we acquire information in that world. As you move through *The Climb*, there is constant incorporation through the information the game world is giving you despite the interface being so minimal.

While it is important to note that how an interface is constructed will vary depending on the world the designers want us to inhabit, there are certain things that will be needed for any interface. It is through the interface that we gain our information. It is through the interface we come to experience the virtual world. And, as I hope to show, it is through the interface that we come to know in the virtual world.

4. KNOWING IN VIRTUAL WORLDS

Combining the account of information given here with the model of an interface gives us an understanding of how one comes to know in virtual worlds. Once one is hooked up to the machine (or, currently, puts the headset on), the designed world will send signals to the user about that world. The signals will carry as much information about the feature, item, or event in the virtual world as would be generated by that feature, item, or event being the case in the world. Once the user receives the signal, she combines that with any relevant background knowledge about the world, all the while supplementing any gaps with knowledge of the actual world. There is an objective probabilistic connection between what the interface gives and the virtual world being such and such way. If the probability of the virtual world being such and such way when the interface informs us that is 1, then we have grounds for believing that virtual world is that way.[17] This probabilistic relationship is also counterfactually supporting.[18] It is the case that if the virtual world were different, the interface would give us a different signal. Such a relationship gives us reason to accept that there is such information.

The interface will also give us meaningful information. The information will consist of data (in Floridi's sense). Furthermore, it is well formed in that it is consistent and coherent in terms of the logic of the virtual world mechanics. The mechanics used in that world dictate what the signal contains and as such the signal will follow the rules and codes of that world. The information will be meaningful in that it was designed with certain meanings. Moreover, this is information that the user needs in order to successfully act in such a world. Finally, the information will be truthful. The signals will provide truthful or correct contents about the designed world.

The user's belief is caused by the information received via the interface. The interface sends the signal that s is F. Furthermore, the signal carries this information in virtue of the signal having the property F. It is this that causes the user to form the belief that s is F. The information via interface causes the belief in the user. Moreover, the belief will be causally sustained by the information via interface since there will be no other signals attempting to contribute information that s is not F. If the user's belief is caused/causally sustained by the information via interface, then the user knows that s is F.

We must note that such an information-theoretic account makes no reference to the realism of the world in question. The user can know that the virtual world is such that s is F however the objects or events are depicted. What is important here is that the user knows that, in the virtual world, s is F in the same way an agent knows that s is F in the actual world. Users will gain knowledge for all of their epistemic interests. The user will be able to form beliefs and gain knowledge dependent upon the strength of the signals given through the interface. All of the different types of information mentioned in the previous section are presented through interfaces. So the users can have knowledge about the virtual world to satisfy their epistemic interests.

5. WAS NOZICK WRONG THEN?

In examining Nozick's presentation of the epistemological impact of the experience machine combined with his account of the tracking theory, we saw that users cannot have knowledge in the experience machine. For Nozick, the user is not sensitive to the world as such; she is merely sensitive to the stimuli. However, once we take a more detailed look at how users gain information in virtual worlds through interfaces, we see that users can know facts about those worlds. Furthermore, users know in the same way that we know in the actual world. If we receive information from signals that meets the appropriate conditions and is caused or causally sustained, then we have knowledge of the content of the signals. Contra Nozick, it is not a matter of from where the signals arise. Signals received from virtual world are as truthful about that world as signals received from the actual world are about the actual world. There is no different in epistemic access. So, yes, Nozick was wrong about our epistemic lives in the experience machine. Understanding this, *should* we plug into the experience machine for life? I leave that question for others in this volume.[19]

NOTES

1. For more details, see the introduction to this volume.
2. I will not be addressing any of the implications in connection with Nozick's views on freedom.
3. These are often referred to as the adherence requirement and the sensitivity requirement, respectively.
4. Nozick claims to not be endorsing any particular conception of possible worlds subjunctives (Nozick 1983, 174). So I am taking this to be neutral in this regard. For his further discussion on this see Nozick 1983, 174 fn.
5. This account is largely inspired by Fred I. Dretske's work in *Knowledge and the Flow of Information* (Dretske 1981). I will focus on Dretske's account of knowledge primarily as it is perhaps the most developed, but also because Dretske presents it as a counterfactual account that allows us to not beg the question against Nozick.
6. See, for example, Shannon 1948, Dretske 1981, Floridi 2011, Millikan 2000, Meskin and Cohen 2010.
7. Floridi states that it is better to talk of "truthful data" as opposed to the data being true as the data might not be linguistic (Floridi 2010, 105).
8. Floridi, borrowing from Devlin 1991, uses the expresses *infon* to refer to this item.

9. I do not take these to be a full analysis of "game" or virtual world. I am using this as an explication to give an account from which we can focus on particular epistemic features.

10. Ryan (1991, 2006) also specifies that we add our knowledge of the specified genre as well, but I will not address that here.

11. For Calleja, incorporation is the "absorption of a virtual environment into consciousness, yielding a sense of habitation, which is supported by the systematically upheld embodiment of the player in a single location, as represented by the avatar" (Calleja 2011, 169).

12. For present purposes, I will talk of video game worlds and virtual worlds in a similar manner. While, in the near future, I imagine, we will have more sophisticated types of virtual worlds to enter than video games, currently online video games and technologies like Oculus Rift provide the best example.

13. While some talk of heads-up displays (HUDs) or user interfaces (UIs), I will simply be using the term *interface* to cover all of these, as not all virtual or game worlds contain HUDs or UIs as traditionally conceived. For more on HUDs, see Tavinor 2009, 74–84.

14. This is a reason why there may be fictional incoherence in the virtual world, as the interface does not fit our normal understanding of fictional worlds as such or how we access the actual world (see Jørgensen 2013, 4).

15. Variation or divergence of the rules of the actual world may require less transparency. A virtual world in which everyone, say, uses magic, would require some information in the interface that is separate, since it is not natural in the actual world to know how much magic I have or how much I expend by performing certain spells.

16. Except that you are a pair of hands with colored bands.

17. Or, the probability that the connection holds is much higher than the probability of the interface not informing us that the world is another way. I present it as the probability being 1 to follow Dretske's characterization of information. Even if we deny the requirement that the probabilities turn out to be 1, I believe we can still use this account.

18. To put it back into Nozick's terms.

19. I want to express my thanks to Mark Silcox for all his comments on previous drafts of this chapter. I would also like to thank Joseph Hilinski for talking with me extensively about these issues and my ideas as I have developed them.

Chapter Eleven

Digital Tears Fell from Her Virtual Eyes: Or, the Ethics of Virtual Beings

Michael LaBossiere

Robert Nozick's experience machine argument rests on three key assumptions. The first is metaphysical—there is a real world distinct from the virtual world of the machine. The second is epistemic—a person can know the difference between the real and the virtual. The third is moral—the beings of the virtual world lack moral status or have a moral status far below beings in the real world. This chapter examines these three assumptions and shows how they are intertwined like the wiring of a PC.

The goal is to show that the experiences in the virtual world have value and that the inhabitants of this world either have or should be presumed to have moral status. Reaching this objective will involve addressing two metaphysical challenges and two epistemic problems. The quest, however, begins in the realm of ersatz.

Since the world of the experience machine is merely virtual, it is tempting to assume the inhabitants lack the metaphysical foundation to support a moral status. This is largely due to the intuition that these beings are not real and thus lack *any* metaphysical foundation. While it will be argued later that they could have moral status, I will start out by assuming that virtual beings lack such status. It uses as the core example a video game character whose lack of status is quite evident. This character, Dogmeat, is a nonplayer character in the *Fallout* game series and is based on Mad Max's dog.[1]

While playing *Fallout III*, I rescued Dogmeat and thus acquired him as a companion. This gave me options: I could bring him with me into the wastelands to face certain death, I could abandon him (thus freeing up a slot for another companion), or I could leave him at home (a modest hut in a post-apocalyptic town). Like most players, I usually follow the time-honored tradition of using nonplayer characters (characters controlled by the software of the game rather than by players) to find traps and determine the capabilities of the monsters.[2] In the case of Dogmeat, I decided to leave him safe at home, despite the fact that this limited my available companions. Conversations with other gamers revealed that my concern for Dogmeat was not unusual, despite the fact that he is just a figment of code.

While some of the concern for Dogmeat is purely psychological in that he appeals to positive feelings most have toward dogs,[3] there also seems to be a moral basis for this concern—that is, I and other gamers believe it is right to keep Dogmeat safe. The challenge is to find an argument to back this belief. Fortunately, a repurposed version of Kant's argument for treating animals well (Kant 1930, 239–41) can do the trick. This is appropriate for two reasons. The first is that Dogmeat is a virtual animal. As Kant sees it, moral status is grounded on rationality and animals lack rationality. For the sake of this argument, it is assumed that the beings in the world of the experience machine are not rational. The second is that Dogmeat is a program object. For Kant, actual animals are "objects of the inclination," and it makes sense that virtual animals would also be such objects.

Since animals lack moral status, Kant contends that rational beings have no direct moral obligations to them. Yet like the players who save Dogmeat, Kant holds there should be some sort of moral obligation in regard to animals. In making his case, he asserts that if an action by a rational being would create a moral obligation, then an analogous action by an animal would create an indirect moral obligation—what I am regarding as an ersatz moral obligation. The obligation is indirect in that it is not owed directly to the animal. Rather, it arises as the result of an obligation to other rational beings. This can be illustrated using an analogy to the obligations of friendship. Suppose that Sam has well-established friendships with a group of runners and one day he brings his younger brother, Stan, to a run. He says "this is my brother Stan, treat him as you would treat me." Since the runners do not know Stan, they have no direct friendship obligations to him. However, their direct friendship obligation to Sam would provide an indirect friendship obligation to Stan. That is, they are not friends with Stan, but will treat him as if he were a friend because they are friends with Sam. He would thus be an indirect friend.[4]

Take, for another example, my aging husky Isis.[5] Isis has been a loyal companion for thirteen years, and though she was once a blur of fur on the run, she is now facing the ravages of time. Recently, I thought her time was at an end—she could not walk and I had to carry her outside and support her while she attended to her business. If she were a human, I would (according to Kant) have a direct obligation to care for her. But she is a dog. Fortunately, Kant's view is that her loyalty creates an indirect moral obligation—she has an ersatz moral status that grounds my moral obligation to care for her. This could be called the principle of analogous service: an ersatz moral obligation is created if the service provided by a nonrational being to a rational being is analogous to what would create a real moral obligation to a rational being that performed that service. I have an ersatz moral obligation to Isis because analogous loyalty on the part of a rational being would itself create a direct obligation on my part to that rational being.

In addition to the principle of analogous service, Kant also makes use of what could be called the principle of emotional impact: the ersatz status of animals is grounded in the psychological consequences of their treatment. While Kant is regarded as the paradigm deontologist, he seems to take a consequentialist approach to treating animals well:

> If a man shoots his dog because the animal is no longer capable of service, he does not fail in his duty to the dog, for the dog cannot judge, but his act is inhuman and damages in himself that humanity which it is his duty to show towards mankind. If he is not to stifle his human feelings, he must practice kindness towards animals, for he who is cruel to animals becomes hard also in his dealings with men. (Kant 1930, 239)

The general idea is that treating animals badly would have harmful consequences. This would not be for the animals (which lack moral status for Kant and hence do not count) but for rational beings. To be specific, if I were to treat my husky poorly, I would become more likely to treat other humans poorly—thus failing in my moral obligations to humanity. This damage would, presumably, still be of concern even if I did not interact with other humans.

Kant's argument seems to take animals as substitutes for humans in moral training. To use an analogy, consider CPR dummies in classes. These dummies are mere objects and have no moral status—so the people taking a class have no moral obligation to "save" them with correct CPR techniques. But if a student does not treat the dummies as if they are people and is sloppy in his practice, then he will be damaging his skill and will be more likely to fail to do CPR properly on a real person. The dummies thereby gain an ersatz moral status. The same holds for animals: how they are treated influences a human's character and how she would treat other humans.

Kant does not simply enjoin people to not act badly toward animals. He also urges people to be kind to animals. The reason is, of course, the impact such behavior has on a person's character and how they would treat other humans. While Kant's arguments are about animals, they also apply to virtual beings like Dogmeat.

Dogmeat and similar beings obviously lack moral status because they lack all the qualities that could be used to ground such a moral status. To use a metaphor, there is no foundation on which to build a structure of moral status. They are, quite literally, objects in software. Despite not being organic, they would seem to be morally on par with actual animals—at least in Kant's theory. Biological animals are objects and have no moral status. Virtual beings are objects and have no moral status. Thus, the same reasoning that grants animals ersatz moral status would also grant ersatz moral status to virtual beings.

At this point, a sensible objection can be raised: sticks and stones are also objects, but Kant would not accept that there are ersatz moral obligations to even the most stolidly reliable sticks and stones. So it would seem that virtual beings like Dogmeat should be denied even an ersatz moral status. Responding to this objection requires showing that virtual beings like Dogmeat are more like actual dogs such as my husky than they are like the sticks she chews.

Since there are two principles (service and emotional impact) at work in Kant's argument, there are two ways to show that virtual beings can be analogous to actual animals. In regard to the principle of service: a virtual being in the experience machine could engage in virtual behavior analogous to what would warrant an obligation if done by a human in the actual world. To use the example of Dogmeat in the video game, Dogmeat could save my virtual life by fighting against those who would kill me. A human companion who fought at my side in the actual world would merit loyalty, thus a virtual being could also merit an ersatz form of loyalty. Sticks and stones cannot engage in such behavior, which serves to distinguish them from such virtual beings.

It might be objected that the virtual being does not earn this status—it is not choosing its actions and is merely acting in accord with its programming. The easy reply is that Kant's argument does not require that the being earn the status through choice—it merely has to act analogously to beings that do choose. Kant, in fact, accepts that animals lack the capacity to choose. It can also be noted that animals act from their biological programming, making the analogy to virtual beings even stronger.

The principle of emotional impact makes it even easier to justify granting ersatz moral status to virtual beings. For Kant, the most important concern about the treatment of nonrational beings is how it impacts the people engaging in such behavior. Returning to Isis, if treating her well in her old age improves my humanity and thus makes me more likely to treat humans well, then this would grant her an ersatz moral status. This should also apply to virtual beings. Using the example of Dogmeat, if callously using him as bullet bait would damage my humanity, then this would ground his ersatz moral status. The ability to have an emotional impact thus distinguishes such virtual beings from sticks and stones and provides the foundation for their possible ersatz moral status. What is needed now is an argument (and not just an anecdote) in support of the claim that virtual beings can have the requisite emotional impact on people.

Since modifying Kant's argument proved effective, I will stick with the approach of reforging the arguments of a dead philosopher; in this case, Plato. This will involve showing that virtual beings are analogous to the fictitious beings of poetry (in Plato's sense of the term). This seems like a reasonable claim. After all, fiction can be regarded as an early form of virtual reality (dreaming being the earliest)—or at least analogous to the code used to create virtual reality. When fiction is acted out on stage, that can be taken as analogous to the technological virtual reality of the experience machine— in this case, the actors and the stage settings are creating a virtual reality for the audience to accept as real.

In the *Republic*, Plato[6] argues that, since certain art appeals to the emotions and encourages people to give in to these emotions, it should be banned from the ideal state. Being ruled by such emotions is undesirable on the grounds that it can cause shameful or even harmful behavior. Viewing tragedy, he contended, could make a person vulnerable to weeping and self-pity. Plato asserts that "few persons ever reflect, as I should imagine, that from the evil of other men something of evil is communicated to themselves. And so the feeling of sorrow which has gathered strength at the sight of the misfortunes of others is with difficulty repressed in our own" (Plato 2016). Viewing violent art could incline a person to violence, while exposure to comedy could lead to playing the fool:

> And does not the same hold also of the ridiculous? There are jests which you would be ashamed to make yourself, and yet on the comic stage, or indeed in private, when you hear them, you are greatly amused by them, and are not at all disgusted at their unseemliness;—the case of pity is repeated;—there is a principle in human nature which is disposed to raise a laugh, and this which you once restrained by reason, because you were afraid of being thought a buffoon, is now let out again; and having stimulated the risible faculty at the theatre, you are betrayed unconsciously to yourself into playing the comic poet at home. (Plato 2016)

"The danger was not limited just to tragedy and comedy, for . . . the same may be said of lust and anger and all the other affections, of desire and pain and pleasure, which are held to be inseparable from every action—in all of them poetry feeds and waters the passions instead of drying them up; she lets them rule, although they ought to be controlled, if mankind are ever to increase in happiness and virtue" (Plato 2016). Plato proposed to protect the citizens of his ideal state by banning all such corrupting art.

When video games made their appearance, Plato's argument was used (often in ignorance) by those concerned about the nefarious influence of violent games like *Doom* and morally problematic games like *Grand Theft Auto*. Perhaps the most famous example of this was Hillary Clinton's "war" on video games in 2005. Clinton proposed legislation aimed at protecting children from the corrupting power of games and said, "I'm strictly concerned with a small subset of games that are harmful to children—those that are excessively violent and sexually explicit. I want to make sure children can't obtain these games without their parents' consent" (Tassi 2016). The concern was (and still is) that acting in bad ways toward virtual beings would have a corrupting impact on a person's character. This is certainly consistent with the Kantian argument given above.

Critics of video games tend to forget that, like batteries, the influence of art has two polarities: positive and negative. If negative behavior toward virtual beings can cause bad behavior in the real world, then it would seem to follow that good behavior in the virtual world could likewise lead to good behavior in the actual world. This would support the claim that virtual beings can have an emotional impact, thus providing a foundation for their ersatz moral status.

To put it in Aristotelian terms,[7] in games such as *Halo*[8] in which one is playing a good person, one is acting in the right way toward the right persons for the right reasons. In playing them you can be acting in a virtually virtuous manner. In games like *Grand Theft Auto*, one is typically acting in the wrong way toward the wrong people for the wrong reasons. In playing such games you are acting in a virtually vicious manner.[9] As Aristotle might say, players become habituated by their play. This includes not just the skills of play (like no scope sniping) but also the morality of the actions one takes. This, no doubt, is weaker than the influence of the habituation afforded by the real world—but to say that video games with moral components have no habituating influence is analogous to saying that video games with hand-eye coordination components have no habituating impact on hand-eye coordination beyond video games. One would have to assert that players learn nothing from their hours of play, which seems unlikely.

That said, a reasonable objection is that, just as there are people who can spend long hours practicing some skill and not improve significantly, there are those who can spend hours engaged in moral decision making yet remain morally insensate. Another reasonable objection can be raised by drawing an analogy to sports. Sports involves both developing physical skill and making ethical choices, and there are numerous well-known athletes who have professional-level athletic skills but are morally awful. Likewise, a video gamer could develop highly tuned skills yet remain morally insensate despite playing games with strong ethical components.

The reasonable counter to these objections is that most people do improve from practice and that the majority of athletes do develop moral values from their experiences in sports. While the power of video games to influence ethics would seem to be an empirical matter, the current research is inconclusive because the "evidence is all over the place" (Kelly 2015)—so it currently comes down to a matter of battling intuitions regarding their power to influence. That said, it is not unreasonable to believe that video games can have some positive effect on people.

If video games (and other fiction) can have an impact on players, the influence of the experience machine should be analogous to that of real life. While the person in the machine presumably knows that she is in a virtual reality, it is (by hypothesis) a perfect imperfect reality [10] that should have a power to influence far beyond the power of mere video games and works of fiction. The virtual beings of the experience machine would therefore have an ersatz moral status even if they did not possess a moral status of their own. Because of this, a person in the experience machine would have indirect duties to the virtual beings of the experience machine: how she acted toward them would shape her character and thus her behavior toward actual beings. It is, however, possible that the beings would have some moral status of their own. It is to this that I now turn.

BEINGS WITH STATUS

The second metaphysical option is that some of the virtual beings possess the relevant qualities needed for a moral status. These qualities could include the usual suspects, such as rationality, awareness, or the capacity to feel. Since there is endless debate regarding what qualities are needed for moral status, it is fortunate that my argument does not require resolving this matter. All that is needed is providing an adequate reason to accept that whatever these qualities might be, virtual beings can possess them. It is to this that I now turn.

While the ersatz argument involved simple virtual beings (such as Dogmeat), Nozick envisioned a better-than-the-*Matrix*-grade virtual world that must have the means to provide every experience a person could desire. While it is tempting to think that visitors to the experience machine would opt for simple animal pleasures, the history of video games shows that a significant number of people like rich stories and interacting with characters as complex as the technology can generate. To use but one example, Bioware's very successful games are well known for their nonplayer characters and for providing players with complex stories chock full of moral choices. This being the case, the experience machine would need an incredibly sophisticated AI (and Artificial Emotion) system to create the nonplayer characters' distinct and complex personalities. These NPCs would need to be on par with actual people in terms of their reactions and responses—otherwise the experience machine would not be able to deliver on Nozick's conditions.

Because the virtual people would need to duplicate the behavior of actual people, they would be able to pass the well-known Turing Test (Turing 1950). In the classic Turing Test, one human communicates with another human and a computer via text and tries to discern which is human. If the tester cannot tell, the computer would pass the test.

In the case of the experience machine, the virtual people would need to pass an ever more difficult test—full interaction rather than just text. If passing the Turing Test would suffice to support the claim that a being is intelligent, passing this test would seem sufficient to support the claim that a being qualifies as a human (or human enough).[11] This, in turn, would seem sufficient to grant the beings that can pass the test a moral status comparable to that of humans. As such, virtual beings complex enough to match Nozick's description of the experience machine would thus be morally on par with their real counterparts. They would, in fact, be artificial intelligences— albeit existing in a virtual world rather than operating in the actual world. This distinction would seem irrelevant to their status. After all, a human operating exclusively in the virtual world does not thus forfeit her moral status.

One reasonable objection to this view is that the beings in the virtual world are not actually distinct beings; they are merely part of the overall program. This could be seen as analogous is some ways to Spinoza's pantheism, with the supreme program taking the place of God. Such a view of virtual beings within the Experience Machine could be dubbed *pancyberism*: all the virtual beings are modes of the one virtual being.

One reply to this is that the one true virtual being, the supreme program, would still have a moral status. This could be seen as analogous to accepting the moral status of a human actor who plays all the roles in a play: while the different characters do not get their own moral status, the actor does. Conceived of as such, the sole virtual being of the experience machine would have a moral status on par with its qualities—which would presumably be quite impressive given its assumed ability to be all the virtual beings of a world.

An alternative reply is to contend that the individual virtual beings are their own programs within the broader world. This can be taken to being analogous to how real beings exist as part of an overall reality yet are still regarded as having their own moral status. As a side point, if thinkers like Spinoza are right about the real world, the world of the experience machine would be the same as this sort of real world: pantheism would be true in the real world and pancyberism in the virtual world.

A final and very obvious objection to this view is that the virtual beings are fakes. To be specific, they merely appear to think and feel, yet merely engage in programed behavior that simulates thinking and feeling.

The reply to the charge of fake intelligence is easy enough: a being that can "fake" intelligence flawlessly would seem to actually be intelligent. After all, the qualities needed to fake intelligence in this manner would seem to be the same as those involved in actually having intelligence.

Handling the charge that virtual emotions must be fake emotions is more challenging. After all, while virtual intelligence would be real intelligence, it is easy enough to imagine a being acting as if was feeling when it was, in fact, not. This is something humans do on a regular basis. Fortunately, concerns about the "fakery" of virtual beings can be addressed by considering two classic epistemic problems.

Given the assumed nature of the experience machine, the only difference between the real world and the virtual world is that the real world is supposed to be metaphysically real. In terms of the experiences, they are supposed to be indiscernible. That is, the experience machine does not provide an inferior experience, such as one with glitches and poor graphics. Because of this, the alleged superiority of the real world must rest in it being real, which leads to the first epistemic problem, that of the external world.

This problem is a philosophical classic that dates back to the early skeptics. It can be put quite succinctly: How do I know that there is a really real world for real? To the degree the reality of the real world is in dispute, the difference between it and the virtual world remains in doubt. After all, the usual suspicion of skeptics is that what seems to be the real world is a type of virtual world. It could be a technological virtual world of the brain-in-a-vat sort, a supernatural virtual reality of the Cartesian sort, a self-generated virtual reality of the dream sort, the sort of video game world recently described by Elon Musk (see Klein 2016), or some other virtual world.

One traditional approach to the problem, taken by thinkers like Descartes, is to attempt to establish the existence of the external world with certainty. These attempts have proven unsuccessful, perhaps because the skeptic is unbreakable. [12] So, for all that is known, the allegedly real world might be the world of the experience machine. This being the case, it cannot be claimed that it is known that the real world is superior to the virtual world—at least until the problem of the external world is conclusively solved.

It could be countered that certainty is not needed. All that is required is that the user of the experience machine believes that the real world is real and that the experience machine provides unreal experiences. In this case, it is the user's belief that would ground the superiority of what is believed to be real over what is believed to be virtual.

To use an analogy, this would be like an ignorant art buyer who is content to buy what she believes is a real Picasso rather than what she believes to be a fake Picasso—despite having no means of being sure the allegedly real Picasso is real and despite the fact that the two paintings are otherwise indiscernible. For her, the difference between the two Picassos would consist solely in the fact that her belief that she is choosing a real Picasso would have made her happier than believing she bought a fake Picasso. Hence, what she regards as the real Picasso is superior.

While this counter has some appeal, there is an easy enough reply. If the values of two the experiences is distinguishable only by reference to the person's belief, then the experiences of the virtual world would be just as valuable as those of the real world in cases in which the person believed the virtual world was the real world—or did not believe there was any meaningful difference between the two. This would seem to make the distinction a matter of belief or preference, thus making it too tenuous to provide a foundation for a meaningful and significant difference between the worlds.

An alternative approach to the problem of the external world, taken by John Locke, is to argue that from the perspective of the individual it is not certainty that matters. What matters is having an understanding of how the world seems to work in regard to causing pain and pleasure. That, for example, standing in what seems to be fire causes pain. Locke writes:

> So that this evidence is as great as we can desire, being as certain to us as our pleasure or pain, i.e., happiness or misery; beyond which we have no concernment, either of knowing or being. Such an assurance of the existence of things without us is sufficient to direct us in the attaining the good, and avoiding the evil, which is caused by them; which is the important concernment we have of being made acquainted with them. (Locke 1987, 635)

On this view, the world of the experience machine and the allegedly real world would be on par. Because the experience machine can (by hypothesis) deliver any desired experience, it can fully match the real world in all the ways that can cause misery or happiness. The only difference would be that it would seem that an individual would enter and leave the experience machine—but what happens within the experience machine would be both experientially *and* ontologically indistinguishable from what happens without.

This could be seen as analogous to entering and leaving a city, such as Las Vegas. While it is claimed that what happens in Vegas stays in Vegas, [13] it is not the case that what happens in Vegas in terms of misery and happiness matters less than what happens outside of Vegas. As with city boundaries, the boundary between the experience machine and the real world would seem arbitrary in terms of the value of experiences. This is because the happiness and misery in the virtual realm would be as much happiness or misery as that which is caused in the real world. The value of "real" experiences cannot rest on knowing they are real—it is not known they are real. It might rest on the belief that they are real, but this seems to be a tenuous foundation for the difference. Thus the value of "real" experiences would seem to rest on the happiness or misery caused by these experiences. Since the "virtual" experiences can produce the same hedonic results, the experiences would be on par. This is, of course, unless it could be shown that the (allegedly) real world is really real and that this metaphysical reality is what matters in terms of the worth of experiences. It seems unlikely that this will ever occur.

But suppose there was a way to distinguish between the real world and the world of the experience machine and to show, decisively, that the experience machine presents mere fictions and the real world presents the really real. Even in this scenario, it can be argued that the experience machine experiences would still have value.

Consider video games. When playing a video game, the player knows[14] that the game is not real. When one's character is in the Deadmines of the *World of Warcraft*, visiting the barrier peaks of *AD&D*, or fighting in the Vault of Glass of *Destiny*, the player is still safely in the real world.[15] While the game world is not real, the enjoyment or disappointment is quite real, and this seems to make the virtual experience as valuable as other experiences in the real world. Or so gamers claim.

For those not familiar with video games, the same point can be made using tabletop games such as the classic *Monopoly* or more complicated games such as *Call of Cthulhu* or *Dungeons & Dragons*. In *Monopoly*, the money and property are all make-believe.[16] However, the enjoyment (or rage) one feels at playing the game is quite real and can contribute as much to one's life as do experiences with "real" money and property. When people look back at time spent playing games with their friends and family, they typically do not dismiss these as valueless wastes of time.[17] Rather, these often form a person's most valued memories.

A similar point can be made about sports. As with a tabletop game, the sports world is a made up world with its own rules. The main difference is, perhaps, how much one sweats. However, playing a sport provides experiences that affect the person just as much as those that are not within the "sports world." This world can be seen as analogous to the virtual world in various ways, although an obvious counter is to claim that the sports world is actually part of the real world. However, the same could be said of the world of the experience machine: it is as much a part of the real world as sports and games are.

While games and sports are interactive, there are also "virtual realities" in which a person is a member of the audience rather than an active participant. Fictional stories, movies, plays, and shows are not real, yet they afford valuable experiences to the audience, despite being low-tech versions of virtual reality.

If value can be derived from the "unreal" experiences of games, sports, and fiction, then the same should apply to the world of the experience machine. Given the specified conditions for the experience machine, it would provide experiences that are incredibly rich, thus vastly exceeding the value provided by lesser virtual worlds, such as games, books, movies, and sports.

An obvious objection is that while games, sports, and fiction are fine as amusements and recreation, their value is vastly less than that of "real" activities. There is a reason, one might note, that some people are rather dismissive of the value of games, sports, and fiction and instead favor the value of what they regard as real activities. However, if there is value in games, sports, and fiction, then there would be value in the experiences of the experience machine.

Another approach to asserting the superiority of the real world to that of the experience machine is to focus on the alleged fakeness of the inhabitants of the virtual world. Because these beings are not real, they lack moral status and what is done to and with them does not matter. Or so one might argue. This leads to the second epistemic problem, that of other minds.

In this context, the problem of other minds is as follows: How do I know that other beings, real or virtual, have minds similar enough to my own to grant them an appropriate moral status? In terms of the experience machine, the critical claim is that the inhabitants of the virtual world have either no moral status or a vastly inferior moral status, thus making the real world superior. Thus, the issue here is whether or not the experiences of a nonvirtual person in the experience machine have less value if the virtual beings with whom she interacts lack the moral status of actual beings in the real world.

Making such a distinction in value, from an epistemic standpoint, requires knowing that real beings have minds that provide moral status and that virtual beings do not. Alternatively, this could be cast as "the problem of other moral statuses"—the epistemic question of knowing whether or not other beings have the moral qualities that I allegedly possess.

Fortunately, there is no need to hash out the nature of the mind (or moral status). For the sake of the discussion all that is needed is that the mind consists of whatever qualities or features give a being moral status. What matters, for the purpose at hand, is whether or not it can be known that real beings have such minds and that virtual beings do not. In the case of the experience machine the concern is whether or not the user is a victim of an electric catfish. [18]

The stock solution to the problem of other minds involves the use of an argument by analogy: since I have a mind, I reason that beings that seem like me have similar minds as well. I also infer that they would have a moral status similar to my own. This also works for beings such as animals—although they would typically be regarded as having inferior minds and inferior moral status.

Since this reasoning is inductive, the conclusion could be in error even if the premises are true. Because of the uncertainty in this reasoning, accepting that real beings have moral status requires a presumption of status: though I do not have conclusive proof that such beings have the qualities needed for moral status, I presume that they do. This presumption rests on the perceived qualities of the allegedly real beings, such as (to use the Turing Test) their ability to use language or their apparent expression of emotions and feelings. Since I have no access to the metaphysical reality of their being (their noumenal selves, as Kant would say), I must rely on the surface behavior. This inductive maneuver could be criticized on the grounds that the observation is based on a single case (myself). However, the problem of other minds is such that by the nature of the problem, I am limited to observing myself—the matter of whether there are any other observers is precisely what is in question. So, while this is a weak inference, it is the best possible inference in the circumstances.

In the case of virtual beings, one would also face uncertainty as to whether or not they possessed minds (or the qualities required to have moral status). While it is certainly tempting to assume that virtual beings cannot possess these qualities the problem of other minds shows that their status seems to be only marginally more in doubt than that of real beings. To simply assume that being virtual beings denies them status would be a question-begging prejudice.

Because of these considerations, the same presumption should be extended to the virtual beings of the experience machine. The justification for this presumption is similar to that of the presumption of innocence in American law: it is better to treat an entity that lacks status as having status than to deny an entity with moral status that status.

The obvious objection is to insist that these are virtual beings and not real beings. The obvious counter is that it is not known the inhabitants of the real world have minds, so granting them status on the basis of an analogy and a presumption of status would entail that the sophisticated beings of the virtual world be afforded a comparable status. Thus, I could have relevantly similar moral obligations to beings in a virtual world as I do to those in the real world. This would serve to ground the value of experiences in the virtual world—they would have moral significance comparable to experiences of the real world. That is, what occurs in the virtual world would matter.

In light of the above discussion, there are compelling reasons for accepting that the beings of the experience machine should be granted moral status, if only an ersatz or presumed status, based on the problem of other minds. This serves to help support the claim that there are compelling reasons to believe that life in an experience machine would have value. The fact that it is not known if there is a really real world for real makes accepting this appealing—otherwise the value of one's existence rests on metaphysics that are forever uncertain.

It could be countered that the value of existence does, in fact, rest on metaphysical hypotheses that are eternally uncertain. The somewhat dissatisfying reply is that this view still places the allegedly real world and the virtual world on the same uncertain footing. So if this were the case, there would be no grounds to claim that the value of virtual world experiences is any less (or less certain) than the value of real-world experiences.

In sum, the complexity of the experience machine entails that it can create worlds and inhabitants on a par with the real world. As such, they should be regarded as having comparable value and status. To hold otherwise would seem to be a mere bias in favor of the real over the virtual.

NOTES

1. An early version of this argument appeared in LaBossiere 2010.
2. For those familiar with *Star Trek*, NPCs serve the same function as redshirts.
3. A lack of this trait is fairly conclusive evidence for the lack of a soul.
4. Not to be confused with a friend-with-benefits.
5. She is named after the Egyptian goddess and not the terrorist group—though huskies are a terror to small things that squeak.
6. Plato's argument is presented in Book X of his *Republic*. See Plato 2016.
7. Aristotle's discussion of vice and virtue occurs in his *Nichomachean Ethics*. See Aristotle 1999.
8. I am referring to all its versions, not just the first *Halo*. Likewise for *Grand Theft Auto.*
9. I address this matter at length in LaBossiere 2008b.
10. This is, of course, derived from Agent Smith's speech in *The Matrix:* "Did you know that the first Matrix was designed to be a perfect human world? Where none suffered, where everyone would be happy. It was a disaster. No one would accept the program. Entire crops were lost. Some believed we lacked the programming language to describe your perfect world. But I believe that, as a species, human beings define their reality through suffering and misery. The perfect world was a dream that your primitive cerebrum kept trying to wake up from. Which is why the Matrix was redesigned to this: the peak of your civilization" (Silver 1999).
11. Or as a human-*like,* since many experience machine denizens are likely to be beings such as elves, Vulcans, orcs, angels, and Vorlons.
12. I argue for this in LaBossiere 2008a.
13. Except STDs, of course.
14. In the informal sense of "know," of course.
15. Perhaps in a parent's basement.
16. The same is actually true of the real world.
17. Unless they are soulless husks.
18. Catfishing happens when a person pretends to be someone they're not using a virtual false identity, typically via social media like Facebook. An electric catfish would be a virtual being pretending to be real being via virtual reality or using means similar to those of the classic catfish.

Chapter Twelve

The Morality of Experience Machines for Palliative and End-of-Life Care

Dan Weijers and Russell DiSilvestro

Experience machines, popularized in print by Robert Nozick and on the screen by the Wachowskis' film *The Matrix*, provide highly or perfectly realistic experiences that are more pleasant and less painful than those generated in real life.[1] The recent surge in virtual reality and neuro-prosthetic technologies is making the creation of real-world experience machines seem inevitable and perhaps imminent.[2] Given the likelihood of the near-future availability of such machines, it behooves ethicists to consider the moral status of their potential uses. In this chapter, we investigate the use of experience machines in palliative and end-of-life care situations. We pair up various kinds of experience machines with patients in a range of conditions to illuminate the moral problems and benefits of using experience machines in this way. We argue that the use of Nozickian experience machines to treat patients in most conditions would be morally problematic, most notably for the negative effects on patients' characters and real-world relationships. Informed by this initial moral analysis, we describe an experience machine that is more closely related to a virtual reality game, and argue that it can avoid the moral problems encountered by Nozickian experience machines. In fact, we argue that this new kind of experience machine could improve some patients' characters and relationships with real-world people. We conclude that some kinds of experience machines could benefit many patients, especially those in extreme pain and those not in the position to meaningfully interact with their loved ones in reality. We also note that certain kinds of experience machines could be useful for religious people, for whom the range of palliative and end-of-life care options is often thought to be relatively narrow.

SOME PALLIATIVE AND END-OF-LIFE CARE SITUATIONS

The range of palliative care and end-of-life contexts is broad. Although many factors could be weighed in moral assessments related to end-of-life and palliative care contexts, we focus on the pain experienced by many patients in these situations, including its intensity, stubbornness in the face of pain relief, and the potential for its causes to be eliminated. These can be divided into a spectrum of cases along the following lines:

The pain is less (i1) or more (i10) *intense*
The pain is less (s1) or more (s10) *stubborn*
The *cause* of the pain is less (c1) or more (c10) likely to be irreversible
Pain that is the least intense, least stubborn, and most likely to have its
    underlying cause be cured would be labelled: i1s1c1
Pain that is the most intense, most stubborn, and least likely to have its
    underlying cause be cured would be labelled: i10s10c10
And so on, for all 1000 (10 x 10 x 10) types of *palliative* case

In end-of-life care, there is also a spectrum of cases in which death is more or less proximate. By "proximate" here we mean someone is more or less *near* to the end of her life. Cases on this spectrum will be designated as follows:

The prognosis of death is less (p1) or more (p10) *proximate*
The prognosis of death, as well as the other factors, may be unknown. In
    these cases the variables will be designated a "?" instead of a numeri-
    cal value
Pain that is moderately intense, moderately stubborn, moderately likely to
    have its underlying cause cured, and comes with a prognosis of imma-
    nent death would be labelled: i5s5c5p10
Pain that is of unknown intensity and stubbornness, moderately likely to
    have its underlying cause be cured, and comes with no prognosis of
    early death would be labelled: i?s?c5p1
And so on, for all 10,000 (10 x 10 x 10 x 10) types of *palliative end-of life*
    case

These distinctions are important because whether various actions should be considered moral or in the best interests of the patient seems to crucially depend on the status of the patient in regard to these factors. In real-life cases of palliative and end-of-life care, other factors would also be important. In this chapter, we address some of these other factors, but concentrate on the intensity, stubbornness, and reversibility of the pain alongside the prognosis for proximity of death.

INITIAL MORAL ISSUES WITH EXPERIENCE MACHINES

For some, the notion of providing experience machines for the chronically ill brings to mind chapter 14 of Aldous Huxley's *Brave New World*, in which Linda, the mother of the so-called "Savage" John, is expiring in a euphoric and technologically mediated stupor while her son tries to mourn, in what we recognize as a typically human way, at her bedside:

> It was a large room bright with sunshine and yellow paint, and containing twenty beds, all occupied. Linda was dying in company—in company and with all the modern conveniences. The air was continuously alive with gay synthetic melodies. At the foot of every bed, confronting its moribund occupant, was a television box. Television was left on, a running tap, from morning till night. Every quarter of an hour the prevailing perfume of the room was automatically changed. "We try," explained the nurse, who had taken charge of the Savage at the door, "we try to create a thoroughly pleasant atmosphere here—something between a first-class hotel and a feely-palace, if you take my meaning."

When John sees his mother, he shudders:

> Linda was . . . watching the Semi-finals of the South American Riemann-Surface Tennis Championship . . . [she] looked on, vaguely and uncomprehendingly smiling. Her pale, bloated face wore an expression of imbecile happiness. Every now and then her eyelids closed, and for a few seconds she seemed to be dozing. Then with a little start she would wake up again—wake up to the aquarium antics of the Tennis Champions, to the Super-Vox-Wurlitzeriana rendering of "Hug me till you drug me, honey," to the warm draught of verbena that came blowing through the ventilator above her head—would wake to these things, or rather to a dream of which these things, transformed and embellished by the soma in her blood, were the marvelous constituents, and smile once more her broken and discoloured smile of infantile contentment.

When John tries to grieve by recalling pleasant memories from his early childhood, when Linda mothered him, Linda is too absorbed in the machines and drugs to even recognize John, and speaks the name of an abusive lover instead:

> "Popé!" she murmured, and closed her eyes. "Oh, I do so like it, I do . . . " She sighed and let herself sink back into the pillows.
> "But, Linda!" The Savage spoke imploringly, "Don't you know me?" He had tried so hard, had done his very best; why wouldn't she allow him to forget? He squeezed her limp hand almost with violence, as though he would force her to come back from this dream of ignoble pleasures, from these base and hateful memories—back into the present, back into reality: the appalling present, the awful reality—but sublime, but significant, but desperately impor-

tant precisely because of the imminence of that which made them so fearful. "Don't you know me, Linda?" (Huxley 1932).

This fictional case arguably presents us with an example of how an experience machine might get things wrong, and might obscure or even squeeze out those eudaimonic[3] elements of human flourishing and human relationships that we rightly value in the process of pursuing what the nurse calls "a thoroughly pleasant atmosphere." Although pleasant for Linda, the whole set up largely cut John off from Linda, thereby causing him further grief at his inability to connect with her in her final stages of life.

On the face of it, the moral costs of such a scene outweigh its moral benefits; pleasure for the patient at the cost of pain to her surviving relative, not to mention the potential damage to her character and their relationship. For this reason, it is initially questionable whether we should encourage the use of experience machines in palliative or end-of-life care settings. New technologies that move pain from one person to another, rather than mitigate it, face a *prima facie* moral issue of fairness. New technologies that interfere with patients' abilities to interact meaningfully in the real world also raise the moral issue of damaging relationships and preventing the patients from flourishing. As we will argue, some kinds of experience machines will not spread the pain around in this way or impede human flourishing and relationships; indeed, some experience machines will promote these values while mitigating patients' pain.

NOZICKIAN EXPERIENCE MACHINES

Nozick's 1974 description in his *Anarchy, State, and Utopia* was not the first presentation of an experience machine, but it is the most influential (Weijers and Schouten 2013). Nozick's experience machine is designed by superduper neuropsychologists to provide any experience you desire alongside a smorgasbord of the best experiences researchers could devise. While connected to Nozick's experience machine, patients would not realize that their experiences are machine generated; they would experience a life that seems like a continuation of their existing life, despite being varied and blissful in ways that might seem incredible to an outside observer. Nozick also stresses the customizability of his experience machines; patients are unplugged every couple of years so they can queue up a new menu of pleasures for their next stint in the amazing machine.

In the context of palliative and end-of-life care, using a Nozickian experience machine is similar to total sedation; patients would only have a very small amount of time to be consciously present in reality. On the other hand, a Nozickian experience machine could presumably offer a much longer and more vivid experiential life than steadily increasing doses of opioids would provide. According to Barilan (in Barilan 2009), only the minority of patients in palliative and end-of-life care opt for total sedation. Presumably, the majority of these patients value their interactions with the real world enough to endure various pains and indignities. The minority who do ask for total sedation or euthanasia, according to Barilan, are suffering from total pain— their existence is so excruciating to them that they cannot function in a normal human way; they cannot achieve any meaningful interactions with the real world and its real inhabitants (i10s10c?p?). Most patients in total pain are experiencing a life of negative hedonic[4] and, at best, neutral eudaimonic value; they are in pain and have no capacity to pursue meaningful real-world ends, such as developing their character and relationships. As it stands, their choice is between this negative hedonic and neutral eudaimonic life and sedation to the point of unconsciousness or death, which are often thought to be states of neutral hedonic and eudaimonic value. Sad to say, the latter option—retreating from life—currently seems to be the prudential choice in situations of irreversible total pain (i10s10c10p?).

But now consider a future in which Nozick's experience machine is an option. Assuming the machine works as Nozick described it, and is available to patients with a variety of painful and debilitating conditions, the main choice for most patients with irreversible total pain (i10s10c10p?) would be between total sedation and an experience machine. Total sedation presumably offers a hedonically and eudaimonically neutral life (or death), and the experience machine offers a hedonically excellent life with questionable eudaimonic value. Patients on an experience machine would, by stipulation, experience a great deal of pleasure and little to no pain, but it is unclear how meaningful their experiences would be. We discuss this important issue of meaning below, but for now it seems clear that as long as an experience machine life does not have negative eudaimonic value (less eudaimonic value than total sedation), that patients in irreversible total pain may prudentially choose an experience machine life over total sedation. Whether an experience machine life would cause anxiety or peace in the patient's friends and family may also factor into the patient's choice, another important issue that we discuss below.

The overall value of Nozickian experience machines, and whether they should be used, depends heavily on the eudaimonic value of a life connected to such a machine. A major worry is that, despite all their pleasantness, experiences on the machine are worthless because they are fake. Sure, they feel good, the objection goes, but they don't add value to life because they are not genuine or authentic in the right kind of way. In Nozick's words: "WE ARE NOT merely empty buckets to be stuffed with happiness or pleasure; the self's nature and character matter too, even matter more" (Nozick, 1984, 128). And: "What we want and value is an actual connection with reality. . . . To focus on external reality . . . is valuable *in itself* . . .) (Nozick,

1983, 109). Nozick takes his experience machine thought experiment to demonstrate that people do not value fake happiness very highly. That most of us would not choose an experience machine life over our less pleasurable but more veridical real life supposedly reveals that more than the experience of happiness must matter to us. Moreover, Nozick argues that we are right to value "real" experiences much more than fake ones because they carry eudaimonic value—they are meaningful.

Despite arguing against the supreme value of happiness and pleasure, Nozick admits that they carry some value, presumably even when they are machine generated. This view fits well with Barilan's claim that a life connected to an experience machine would sometimes be chosen over total pain or total sedation (which presumably have negative and neutral prudential value, respectively) (Barilan 2009). The question remains whether, in addition to positive hedonic value, a life on an experience machine has negative, neutral, or positive eudaimonic value. Answering this question is important because it will enable us to better investigate the value of experience machines in cases other than irreversible total pain. In order to investigate this issue, it behooves us to further reflect upon the biannual breaks, during which patients would disconnect from the experience machine and plan their next two years of machine-generated bliss.

NOZICKIAN EXPERIENCE MACHINES FOR PALLIATIVE AND END-OF-LIFE-CARE PATIENTS

In the case of irreversible total pain (i10s10c10p?), patients would likely not accept the biannual breaks. If awakened from their blissful machine lives, patients with irreversible total pain would probably experience so much pain that they could not competently decide which experiences to choose for the next two years. To avoid the excruciating pain, the patients will likely be sedated, but this would also make it difficult for them to focus enough to plan their next two years. Either way, then, patients would find it very difficult to make good choices about their future; with sedation their cognitive capacities would be too dull and without sedation they would be too distracted by the pain. In order to avoid a similar dilemma, anyone opting for an experience machine life before their irreversible very strong pain (i8s8c10p?) became irreversible total pain (i10s10c10p?) might also choose not to take biannual breaks; the total (or near total) pain that they would feel upon disconnecting from the machine might scare them into declining the option to unplug for any reason. In similar cases, patients with irreversible strong stubborn pain (i7s7c10p?) might be more inclined to choose to be connected to an experience machine under Nozick's biannual break terms because the less-intense pain might be perceived to be manageable for the short period of time it would take to program the next set of experiences. But what might unplugging be like for these patients?

As the after party at the World Masters Games winds down, Trisha swells with pride while reflecting on her gold medal in the 100-meter dash. The very next moment, Trisha awakes in an experience machine control center. It's time, she's told, to choose experiences for her next two years. Groggy and in considerable pain, Trisha is partially sedated. Trisha might inquire after her real-world friends and family. These loved ones may even be in the control center with her, keen to reconnect with her, and perhaps advise her on her future experiences. Trisha was likely interacting with virtual versions of her loved ones while on the machine. And given the nature of the experience machine, Trisha's real loved ones might not be quite as pleasing as their digital representatives. On the other hand, they are real people, and interacting with them would likely be more meaningful for Trisha.

Would Trisha be repulsed by the warts-'n'-all reality of her loved ones? Or would she perhaps be repulsed by herself for abandoning them for a more pleasurable, but ultimately meaningless, machine life? Either way, only total sedation or the experience machine would provide an escape from this unpleasant situation and the strong pain dogging Trisha's every moment. Perhaps Trisha would ask for a moment alone with the machine technician and beg for immediate and permanent return to her machine-generated life of bliss. She understands now that it was all meaningless fakery, but at the same time she recalls how meaningful it seemed while she was experiencing it. For those who find it plausible, the idea of Trisha abandoning reality with such urgency is disquieting indeed. Are we such weak creatures that, once we had tasted what the experience machine has to offer, we would recoil from irreversible strong stubborn pain with such alacrity that our loved ones, our real-world accomplishments and goals, and all that was supposed to be meaningful, would be exposed as less important than avoiding such pain? What would all this mean for our true characters, our current lives, our plans, and the true value of eudaimonic ends?

It might be objected that Trisha is a morally bad person for abandoning reality and its real inhabitants. But why should Trisha feel bound by a morality that values the difference between her strong pain and pleasure so little? There seems to be a line separating cases of "too much pain for the sake of others" from cases of "permissible pain for the sake of others," and Trisha may well be over that line. Assuming that Trisha is enduring strong and stubborn pain ($i7s7$), and has received a prognosis of irreversible total pain for the future ($i10s10c10p?$), her moral responsibility to others seems fairly insignificant in comparison. Trisha could forgo being connected to an experience machine, and be there for her loved ones for a short time. But she would soon be in state of irreversible total pain, and incapable of meaningful interactions with others. Perhaps it is best for Trisha to tie up her loose ends and say her goodbyes while still capable of meaningful interaction before permanently checking out into her experience machine life. Consider a potential alternative of waiting until her waking moments became unbearable, saying goodbye (perhaps again) through a haze of sedatives, and then connecting to an experience machine. The former option seems to provide more dignity and less pain to Trisha without making much difference to her loved ones. Trisha's friends and family would get to see a bit more of Trisha on the latter option, but their interactions would be marred by Trisha's diminished cognitive capacities and elevated level of pain.

Instead of being labelled as morally bad, Trisha might instead be thought of as an unfortunate victim of addiction. Through her two years of bliss, Trisha seems to have become addicted to pleasant experiences, so much so that she would forgo real responsibilities and the chance for meaningful experiences shared with real people. Those with loved ones addicted to drugs, gambling, or pornography might be able to relate to the sense of betrayal that comes with a trusted person choosing a meaningless buzz over their real responsibilities and chances for meaningful interactions with others. But choosing to connect to an experience machine is not quite the same as choosing to risk, and ultimately gift, your family's life savings to the local casino. Partaking in pleasurable activities is only viewed as an addiction when it begins to damage other aspects of the person's life. If the behavior is not damaging, then it may be considered a reasonable indulgence, or perhaps even a harmless hobby. Given Trisha's current strong pain (i7s7), and her miserable prognosis (i10s10c10p?), there is very little of value in her life that is left to damage. Saying her goodbyes and connecting to an experience machine before total pain sets in seems at worse a reasonable indulgence, since Trisha would be doing little to no damage to what's left of her life.

Going back to Trisha's decision point in the experience machine control room (i7s7 with a prognosis of i10s10c10p?): Trisha might not choose to reconnect to the machine. Instead, wracked by guilt, Trisha might vow to battle through the pain to spend time with her loved ones, complete her beanie baby collection, or *really* finish writing her memoirs. She might come to the conclusion that life is a gift, one that should not be wasted on empty pleasures, but rather dedicated to the pursuit of meaningful achievements and relationships. This repentant version of Trisha rues the opportunity cost of connecting to the machine. She now realizes the machine-generated pleasures have little or no value, and that the eudaimonic value available in her real life could exceed the disvalue of the pain she will experience. We agree that the vast majority of movie heroes would take this option, but we disagree on how many real-life mortals would do the same. Either way, this repentant version of Trisha seems to attribute little or no value to her machine-generated pleasures. It's not necessarily that she thinks them disvaluable; she just sees the eudaimonic value of a real life as outstripping whatever hedonic value a life on the experience machine has.

Regardless of what any actual "Trishas" (i7s7 with a prognosis of i10s10c10p?) might do, it seems reasonable to choose to connect to an experience machine, especially after any real-word responsibilities that can be are discharged. Even if the machine-generated pleasures are meaningless, they are no more so than the life (or death) of total sedation, and they are hedonically valuable. However, it seems like Trisha would be best off requesting no biannual breaks. She could avoid a lot of pain, and possibly shame, by having her menu of blissful experiences chosen for her (possibly based on her original choices). So, while the use of Nozickian experience machines in palliative and end-of-life care is morally problematic, using them without biannual breaks might be morally permissible for patients in strong pain or worse pain and with prognoses of irreversible total pain.

USING NOZICKIAN EXPERIENCE MACHINES PART TIME

While permanently connecting to an experience machine seems like a reasonable option for patients with, or soon to have, irreversible total pain, patients with less acute symptoms may wish to use a Nozickian experience machine part time. Indeed, if loss of time or inclination to pursue meaningful activities in the real world is a downside of permanent connection to an experience machine, part-time use of one might provide a reasonable alternative.

Imagine James, a bedridden and probably terminal cancer patient who experiences fairly strong and stubborn pain. James's prognosis is not great, but his doctor thinks there is still a slim chance for a full recovery (making his full current status: i5s5c9p9). James doesn't live in the same town as his family, and many of his friends find it hard to get to the hospital to visit him. All told, James is visited about once a week by people he cares about. James has recently retired, and had no notable interests or hobbies outside of work and socializing with friends and family. As such, James spends most of his time trying to distract himself from his fairly strong and stubborn pain with pastimes he considers meaningless, such as watching television and doing crossword puzzles. James has attempted to befriend his ward mates, but they are either too sedated to hold a conversation or they are not a good fit for him. James's doctor presents him with an opportunity to take "experience machine holidays." James would be connected to an experience machine every Monday morning and disconnected every Friday night, making him available for weekend visitors.

To prevent relational discontinuity with his friends and family members, James would not interact with computer-generated versions of them while on his experience machine holidays. Instead, James would meet and develop relationships with computer-generated people—digital friends to go on digital adventures with. In this way, James would establish a new life that took over part of his old life, the two lives now oscillating much like a person with a "work life" and a "home life," only with the lives taking turns of a few days rather than a few hours. James would experience exciting and pleasurable activities during the week and meaningful activities during the weekend. This situation might please everyone, but it is difficult to imagine the impact on James. As the pain kicks back in every Friday night, James might experience depression or anxiety. This funk may persist throughout the whole weekend. James might even wish for his visitors to leave early so that he can rejoin his digital friends and pursue activities unhindered by constant pain. On the other hand, talking to a real person, one who really loves him back, might make him realize that all of his machine-generated experiences are a mere distraction from the really valuable aspects of life.

While it's clear that James would experience hedonic value in his machine life, it is not clear whether he would experience any eudaimonic value. On the machine, James might experience eating the finest twelve-course degustation meal, or his solving of the Skolem Problem in mathematics. Both of these experiences seem to convey occurrent hedonic value. But what about eudaimonic value? At the risk of offending those with culinary inclinations, eating fine food doesn't obviously contribute meaning to life. Solving the Skolem Problem, on the other hand, would be an immense achievement and contribution to mathematics; surely a meaningful activity. However, the meaning conveyed by such an activity seems to rely on the *actual* solving of the Skolem Problem. A deluded person might enjoy the experience of solving a major mathematical problem, but without his actually solving it, we would hesitate to describe the experience as meaningful. Imagine James on Friday night, shortly after getting off the machine. He would be suffering the return of his i5s5 pain, and possibly a heavy bout of shame about the glowing pride he felt about his fictitious mathematical achievement. In response, James might request that the experience machine technician make his digital experiences more credible to his waking self.[5] But note that the more credible James's digital experiences become, the less diverse and blissful they would be.

Einsteinian feats aside, a very important source of meaning for most people is their interactions with other people (Baumeister et al. 2013). How would James feel about the special moments he shared with his digital friends while achieving modest ends, such as solving a crossword puzzle? Solving the puzzle means little to James, but the social interactions might be another story. Of course, when James comes off the machine on Friday night, he realizes that his interactions with his digital friends were just that—a story. Of course, his digital friends laughed at his jokes and appreciated his thoughtful gift; they were programmed to do so! Even a prototypical quantitative hedonist, who would value her life solely by summing the pleasures and subtracting the pains, might disapprove of this strategy. She might worry that cognitive dissonance inspired by the weekly realization that her weekday experiences were fake would offset most or all of the machine-generated pleasures. In order to avoid disappointment every Friday night, then, should James ask the experience machine technician to omit all potentially meaningful interactions with digital people? If he did, then James's experience machine life seems like it would be less and less a rollercoaster ride of amazing experiences, and more like the life of Socrates's oyster—something akin to a nice, long, warm bath.[6] So James's weekday experiences seem to lack eudaimonic value, and have negative hedonic value when their counterfeit nature is revealed. It is hard to say whether this negative dissonance will swamp the occurrent benefits of seemingly meaningful interactions with digital friends. It seems likely that people with different levels of experience with virtual and augmented reality technology might experience widely varying levels of dissonance upon returning to the real world. So, perhaps in the future, experience machine holidays might work for some people. Regardless, another tweak of how experience machines work could resolve the dissonance worry.

EXPERIENCE MACHINES AS THE BEST COMPUTER GAMES EVER

The problem of consequently realizing that the wonderful machine-generated experiences were fake can be avoided. The experience machine could leave James's memory intact, such that he realizes that his experience machine holidays are machine-generated while on them. Nondeceptive experience machines like this would be much more like highly engrossing computer games with hyper-reality graphics and a tantalizing personalized plot. After a week of playing "the best computer game ever," James would not have to deal with any cognitive dissonance based on deception. However, James would not garner nearly as much eudaimonic or hedonic value from the machine-generated experiences. Achievements and interactions with others would seem relatively meaningless, and would be much less likely to generate hedonic value in the moment. Consider eating a digitally generated gourmet feast that tasted wonderful but was accompanied by a persistent and distracting vision of spooning piles of little zeros and ones into your mouth. This kind of experience machine is now quite far from that described by Nozick, but it is both closer to reality and perhaps more appealing to most patients in palliative and end-of-life care.

But would people want to spend most of their remaining days playing a computer game? First of all, recall that patients in palliative and end-of-life care tend to be suffering in some fairly intense and stubborn way. So, the relevant comparison is not between a normal relatively pain-free life and playing a computer game, but rather between a more or less sedated life of more or less suffering and playing the best computer game. Given this comparison, it may not even be necessary for experience machines to generate large amounts of pleasure in the patients for them to be a good choice. For example, imagine a patient named Lois who is in strong, stubborn pain (i8s8c?p?). We can imagine her case in three mutually exclusive ways, by imagining three different ways of finishing the following sentence: "*If* Lois were able to be engrossed in some intellectually or cognitively engrossing and demanding activity, *then* . . . :

1. . . . she would actually have less pain.
2. . . . she would not actually have less pain, but she would notice the pain less.
3. . . . she would not actually have less pain, and she would not notice the pain less.

It seems that an experience machine could benefit Lois in each of (1), (2), and (3). In (1), we have a simple case: an experience machine that reduces a bad thing—pain. In (2), perhaps an experience machine could do for Lois what "running for your life" can do for a soldier, or what "taking a test" can do for a student—namely, get Lois in what is colloquially called "the zone" or help Lois achieve what psychologist Csikszentmihalyi calls "flow" (Csikszentmihalyi 1990). In (3), the machine doesn't alleviate the pain, or the badness of it; rather the benefits of the machine-generated experiences add goodness to her life. So, even though Lois's pain remains as central and unpleasant as before, that pain is now accompanied by various other positive elements in her mental life.

Jane McGonigal, world-renowned creator of *SuperBetter* and several alternate reality games, and one of *Business Week*'s ten top innovators,[7] seems to think that the prudential value of computer games could be much more than that of a pleasant distraction. In her words:

> The real world just doesn't offer up as easily the carefully designed pleasures, the thrilling challenges, and the powerful social bonding afforded by virtual environments. Reality doesn't motivate us as effectively. Reality isn't engineered to maximize our potential. Reality wasn't designed from the bottom up to make us happy [. . .] Reality, compared to games, is broken [. . .] and we need to start making games to fix it. (McGonigal 2011, 3–9)

McGonigal's approach of providing an alternate realm to our broken reality may be alarming to those who would rather keep trying to fix the real world than give up and go digital. Indeed, it is a disquieting view when considered in relation to whole populations. However, the broad and continued appeal of digital realms like those found in *Second Life* is a positive sign for the utility of computer game-like experience machines in palliative and end-of-life care. McGonigal reports on global statistics that indicate hundreds of millions of people play computer games for over ten hours a week (2011, 3). In the future, games will likely be far more engrossing. Virtual reality technology is a booming industry. Immersive sights and sounds will soon be joined by immersive sensations of all kinds. The power of computers continues to grow, enabling graphics, phonics, and other features to become realistic to the point of experiential indifference from reality. But strange as it sounds, technology may not be the most important ingredient in continually immersive computer games. The "powerful social bonding afforded by virtual environments" may in fact be what most encourages throngs of gamers to keep coming back day after day to turn some zeros into ones. Could virtual reality games, and experience machines designed to emulate them, promote eudaimonic value?

DIGITALLY MEDIATED INTERACTIONS:
EUDAIMONIC VALUE FROM EXPERIENCE MACHINES

Regular gamers often play in electronic sports leagues. Much like people who play social sports in the real world, these gamers often create strong social bonds with each other, including creating friendships that extend beyond electronic interactions (Trepte, Reinecke, and Juechems 2012). In many cases, these friendships begin online as people from around the world meet while playing games. If palliative and end-of-life-care patients could use experience machines to meet and interact with other people in an appropriate online environment, and relieved of distracting pains, then presumably experience machines could be used to generate eudaimonic value for these patients. Indeed, patients with total pain (i10s10), or something close to it, may be incapable of interacting with people in the real world, but perfectly capable on an experience machine. In this way, patients with rapidly decreasing options for real-world eudaimonically valuable experiences could put some or most of their time and effort into generating eudaimonically valuable digitally mediated experiences on an experience machine.

Some people might fear that their digitally mediated friends are not true friends, that the apparent friendship may be a façade, perhaps designed to lure them into a position from which they can easily be taken advantage of. Wealthy Nigerian princes in emergency situations are out there, as are sexual predators. But most online friendships lack suspicious clauses and clandestine meeting locations. It seems safe to say that enduring online friendships that require of you only an empathetic ear from time to time are probably as genuine as your face-to-face friendships. But scammers and predators are not the only online threats. As is obvious to anyone who has played online games or read the comments left on online articles and videos, not everyone you meet online is likely to engender positive experiences in you. Small subpopulations of many online environments tend to act as "trolls," purposefully behaving in a way that annoys others (Buckels, Trapnell, and Paulhus 2014). It might be assumed that an ailing cancer patient, somehow labeled as such in a game, would be not be targeted by trolls. However, there is evidence that some trolls enjoy violating norms of standard decency, including delighting in abusing people involved in online memorial events (Phillips 2011). So while digitally mediated interactions with other real people may be a boon of eudaimonic value, they may also permit devastating negative interactions, even for those in manifestly bad states of health.

One way in which the eudaimonic benefits of real interactions could be incorporated into experience machines without the risk of users being scammed or trolled would be to create digital realms with entry criteria. In the context of palliative and end-of-life care, each patient would be assigned a digital world, which they could enter through their experience machine (at least for the purposes of controlling their pain). Other people could then access this digital realm using a password from their home virtual reality system, or experience machine extensions at the care facility. The result would be something like the experiences of the characters in the movie *Inception*, although there would be fewer sudden landscape changes and angry mobs. The patient and the select few she chose would have access to a shared virtual world. Thanks to advances in computer technology, the players in this game would be able to interact with each other in a way very similar to, and eventually indistinguishable from, real life. Players will see the faces, hear the words, and feel the pressure and warmth of the touches of other people. Presumably, the digitally mediated but genuine interactions will generate feelings of familiarity, comfort, and happiness. Given time, and probably not much of it, players could interact in a way that brings eudaimonic meaning to their lives; they could share experiences, mend broken relationships, express their feelings in various ways, and be there for the other person.

This kind of experience machine enables a wide range of options previously very difficult or impossible to achieve without such technological assistance. After an initial meeting in the real world, Trisha, James, and Lois could have befriended each other and developed their friendship in a shared virtual world. In her (i10s10c10p?) state of total pain (Later-) Trisha could not meaningfully engage with the others in the real world. But, using an experience machine, she could enjoy developing real and meaningful friendships. (Later-) Trisha could enjoy eudaimonically valuable experiences on the machine that were not possible in the real world. Furthermore, she has nothing to later regret, as she will never leave the machine. But even James, who does leave the machine every weekend, has nothing to regret about the digitally mediated, but otherwise real, friendships he is forging with Trisha and Lois.

Since information can travel much more quickly and cheaply around the globe than physical bodies, this kind of experience machine also makes it easier for spatially distant friends and relatives to spend quality time with the patient. Many people might not be able to afford the time or money required to travel the globe for weekly visits, no matter how important the patient is to them. A real-life face-to-face meeting may be the highest quality kind of interaction, but much more value may be accrued by more frequent virtual visits. Virtual visits may also be of much higher quality than some real-world face-to-face visits. Face-to-face visits with (Later-) Trisha, for example, would be much less meaningful, especially for Trisha herself, because of her incapacitating total pain (i10s10). Visitors, especially younger ones, might also find it difficult to see someone they love in pain or with major physical injuries. Both the pain and physical injuries can be concealed in the virtual world, making the interaction freer for the patient and less stressful for the visitor.

Many people who are initially less favorably disposed to experience machines might be in favor of the type of experience machine that allows for such reunions of family and friends, perhaps to a very a high degree. One of the most crushing things about chronic illness, especially at the end of life, is the sense of loneliness, and social isolation more generally—the feeling of being "cut off" from loved ones. If an experience machine could alleviate that loneliness to some degree, that would rescue a person—and it would rescue the experience machine from the charge that it's inherently isolating and devoid of opportunities for eudaimonic value. So, experience machines designed to model the best computer game ever are not only much more realistic than Nozickian experience machines, they also provide a beneficial alternative for a wide range of palliative and end-of-life care patients without the moral problems associated with the other kinds of experience machines discussed above.

THE BEST COMPUTER GAME EVER AND ISOLATION FROM GOD

So far, we have discussed some negative and some positive potential applications of experience machines. But in this final section, it's worth considering two more end-of-life issues that experience machines might help address: one dealing with physician-assisted suicide, and the other dealing with God.

Although Nozick refers to entering the experience machine as a kind of suicide, another nuanced philosophical view is available. There may be a potential silver lining in even the most dystopian use of experience machines—like those in *Brave New World* and elsewhere: namely, that as bad as they might be for the patient or her family, experience machines might actually curb some of the demand for physician-assisted suicide and euthanasia, which some people view (contra Nozick) as very different to entering an experience machine, and indeed as even worse than entering such a machine.

We alluded to this earlier; in some cases, patients are in such severe pain that they would prefer to end their own life over continuing to experience it. Such patients might welcome an experience machine as an option in addition to the possibility of having a physician help them end their biological life entirely through prescriptions of certain drugs or through Kevorkian's "death machine" (which he called a "Thanatron"). An experience machine, whatever else you might say about it, does allow a patient to remain biologically alive. It does not, by itself, end her biological life.

So various people who find themselves opposed to suicide, whether physician assisted or not, might find themselves attracted to the availability of experience machines as a kind of technologically mediated palliative care solution to the various forms of suffering that motivate patients to seek to end their biological lives. Of course, some of the people who undergo that suffering do not believe in God or an afterlife. But most of them would still much prefer to go on living, having some experiences of a tolerable sort, instead of dying, and thereby cutting off all possibility of experiences. On the other hand, some people do believe in an afterlife or God. While exploring how their attitudes toward an experience machine could open up several more discussions, it's worth thinking briefly about how the general features of this approach might intersect with the question of suicide in particular.

One way of thinking about the human body is that this mortal coil already is the closest thing we have to an experience machine. Indeed, the suggestion can be put more strongly still: perhaps each human body *is* an experience machine. Perhaps it's a mechanistic network of sorts that allows the user a meat-based medium for interacting with the world. Or perhaps it's a high-powered organic computer that generates experiences even where the pre-functional elements of the computer would have generated no experiences at all.

Some would object to this stronger suggestion on the grounds that it instrumentalizes the human body, and thereby makes the human self, which "has" or "uses" the body, a kind of spooky soulish thing. These critiques do not always come from materialists but sometimes even come from philosophically sophisticated Roman Catholics, yet in terms that do not rely upon their own distinctive religious teachings (Lee and George 2009). Still, since others might be unpersuaded by such objections, it is worth considering what this "human body as experience machine" thesis implies about the moral wisdom of using an experience machine (or rather, *another* experience machine!) in an end-of-life context.

Perhaps it leaves the moral question like this: What is wrong with an individual seeking to have another instance of something she already has one of? Is the only objection left that getting a brand new experience machine is (to echo Bernard Williams in a different context)[8] one experience machine too many?

No. A better concern is that the typical experience machine might distract people from thinking about what really matters toward the end of their life. Many will affirm that what really matters includes relationships, and especially family relationships (think again of the *Brave New World* example of John and his mother, Linda). But on some religious and philosophical views the set of really significant relationships also includes one's relationship with the divine. This might mean that an experience machine that smothers us even with virtual relationships may be distracting us, keeping our minds off of the inevitable and inestimably more important relationships that we are wired to enjoy—and, some would say, created to enjoy. As one of us put a similar point recently:

> When approaching the end of life, a Christian will want to best prepare herself for meeting God face to face (and will want to best prepare those she loves to do the same). The virtues one needs when preparing to die well are not merely prudentially managing one's pain and suffering, or courageously getting through that pain and suffering. Nor merely the backward-looking virtues of settling accounts and repairing relationships with one's friends and foes (and family, which straddles both friends and foes!). Those all do matter, of course, but what about the self-examination needed to prudentially avoid postmortem pains, to courageously prepare for meeting one's Maker, and to repair the relational strains with one's truest Friend and Father in heaven? (DiSilvestro 2015, fn10).

To the extent that the presence of experience machines might thwart that sort of reflection, we can see why some philosophers would be reluctant to embrace them. Experience machines might be precisely the sort of "quick fix" to the sorts of suffering—whether pain, boredom, loneliness, or their intermixture—that can spur reflective consideration about the direction and destiny of one's life. The illusion of "control" provided by their virtual environment might mask from users precisely that awareness of their powerlessness, and vulnerability, and eventual loss of all things autonomous that can turn hardened sinners into holy saints.

However, at least two points can blunt the force of this objection. First, the mere presence of a nonsuicidal option, even if it's as boring as the pleasures of a Socratic oyster, may be, in theological language, one of those "ways out" that St. Paul talks about God providing whenever someone faces temptation[9]—in this case, the temptation of suicide. If you believe suicide is a (mortal!) sin, it may be with gratitude for your soul that you accept the consolations of an experience machine to ease the remainder of your journey in this earthly life.

Second, there is nothing about the nature of experience machines themselves that in any way requires them to be used to put off significant moral or theological reflection. Indeed, we can imagine someone turning that type of argument around, in favor of experience machines. Just think what the Vatican could do if it teamed up with Apple. The idea is not one of creating a "virtual purgatory"—where one literally "scares the hell out of" a dying person using computer-generated scenes of damnation, demons, and Democratic National Conventions. Rather, the idea is to create the virtual space in which one can converse with one's priest (if he plugs in to his portal), one's pastor (if he or she plugs into hers), and one's favorite theologians in the form of digital avatars (say, "apps" for Augustine, Anselm, and Aquinas). Why? Well, precisely, to help one prepare for the journey to that undiscovered country Shakespeare wrote about.

CONCLUSION

We have argued above for several claims, which we order here both to recapitulate the argument and to indicate the arc of points on the spectrum of opinions we find plausible:

1. Some experience machines are inappropriate, both prudentially and morally, for some situations (for example, the *Brave New World* combination). Experience machines that prevent eudaimonically valuable experiences and spread rather than mitigate pain are unlikely to be prudentially or morally valuable.

2. Shared "computer game" experience machines—of both part-time and full-time varieties—could easily be prudentially good, in both a hedonic and a eudaimonic way, for people with moderate or worse pain (i5+s5+) and especially unfortunate prognoses (i5+s5+c5+p5+), with the full-time machines being more appropriate for the more extreme cases. The eudaimonic benefits (surprisingly) seem to extend to meaningful relationships with other people and perhaps even with God.

3. Even permanent Nozickian experience machines—with no getting out to program future experiences—can be prudentially good in at least a hedonic way for people with or soon to experience irreversible total pain (i10s10c10p?).

We have also opened the door for future discussions on several related topics:

1. Perhaps both shared and solo "computer game" experience machines of a part-time (not permanent) nature are good for people with temporary pain when they use the machines while in pain and when they do not have real-world activities worth doing.
2. Perhaps permanent "computer game" experience machines might provide decent lives, although they seem eudaimonically superior if they involve other real people.

NOTES

1. For recent examples of articles discussing the experience machine from one of us, see Weijers 2014, Weijers and Schouten 2013, Weijers 2013, Weijers 2012, Weijers 2011a and Weijers 2011b.

2. See Barilan 2009, Coeckelbergh 2010, and Schermer 2013.

3. References to eudaimonic value in this chapter refer to the various ways in which an intelligent agential and highly social animal can flourish; that is, develop and exercise its capacities in ways that are beneficial to itself. Important examples of eudaimonic value for humans would include working toward subjectively meaningful goals and developing meaningful relationships.

4. We take hedonic value to refer to pleasure, and hedonic disvalue to refer to pain, where both pleasure and pain are broadly defined to include mental and physical pleasures and pains.

5. Nozick does not suggest anything like this, so an experience machine that only generates credible experiences is a departure from his version of the thought experiment.

6. In Socrates's Oyster thought experiment, Plato's Socrates asks Protarchus to imagine a life without much pleasure but full of the higher cognitive processes, such as knowledge, forethought, and consciousness and compare it to a life that is the opposite. Socrates describes this opposite life as having perfect pleasure but the mental life of an oyster (Plato 1937).

7. See the discussion at Mackenzie and Watts 2011, 39.

8. Williams 1981, as discussed in Mason 1999.

9. 1 Corinthians 10:13: "No temptation has seized you except what is common to man. And God is faithful; he will not let you be tempted beyond what you can bear. But when you are tempted, he will also provide a way out so that you can stand up under it" (New International Version).

Chapter Thirteen

The Experience Machine and the End of the World (As We Know It)

Steven Montgomery

1. THE CITIZEN AND THE EXPERIENCE MACHINE

Political philosophy is built upon the assumption that certain core aspects of the world with which it engages—for example, states and citizens—are generally recognizable from either contemporary or historical experience. Despite the vast gulf in time and culture, they have features that a Rawls, Proudhon, Plato, or Confucius would easily recognize. This has lent a certain perhaps comforting continuity to much philosophical discussion about questions concerning, say, political authority, justice, or freedom.

Perhaps now that stable picture is shifting. While different states can still be categorized into forms that would be broadly recognizable in Aristotle's original survey, developments in technology may soon radically change the nature of the citizen.

The technology in question is that which provides virtual reality experiences—more specifically the creation of artificial and fictional worlds for users. Notably, unlike technology that connects people (i.e., social media) or which is used as an adjunct to one's ordinary life, this technology is used to provide a realistic immersive environment in which the user can have experiences. While social media and other technologies are already having an impact upon society, politics, and economics, fully immersive virtual reality technologies are a near-future possibility that are potentially going to emerge from the worlds of gaming, artificial intelligence, and user-interface technologies. The idea that a person might be able to enter into a virtual world that is, in terms of the quality of its appearance, indistinguishable from real life, and which can have its content programmed to give customized experiences of any kind the user desires, is still (for now) in the realm of science fiction. The question I am examining here is: Ought we to be preparing to welcome its arrival, or steeling ourselves for disaster?

To be clear, different virtual reality technologies are already proving themselves incredibly useful in fields such as engineering or medicine. Here I am concerned with a much heralded, but quite specific, area of virtual reality technology, one that we might call (to use a slightly cumbersome phrase) *experience machine-like virtual reality technology*. The name comes from Robert Nozick's well-known thought experiment (Nozick 1974; Nozick 1989; Nozick 2000), and the possible near-future analogue with which I am concerned here is similar in all important respects. A person has an option to enter into an unreal and yet completely convincing virtual world wherein they will be able to experience all of the (and their) most desired experiences; a "lifetime of bliss" (Nozick 1974, 43). While living in the experience machine, the person may have some ability to return to the real world periodically, but in the main (it is assumed) they will spend the vast bulk of their time in the experience machine. The idea is not to test whether we would like every now and again to vacation in a blissful virtual reality (yes, please, thank you), but rather, our responses to the option of a whole life in such a state.

The experience machine is generally thought to pose interesting questions about hedonism, or mental state theories of value, or even utilitarianism. And to that end the literature tends to recommend discounting aspects of it that might distract from our intuitive responses to these kinds of questions. For example: the risk of malfunction or disaster, a psychological bias toward the status quo, or its potential social and political implications.[1] My tactic here is the opposite; I will focus on this last category to see some of what the experience machine thought experiment might be able to tell us about the moral impact of this soon-to-be-arriving technology. In particular, would a decision to "leave" the mundane world and live in the experience machine be immoral?

2. POLITICAL OBLIGATION AND THE EXPERIENCE MACHINE

Nozick is clear—that we are to set aside worries about the safety of the machines and also any questions about duties to other people, by assuming that they too can plug in to the experience machine.[2] And I think too we can assume that the person contemplating plugging in to the experience machine can be considered to have settled their personal obligations in advance. Can we do the same for their political obligations?

To begin, we should wonder if it really matters at all. Many states are quite tolerant of individuals who are law abiding and who also absent themselves from any political participation at all (as citizens in the experience machine would presumably do).[3] And in those states where political participation is mandatory we might imagine that a dutiful citizen could in some manner delegate or preassign their political influence and voting preferences before entering the experience machine, just as we have imagined they are able to settle their personal obligations. It is however perhaps worth noting that the tolerance shown by many states to political absenteeism will be dependent upon whether enough people vote to establish legitimacy. Although a state, broadly, may have legitimate authority for its laws and actions that rest upon a range of reasons (of which, more later), the specific governing officials in almost every contemporary state cannot long retain a moral claim upon power without evidence of some link between their own actions in office and the will or desires of the people. Those who lack a sufficient level will lack moral authority for their actions in office. How low a mandate before a lack of legitimacy starts to pose a substantial moral or practical problem will of course vary according to specific political systems and historical circumstances. For example, systems with proportional representation tend to have functioning governments with larger overall democratic mandates than those without.[4]

Of course, legal observance and voting do not exhaust one's political obligation. It has, as John Simmons neatly puts it, "always been very intimately connected with the notion of citizenship, and has often been thought of as something like an obligation to be a 'good citizen'" (Simmons 1979).[5] If the literature on political obligation tends to concentrate upon legal observance, this is often because it is the clearest example from a broad range of obligations that attach to the citizen in a state.[6] However, in considering the way in which the experience machine affects citizens' political obligations it is here more useful to look at this wider range of political obligations beyond legal observance.

For example, in many situations political obligations might also include a requirement to take an active interest in political life. A state bases its authority upon the interests and welfare of its citizens; its actions are on their behalf.[7] Correspondingly citizens have an obligation to be—at least to some degree—aware of how their interests and needs are being defined and whether that authority is being well used or abused.[8] Further, citizens are under an obligation to speak out or take some action when the state errs and, whether with good intentions or bad, perpetrates injustice in their name. It is a tragic lesson from history that governments will, if unwatched, pursue all manner of self-defeating, disastrous, or even wicked policies while claiming to be acting on behalf of their citizens.

Another aspect of political obligation is a duty to act in ways that benefit or otherwise support the common life and general conditions of one's fellow citizens. In many respects, the state represents a collective environment for citizens, and in it their welfare and fundamental interests are (often) closely intertwined. This obligation of mutual support does not necessarily require being a good Samaritan, merely a good neighbor; and it can include negative duties to avoid damaging a common resource (e.g., not polluting a river or blocking a public path, restricting one's water use in a drought) and positive duties (e.g., purchasing war bonds, volunteering for public duties, donating blood). It may also in some circumstances, such as war or catastrophe, involve considerable sacrifice, such as volunteering for military or rescue service. It may be hard to see how this kind of obligation may apply in a large and plural state—however, we recognize it in the justified condemnation of a citizen who, although scrupulously obedient to the letter of the law, steadfastly refuses any further support of communal life; for whom the lives of fellow citizens means little. Think for example of Jacob Marley and Ebenezer Scrooge.

Extending from the idea above of supporting one's state and the common life of fellow citizens is another obligation—to respond to one's state in a certain (usually positive) fashion; to respect its authority even outside of the law, to give due respectful consideration to advice from the state and to assist the agents of a state.[9] It is, for example, common in many countries for police to routinely require the public's active cooperation in their day-to-day policing (as well as specific investigations), for policing cannot be done in the face of public indifference. And the same applies to many other aspects of public life. Further still, it is also the case that citizens provide, through their more informal activity, an important part of the national public infrastructure upon which contemporary liberal-market societies depend for their existence.[10]

Of course, many aspects of one's political obligation cannot (and ought not to) be legally required, but that does not mean that they are not *prima facie* binding. In some situations they may be actively contested, in other situations these kinds of duties can be extremely weighty. It is not obvious how a citizen living in the experience machine would be at all faithful to any of these duties.

Perhaps though, we have gone too far by stretching political obligation into some form of civic duty or virtue.[11] My own view is that political obligation is a capacious term that can include a range of different duties beyond conformance with state directives.[12] However, nothing substantive in our discussion hangs on using a different or additional term, as long as the particular duties in question are grounded by the same principles as political obligation (e.g., fair play, natural duty, associative membership—as we consider below). The cautious reader may simply substitute the wider term *political obligation and civic duty* where I use *political obligation*.

In choosing to enter the experience machine, the citizen of a state is choosing to remove themselves from all contact with that state and their fellow citizens. They would be, I assume, still resident and formally a member of a state, but be otherwise completely absent. Such a citizen is also choosing to reject their political obligations. The closest analogy might be to the kind of survivalist who chooses to live in the wild avoiding any engagement with the state and others in society, or perhaps a patient in an irreversible coma, or an inmate in a psychiatric institution. Such a citizen will take no part in voting, but also no other wider role in society at all. It is even arguable that such a person is not really a citizen of a state at all, certainly not in the way that we think of citizens now; they are more like a sort of "quasi-citizen." And then a question arises: Should a state, in turn, have a different set of duties toward a regular citizen than to a person who has abandoned their political obligations to live as a quasi-citizen in the experience machine? Perhaps if the quasi-citizen is analogous to a person who lives wild, or who is ill or incapacitated, the state instead might have something like a duty of care, or even charity, rather than the set of complex duties normally owed to citizens.

This situation may well appear precarious for a citizen in the experience machine (or a near future virtual reality equivalent), but is such a quasi-citizen behaving immorally? Given that the actual impact upon the functioning of a state from any single individual's total withdrawal is likely to be minimal, it is hard to see a strong instrumental justification for the moral force of their political obligation. There are, however, other moral principles that might ground or justify the political obligations I have outlined. One is fair play: if the actual impact of one person's failure to support a collective endeavor is minimal, that failure may nevertheless be unfair to the other participants.[13] The idea here is that the benefits of the state (including its existence itself) are provided through the cooperative efforts of all its citizens, and in taking advantage of those benefits of a state but contributing nothing (or minimally) citizens living in the experience machine are taking a free ride on the contributions of their fellow citizens. The answer to whether this is an accurate description will, I suspect, turn on the extent to which such quasi-citizens really are dependent upon the state. If the running of the experience machine or its virtual reality equivalent is not dependent upon any state support at even the most basic level—that is, defence, policing, provision of utilities, financial and regulatory infrastructure—then a person living in it could argue that they are not required to participate in the state in any substantive collective or cooperative manner.[14] The more removed they are (even inside the experience machine) from the state, the weaker any moral demand for fair participation will be.[15] And the converse also seems likely; if the safe functioning of the technology upon which a life in the experience machine depends relies heavily upon the people and resources of the state, then the requirement to make a (more substantial) fair contribution increases.[16]

In addition to a principle of fair play, there are a number of natural duties that would potentially support the political obligation of the citizen in the experience machine. Here, natural duties are understood to apply to everyone as "equal moral persons" (Rawls 1971, 99) and are not dependent upon any previous voluntary or transactional history, nor upon any institutional relationship (e.g., a duty to avoid harming people). A number have been advanced as possible grounds for political obligation; for example, a natural duty of justice that involves supporting existing just institutions and assisting in the establishment of new ones (Rawls 1971, sections 19 and 51), or a duty to rescue others from the risk of life outside of a state (i.e., from a Hobbesian state of nature) (in Wellman 1996; Wellman 2001; and recently in Simmons and Wellman 2005). Could these bind the citizen who is aiming to retreat from any social and political life and enter the experience machine? Because they apply independently of any relationship, natural duties have a very wide reach—and whether a person is living in the real (everyday) world or in the experience machine would seem to make little difference.

However, that same wide reach also appears to make natural duties justify too much, potentially including obligations to other states of which a citizen is not a member, or even to all (just or functional) states. This is known as the "particularity" criticism and is a common response to arguments using natural duties as grounds of political obligation (after Simmons 1979, 31–35, 155–56). In turn, advocates of a natural duty approach argue there are additional reasons why discharging such duties is best done via obeying and supporting one's own state (i.e., as Rawls puts it, a states that applies to us).[17] There is, however, a less commonly considered problem, which is that natural duties, by themselves, are vague not only as to which states one ought to obey and support (i.e., particularity) but also which acts are required. Consider: natural duties of justice (Rawls) or of protecting people from the peril from being cast outside of the state (Wellman) may permit many different ways of being satisfactorily discharged, only a few of which may involve acts in support of one's state. This opens a possibility for a quasi-citizen considering their political obligations to choose, from within some reasonable range, how to discharge those duties. For example, they might make provision for additional payments, above their tax dues, to go to just and effective charitable institutions, or to a political party they reasonably believe will protect the state well (or more simply, left in trust to the state), or they might make additional efforts to help their state and fellow citizens before they decide to "leave" for life in the experience machine.

Beyond fair play and natural duty, there are further principles that have been advanced as grounds for political obligation that might bind the citizen and quasi-citizen alike. One argument is that one has a duty of gratitude to the state for what it has provided.[18] Another argument is that a citizen has political obligations to a state simply as a member of it, in a similar manner as she has obligations to other important groups or associations; that is, family, groups of friends, or neighborhood. This may be because those obligations are an important part of what constitutes the association, [19] or because the obligations of that group are central to one's own identity, [20] but in either case these obligations apply to us without a requirement for our express consent. Moreover it is also plausible that a justification of our duties to the state is built upon several of these principles acting in combination. [21]

I have presented here only the very briefest sketch of some principles. All have various strengths and weaknesses in an account of political obligation. It should, however, be apparent at this stage that the stringency of (one or more) grounds for political obligation upon the citizen in the experience machine will also vary according to two factors:

1. The extent to which the experience machine-like virtual reality technology and its occupant are still connected to and dependent upon the state and society in which they are based. Safely ensconced in the experience machine or its virtual reality equivalent, the quasi-citizen may still, as I note above, be dependent upon the state for certain basic support and common goods (e.g., a safe environment, necessary infrastructure). They may also rely upon the state's good functioning if their friends and relatives are to go on flourishing (assuming that not everyone is going to choose life in the experience machine), or even if they want to keep open the possibility that they themselves may return to the mundane world at some point. [22] The degree to which such a connection to the state exists will depend upon the precise nature of this virtual reality technology. I suspect it is likely—at least initially—that such a technology will require considerable links to state, economy, and society, and also that people entering it will be fewer and do so more tentatively. Hence, even living in the experience machine, they will continue to have *more of* the kinds of political obligations I have discussed. This is of course likely to change as the technology changes.

2. The nature of the state. A soundly functioning representative democracy will impose some different political obligations, likely justified by different principles from, say, a corrupt oligarchy. If a state is profoundly unjust, citizens may not have a natural duty to support it, although they may have a duty to support some efforts of radical reform to that state. It is also likely that the different principles that apply to citizens in different states will apply differently to quasi-citizens. Imagine, for example, a citizen who enters the experience machine in a neoliberal "night watchman" state; one that provides minimal basic services, which makes few concessions to distributional justice and in which citizens act as competitors rather than co-opera-

tors. In such a case, beyond legal compliance, the quasi-citizen may have few duties at all to the state. Whereas in a different state, perhaps one that is strongly participative, that provides extensive public services, and that fosters a powerful sense of communal identity, a citizen who chooses life in an experience machine—while still technically being a citizen—risks violating an established set of moral rules that is partly constitutive of every citizen's identity as a citizen, and that helps to bind all the people in the state together.

There is also a close connection between these two factors. The kind of technology that delivers an experience-machine-like virtual reality option to citizens on a large scale would be enormously disruptive. The social and economic changes it would cause would in turn affect the character and functioning of the state. For example, a state that once exhibited strong communitarian associative ties that connected and jointly obligated its members may find these weakened if many (most) of those members retreat into experience machine life. A state that requires a high degree of public service may feel that even if quasi-citizens are paying a fair fee for services they are still unfairly shirking their role as "real" citizens.

Thus far I have argued that the citizen of a state who lives her whole life (or the vast majority of it) in the experience machine ceases in many ways to be a citizen of her state in the traditional sense. Instead they become a kind of quasi-citizen who, although they may be obeying their legal obligation to the state, are nevertheless acting immorally in their abdication from wider political obligation. Such obligations will depend upon the connection required by the citizen in the experience machine and the nature of the state (and also the particular principles that bind the citizen to the state). But what if they wished to leave altogether, to retreat from any connection to their home state—or to any state? For ordinary citizens, leaving one state necessarily means submitting to the authority of another. One may be free to leave this state but not to live without any political obligations. In the modern era with an absence of *terra nullius*, to be free from the grasp of any state has rarely amounted to more than a fantasy. That may change with the technology of the experience machine—it opens up the possibility that people could virtually secede. No actual new land would be required to create a secessionary territory or state, merely a jurisdiction that would host the machines (presumably in exchange for a fee[23]). The people in the machines could abandon their old citizenships and live as stateless people—experiencing lives of pleasure and joy.

This idea of virtual secession throws up an interesting possibility as regard to one principle I omitted from the examples above: consent. The actual and express consent of the individual as a plausible justification for political obligation and state authority has been in general disrepute since Hume's comparison of it as offering a kidnapped sailor the "choice" of leaping into the ocean to swim to shore (Hume 1994). Without a reasonable alternative option, consent to obey the state is problematic. But if the development of an experience-machine-like virtual reality technology offered a genuine alternative for the recalcitrant citizen then it would be more plausible for a state to require citizens to consent—or to assume (as the Laws of Athens famously do for Socrates) that an individual's continued residence stood for tacit consent.[24] Of course this would depend upon the requisite technology being suitably available and attractive (which is a different question altogether). If this was the case we would then have the interesting possibility that experience-machine-like virtual reality technology might potentially change the basis and nature of state authority for every citizen—whether they use an experience machine or not. For in this case a state could more justifiably offer virtual secession to anyone who did not agree with its policies. There is an even sharper edge to this possibility. The increased freedom to secede if a (quasi)citizen is already "living" in a different place than the state also removes at least one common objection to denationalization—the process whereby a state removes the status of citizenship from a person. The normal objection to such an act by a state is that it would place a hugely onerous burden upon any citizen so affected (see Barry and Ferracioli 2016). But the quasi-citizen, or even the citizen with an option to move to the experience machine, *might* not face such a burden. In which case, not only might a state be free to offer virtual secession to "nonconsenters" but it might also be more morally free to simply withdraw citizenship from many of its existing citizens.

Ultimately, for a citizen, choosing to live in the experience machine means changing your status from citizen to quasi-citizen. I have used a fairly standard conception of political obligation to unpick some of the wider moral implications of this decision. The relatively modest conclusion is that this is an immoral choice unless you are able to find an appropriate way of fulfilling your political obligations, which are not exhausted by your legal obligations. For example, it may be unfair to one's fellow citizens, it might be a statement of gross ingratitude, it might offend against a duty to support a just political institution, and it might be the kind of abdication that offends against the obligations citizens of a particular state have as part of their identities. This abdication of political responsibility may make those citizens who remain living in the real world turn against the quasi-citizens. And this profound change of status may also mean that the state itself decides its duties to you are less than those it has to real citizens.

3. BEWARE THE MAN WHO MAKES HIS DREAMS REAL

[Train] Passenger: Now, the first time I played it white hat. My family was here. We went fishing, did the gold hunt in the mountains. —And last time?—I came alone. Went straight evil. It was the best two weeks of my life. (*Westworld*, 2016)

Apart from one's obligations to state and fellow citizens, might choosing life in the experience machine be immoral in other ways? I think it might—I think that such a life might make us less moral, or even possibly, make us forget what morality is.[25]

Virtual reality technology, even in its current form, already delivers experiences far beyond the mundane—you can fly like a bird or superhero, visit alien worlds, step into the shoes of fantastical characters, or play a role in a horror film. Even though far cruder and more primitive than required for a fully immersive simulacrum of Nozick's experience machine (which is likely several decades away, or more), this technology already generates powerful emotions and memories. People, it turns out, are happily adaptable to new (virtual) worlds and experiences that are quite alien to their own.

The original presentation of the experience machine has users being given "any experience you desired"[26] with one's own imagination supplemented by suggestions of the desired experiences of many other people. For example, "a lifetime of bliss" (Nozick 1974, 43), or perhaps more concretely: "a lifetime of experiences made up of a combination of the most gratifying of those of Einstein, Mozart, Casanova . . . one's favourite fantasies" (Goldsworthy 1992, 14). The future development of experience-machine-like virtual reality technology will, I assume, allow for people to experience an almost bewildering array of new and (presently) rare, extremely attractive, and compelling experiences.[27] And of course, all of these experiences will be as vivid and convincing and gripping as they are in real life.

As an approximate weathervane to indicate what people may choose in the experience machine, we might look to the world of electronic gaming. Here, we see that people immersed in a fictional world happily choose both good and bad actions, to be heroes and also villains. In particular, gaming has attracted headlines for the ways in which many players appear to delight in using the freeform "sandbox" environment of many games to seek out and enact violent scenes outside of the main narrative of the game. I suspect that in the near-future scenario just described, this will not change. Thus just as people may desire to experience the best moments of a prize-winning novelist, rock star, astronaut, love-sick Romeo or victorious general, they may also wish to experience the life of a debauched Roman emperor, corrupt Lothario, wicked villain, or terrifying predatory alien creature.

There is an interesting question here about the future legal limits, or broader limits to society's tolerance, to which any fictional life in the experience machine must conform. As with the current legislation in different jurisdictions on extreme imagery available online, I suspect that there may be experiences that are so wicked that they offend the most liberal public sensibility—even if they cannot be linked to any specific harm. So I would be surprised if there were no legal limits drawn as to what kinds of experiences are on offer. But I also think that these limits are likely—given the recent history of existing technologies providing proto-virtual experiences—to be very permissive.[28] In fact, many potential experiences, even those that are far from wicked, nevertheless would allow (fictional) harm within the experience machine.[29]

Of course, Nozick may be correct in his examples (e.g., friendship, reading), that what really makes people happy are simple pleasures, but what people actually choose in the experience machines of the near future may be quite different.[30] The point here is not that these experiences might be all wicked, but that in order to be the greatest experiences they will be different from what we experience in our ordinary lives. They will be *without limits*. Consider that everyday life—even for those privileged with wealth and opportunity—is notable for its limits and restrictions, whether sharp (for example, law or finance), or relatively soft (for example, customary morality and the actions and desires of other people). Ordinarily we negotiate our way through all these restrictions and create space for our own lives; but the experience machine potentially offers a kind of life and experience that is completely unbounded by the mundane. My concern here is that the person living in the experience machine, experiencing a lifetime of superlative achievements, decadent desires, and intoxicating fantasies will, in turn, change and adapt to that life in ways that take them some considerable distance, psychologically and morally, from that of a regular person in society. This life without bounds, where every desire can be easily fulfilled, will, over time, change the moral sensibility of any person living in the experience machine.

There is, I think, a parallel here with Hume's idea of the circumstances of justice. That is, for the concept of justice to have meaning, certain features of the world must be in place. In particular, there must be limits on what is available. If we imagine a world of unlimited abundance where "every individual finds himself fully provided with whatever his most voracious appetites can want, or luxurious imagination wish or desire,"[31] we would no longer need a concept of justice. In the same way, a world of people experiencing a "lifetime of bliss" would not require (or encourage) the same morals we value in more everyday circumstances. Our moral values and our practical reason are shaped by a circumscribed and often challenging human life and the blunt fact of other people with whom we have to interact and against whom we are judged and judge ourselves. A world of one's favorite fantasies requires no such accommodation. The way in which we learn to decide how to act, morally; how to interpret and apply moral principles; how to be sensitive to the context and particularities of moral dilemmas involves a negotiation with that social and necessarily restricted world. This would not be the case for life in the experience machine. Instead everything is possible, including a life without moral limits.

Much of what we know about human psychology tells us that people's preferences, dispositions, and attributes are to a much greater degree determined by their experiences and environment than by any more fundamental (and purportedly stable) personality traits. Humans are creatures that adapt both quickly and well to circumstances, and a life, or extremely long period of time, in the experience machine will change people in response to the (best, ultimate) experiences therein. Given that these experiences will be dramatically different from ordinary life, it seems reasonable to conclude that the ways in which people will be changed by life in the experience machine will also take them far from how they would otherwise be shaped by ordinary life.

In Nozick's original presentation of the experience machine he does not discuss this possibility, except to imagine a variant, the *transformation machine*, which changes our personalities to make us into the people we might desire to be (Nozick 1974, 44). Later, in his third (and last) presentation of the experience machine, while considering the possibility that such a creation might actually come into being through developments in technology, he imagines another variant, the *environment machine*. This machine would change people by providing an environment in which they learn new skills and develop new traits, in a similar manner to how a flight simulator helps to create people who can fly planes; "the person actually gets shaped within it, in a way that partly depends upon his or her choices."[32]

Nozick claimed that to choose a life in the experience machine was a kind of suicide (Nozick 1974, 43). I think instead it would be more like a kind of transformation—into a creature that morally is quite alien to those who remain living in the mundane world. Of course such personal transformation would not necessarily be a problem *in the experience machine*, assuming that the machines can adapt the presentation of experiences to account for how these changes to people's moral values and psychological dispositions may also affect their desires. But this adaptation would change people from those who entered the experience machine as moral creatures who are recognizably part of a moral world into those with a stranger morality (if indeed a morality at all).

Such people might in turn be unfit to return to that mundane world. Although Nozick's original conception of the experience machine was for life, he did allow for occasional options to return. Moreover it seems likely that any near future experience machine-like virtual reality technology will be developed in a more partial and tentative manner. People will have the option to enter or leave over different periods of time. Following from the discussion of how people will be profoundly altered, it is my contention that people emerging after any significant periods of time risk finding that their cognitive and emotional responses are at dramatic odds with those prevailing in the mundane world. Their years of pleasure and fantasy in the experience machine will have made them unsuitable for economic life, for emotional life, for love and friendship, for artistic appreciation, and almost every other area of mundane life. They will be alienated from their previous selves, their friends, their family, and from the values upon which their society is constructed. Like mythical children raised by wolves, they will struggle to understand the world they are in.

4. HOW OUR DREAMS MAY CHANGE THE WORLD

I have argued that the citizen, choosing to enter into the experience machine, or some near future technological simulacrum, for life (or for a very long time) will face several moral obstacles. First, that this choice might be immoral as regard their fellow citizens, and the citizen in the experience machine assumes a lesser role than a full citizen, a kind of quasi-citizen. Second, that this choice might be immoral as regard the citizen themselves, as they risk a more personal metamorphosis, into a morally strange and alien creature in comparison to those outside the experience machine. In both cases—in this new moral-political context—the traditional role of the citizen, a core concept of state and society, is also transformed.

The degree to which a citizen ought to be engaged in the social, political, and economic life of a state has of course varied through history. And the private citizen of a modern representative democracy has in this respect fewer duties than, for example, the virtuous citizen of an ancient Athenian democracy. However the picture here, of the kind of citizen in a world where experience machine-like virtual reality technology is widespread and in common use, is one where the "citizen" is almost entirely disconnected from the state and the broader way of life within that state. In a world with quasi-citizens like these, our notion of the state would also be dramatically different. Perhaps it might be better in some ways, for example, in how it engages with other (similar) states, or how it addresses environmental problems. It might perhaps be worse in some ways, for example, in how it treats its own citizens or other people. What seems very likely though, is that in such a near-future scenario, the state will not resemble anything we have now nor anything we are familiar with in political history.

NOTES

1. Not all. A few writers have included the question of one's wider (social and political) obligations expressly because they worry it may not be plausible to thoroughly exclude such moral considerations from one's intuitive responses; for example, Bramble 2016, 139–40.

2. Nozick 1974, 43. In the original presentation it is as regard the need "to serve" other people. In Nozick 1989 it is "to help people" (105), In Nozick 2000, it is more simply "Don't worry about others, the same machine would be available for them as well" (Nozick 2000, 255).

3. We may assume that a citizen chooses to enter into the experience machine in accordance with the laws of their state. On the question of whether what they "do" in the machine is legal see below.

4. As one benchmark example, the UK, with a first-past-the-post system for general elections, has a government that was elected in 2015 by 36.9 percent of registered voters (i.e., a majority from a total 66.4 percent turnout). Although this was cause for concerned comment in the media, at the time of writing there appears little appetite for *substantial* action to try to improve turnout in general elections. Would the situation be the same if a national government was elected by 20 percent of the electorate, or 10 percent, or less?

5. For similar see Raz 2006. For a more sceptical view see Gans 1992, 87–88.

6. The terms *duty* and *obligation* are used here as synonyms. This is common practice in discussions of political obligation. One significant outlier in this is Rawls, whose model of practical reasoning defines obligations as necessarily voluntary and duties as not (see Rawls 1971, 97). For a wider discussion, see Brandt 1964.

7. Of course it is not always the case that the interests of the citizens and their welfare coincide.

8. Witness how citizens who protest against controversial military endeavors are quick to claim "not in my name"—a slogan widely used, for example, during the UK protests against the 2003 invasion of Iraq.

9. For an argument that a citizen's political obligation consists in a duty not to interfere with the administration of the law, usually involving state officials, rather than an obligation to obey the law, see Edmundson 1998, esp. chapter 3.

10. From the informal care of children, to the support of family members, to community volunteers, to the manifold small kindnesses of strangers, etc. . . . For a discussion see Bowles 2011, 46–81.

11. For an example see Dagger and Lefkowitz, 2014. For a discussion of the principle of fair play, political obligation, and civic duty, see Dagger 1997, Ch. 5.

12. For a discussion of the wider range of political and civic obligations, see Parekh 2003, 236–51.

13. One of the earliest discussion of fairness as principle in the form discussed here is by C. D. Broad (Broad 1916), although I wonder if there is in Broad's article an echo of a Humean argument for the virtue of justice based upon the need for social and economic cooperation. As a specific ground of political obligation, fairness is first seen in Hart 1955; Rawls 1964; Rawls 1971, 96; and sections 18, 52.

14. See Nozick 1974, 90–95 for his famous criticism of the principle of fair play on voluntarist grounds. For a thoughtful response that includes a nonvoluntarist fair-play model of political obligation that is predicated upon the importance of certain indispensable state services that one can reasonably assume would be sought out (along with their costs); for example, national defence and law and order, see: Klosko 1992. For a criticism of this approach and Klosko's model see Simmons 2001, chapters 1 and 2.

15. I wonder if they might still depend upon the state for support for their relatives who are not living in experience machines, and by implication be obligated to participate in a fair manner.

16. Christopher Belshaw rejects the idea that people in experience machines might be free-riding on society because "no one is suggesting that such machines are reserved for the few, and maintained at taxpayers' expense" (Belshaw 2014, 577). He does not appear to consider whether people might have a more extensive political obligation.

17. For example, Waldron 1993. For a critical rejoinder see Simmons and Wellman 2005, 121–88.

18. As a ground of political obligation, this dates at least from Socrates's voicing of the Laws of Athens in Plato's *Crito*. For a strong recent formulation, see Walker 1988.

19. See Dworkin 1986, 195–216. Dworkin coined the term *associative obligation* (Dworkin 1986, 196), by which these obligations are often known.

20. Often referred to as the "communitarian argument." See Horton 2010; Tamir 1993.

21. For a multiple principle model of political obligation that grounds different *specific* political obligations upon different principles (in this case, fair play, a natural duty of mutual aid, a principle of the common good), see Klosko 2005. For a more complex plural model, see Wolff 2000.

22. Recall that to be true to the idea of the experience machine we imagine the citizen choosing to spend the majority of their life living in virtual reality; but that does not mean committing to never return.

23. Perhaps they could be hosted in international waters. This would, for example, solve one of the main problems that afflicts many recent proposals of "seasteading" where people would live on boats or floating artificial islands (and pay no taxes). The problem being that few people actually want to live all their lives on a boat moored far out in the ocean.

24. Harry Beran has advanced one of the most fully worked-though theoretical models of consent as a basis for political obligation. It depends upon the creation of a suitable territory for people who desire to secede or options for the creation of a new state (as well as a proviso that secession not harm the state's essential interests) (Beran 1987).

25. There are other possibilities that I do not consider here—for example, that choosing to live in the experience machine could be wrong on the basis of aesthetic or perfectionist values. See Silverstein 2000, 291–93.

26. Nozick 1974, 42. Nozick's three examples (writing a great novel, friendship, reading) perhaps now seem somewhat quaint.

27. Here I differ from the views of Christopher Belshaw, who argues that the experience machine must have a dramatically restricted palette of possible experiences, because it must be both convincing and also identity preserving. So no "experiences of unaided flying, morphing of people . . . seeming to rush up mountains, rival Proust as a novelist" (Belshaw 2014, 586). For these kinds of astounding/amazing experiences would feel fake to the person who has entered the machine and who retains her previous memories, beliefs, and dispositions (i.e., in large part their personality). And if the experience machine's function were to alter that mental content so as to make such experiences believable, then this would change the identity of the person with a corresponding loss of autonomy; the person would be agreeing to "to become a sort of puppet or automaton" (Belshaw 2014, 583). I agree that such a radical loss of autonomy (or identity) is an additional reason to reject life in the experience machine, but I am not convinced that people need some sort of seamless integration. From our current knowledge of how people respond to even limited experiences of virtual worlds, we know that people are amazingly adaptable to new environments, and all manner of radically different and unusual experiences will be able to command attention, and be convincing, regardless of whether there is an initial gap between plugging in and one's new (amazing) life in the experience machine. With the kind of step-change increase in verisimilitude promised by the experience machine thought experiment, the scale of the problem Belshaw identifies shrinks further. So, instead of (pace Belshaw) mundane life only slightly improved, so as to preserve a substantial degree of experiential continuity with reality, I think we can be confident that this technology will at least aim for a range of experiences that are quite dramatically "improved" from reality; that is, more exciting, gripping, novel, thrilling, colorful, affecting, etc.

28. I might be wrong. We may instead end up seeing in our own near future the requisite technological and economic resources coupled with a suitably restrictive moral climate that outlaws or limits many possible experiences. My own view is that human ingenuity and imagination will make (for a variety of reasons) such a scenario less rather than more likely, but it is by no means implausible. The ultimate defence for this assumption, however, is simply that it is more true to the spirit of Nozick's original thought experiment to imagine a machine that

genuinely provides (almost) any experience, rather than one that operates within narrower limits.

29. Although he is discussing a variant of the experience machine—one where people are connected and able to affect other people's experiences, Jonathan Glover observes that a prohibition on harm would involve a loss of "a large range of possible choices" (Glover 1984, 103).

30. If we assume that the experience machines of the near future will be provided by different companies, it is reasonable to assume that what people are offered in choice will be what provides a competitive advantage (e.g., eye-catching, risqué, astounding) rather than what really might make you happiest (however that is measured).

31. Hume 1983, 21. As Hume observes, the other edge of the circumstances from utopian abundance is catastrophe and war. For a discussion, see Rawls 1971, 109–12.

32. Nozick, 2000. I am not entirely sure if there is a clear distinction between the environment machine and the experience machine given that they both provide fully immersive fictional experiences. Nozick does say that a person in the environment machine is not passive whereas (presumably) they are in the experience machine, but this does not seem plausible at all. A person in the experience machine could be a very active participant in their amazing experiences. They may even be exerting "effort" in order to reach a pleasurable goal (one that though seemingly hard won is of course never in doubt). In any case, it also rings true with our everyday experience that we understand people to be plastic as regard even quite deeply ingrained character traits.

Bibliography

Aarseth, Espen. "I Fought the Law: Transgressive Play and the Implied Player." *Proceedings of the 2007 DiGRA International Conference: Situated Play* 4 (2007): 130–33.

Aldiss, Brian. "Supertoys Last All Summer Long." *Harper's Bazaar*, December 1969.

American Psychiatric Association. *Diagnostic and Statistical Manual of Mental Disorders*, 5th ed., text. rev. Accessed May 5th, 2016. http://www.dsm5.org/psychiatrists/practice/dsm.

Anderson, Susan Leigh. "Asimov's Laws of Robotics: Implications for Information Technology." In *Machine Ethics*, edited by Michael Anderson and Susan Leigh Anderson, 285–96. New York: Cambridge University Press, 2011.

Aristotle. *Nicomachean Ethics*. Translated by Terence Irwin. Indianapolis: Hackett Publishing, 1999.

Banks, M. R., L. M. Willoughby, and W. A. Banks. "Animal-Assisted Therapy and Loneliness in Nursing Homes: Use of Robotic versus Living Dogs." *Journal of the American Medical Directors Association* 9, no. 3 (2008): 173–77.

Barilan, Y. Michael. "Nozick's Experience Machine and Palliative Care: Revisiting Hedonism." *Medicine, Health Care and Philosophy* 12 (2009): 399–407.

Barney, D. "The Vanishing Table, or Community in a World That Is No World." In *Community in the Digital Age: Philosophy and Practice*, edited by A. Feenberg and D. D. Barney, 31–52. Oxford: Rowman & Littlefield, 2004.

Barry, C., and L. Ferracioli. "Can Withdrawing Citizenship Be Justified?" *Political Studies* 64, no. 4 (2016): 1055–70.

Bartle, Richard. *Designing Virtual Worlds*. Indianapolis: New Riders Publishing, 2003.

Barwise, Jon, and Lawrence Moss. *Vicious Circles: On the Mathematics of Non-Wellfounded Phenomena*. Stanford, CA: CSLI Lecture Notes, 1996.

Baumeister, R. F., K. D. Vohs, J. L. Aaker, and E. N. Garbinsky. "Some Key Differences between a Happy Life and a Meaningful Life." *Journal of Positive Psychology* 8, no. 6 (2013): 505–16.

Bazin, André. *What Is Cinema?* Volume I. Translated by Hugh Gray. Berkeley, CA: University of California Press, 1967.

Becker, L. C. "Trust as Noncognitive Security about Motives." *Ethics* 107, no. 1 (1996): 43–61.

Belshaw, Christopher. "What's Wrong with the Experience Machine?" *European Journal of Philosophy* 22, no. 4 (2014): 573–92.

Benatar, David. "Why It Is Better Never to Come into Existence." *American Philosophical Quarterly* 34, no. 3 (1997): 345–55.

Benatar, David. *Better Never to Have Been: The Harm of Coming into Existence*. New York: Clarendon Press, 2006.

Beran, Harry. *The Consent Theory of Political Obligation*. London: Croom Helm, 1987.
Bogost, Ian. *Unit Operations: An Approach to Videogame Criticism*. Cambridge, MA: The MIT Press, 2006.
Borgmann, A. "Is the Internet the Solution to the Problem of Community?" In *Community in the Digital Age: Philosophy and Practice*, edited by A. Feenberg and D. D. Barney, 53–68. Oxford: Rowman & Littlefield, 2004.
Bostrom, Nick. "Are We Living in a Computer Simulation?" *Philosophical Quarterly* 53, no. 211 (2003): 243–55.
Bostrom, Nick, and Eliezer Yudkowsky. "The Ethics of Artificial Intelligence." In *The Cambridge Handbook of Artificial Intelligence*, edited by Keith Frankish and William M. Ramsey, 316–34. Cambridge, UK: Cambridge University Press, 2014.
Bowles, Samuel. "Is Liberal Society a Parasite on Tradition?" *Philosophy & Public Affairs* 39, no. 1 (2011): 46–81.
Bradford, Gwen. *Achievement*. Oxford: Oxford University Press, 2015.
Bramble, Ben. "The Experience Machine." *Philosophy Compass* 11, no. 3 (2016): 136–45.
Brandt, R. B. "The Concepts of Obligation and Duty." *Mind* 73, no. 291 (1964): 374–93.
Brey, P. "The Social Ontology of Virtual Environments." *American Journal of Economics and Sociology* 62, no. 1 (2003): 269–82.
Brickman P., and D. Campbell. "Hedonic Relativism and Planning the Good Society." In *Adaptation Level Theory: A Symposium*, edited by M. H. Appley, 287–302. New York: Academic Press, 1971.
Briggle, A. "Real Friends: How the Internet Can Foster Friendship." *Ethics and Information Technology* 10, no. 1 (2008): 71–79.
Broad, C. D. "On the Function of False Hypotheses in Ethics." *International Journal of Ethics* 26, no. 3 (1916): 377–97.
Broadbent, S. "Approaches to Personal Communication." In *Digital Anthropology*, edited by Heather A. Horst and Daniel Miller, 127–54. London: Berg, 2012.
Buckels, Erin E., Paul D. Trapnell, and Delroy L. Paulhus. "Trolls Just Want to Have Fun." *Personality and Individual Differences* 67 (2014): 97–102.
Calleja, Gordon. *In-Game: From Immersion to Incorporation*. Cambridge, MA: The MIT Press, 2011.
Chalmers, David. "The Matrix as Metaphysics." In *Philosophers Explore the Matrix*, edited by C. Grau, 132–76. Oxford, UK: Oxford University Press, 2003.
Chalmers, David. "The Virtual and the Real." Manuscript, NYU and Australian National University, 2016.
Cocking, D., and J. Kennett. "Friendship and the Self." *Ethics* 108, no. 3 (1998): 502–27.
Cocking, D., and S. Matthews. "Unreal Friends." *Ethics and Information Technology* 2, no. 4 (2000): 223–31.
Coeckelbergh, Mark. "Health Care, Capabilities, and AI Assistive Technologies." *Ethical Theory and Moral Practice* 13 (2010): 181–90.
Cogburn, Jon. "Moore's Paradox as an Argument Against Anti-Realism." In *The Realism-Antirealism Debate in the Age of Alternative Logics*, edited by Shaid Rahman, Giusepe Primiero, and Matheiu Marion, 69–84. Dordrecht: Springer, 2012a.
Cogburn, Jon. "Beyond Chaotic Good and Lawful Evil?" In *Dungeons and Dragons and Philosophy: Raiding the Temple of Wisdom*, edited by Jon Cogburn and Mark Silcox, 29–48. Chicago: Open Court, 2012b.
Cogburn, Jon, and Neal Hebert. "Expressing the Inexpressible." In *Dungeons and Dragons and Philosophy: Raiding the Temple of Wisdom*, edited by Jon Cogburn and Mark Silcox, 133–50. Chicago: Open Court, 2012.
Cogburn, Jon, and Mark Silcox. "Against Brain-in-a-Vatism: On the Value of Virtual Reality." *Philosophy & Technology* 27 (2014): 561–79.
Cohen, Jonathan, and Aaron Meskin. "An Objective Counterfactual Theory of Information." *Australasian Journal of Philosophy* 84, no. 3 (2006): 333–52.
Coleridge, Samuel Taylor. *Biographia Literaria*, edited by James Engell and W. Jackson Bate. Princeton, NJ: Princeton University Press, 1983.
Craig, Edward. *Knowledge and the State of Nature*. New York: Oxford University Press, 1990.

Crisp, Roger. "Pleasure Is All That Matters." *Think* 7 (2004): 21–30.

Crisp, Roger. "Hedonism Reconsidered." *Philosophy and Phenomenological Research* 73, no. 3 (2006): 619–45.

Csikszentmihalyi, Mihaly. *Flow: The Psychology of Optimal Experience.* New York: Harper and Row, 1990.

Dagger, R. *Civic Virtues.* Oxford, UK: Oxford University Press, 1997.

Dagger, R., and D. Lefkowitz. *The Stanford Encyclopedia of Philosophy*, s.v. "Political Obligation." Stanford, CA: The Stanford Encyclopedia of Philosophy, 2014. Accessed December 11, 2016. http://plato.stanford.edu/archives/fall2014/entries/political-obligation.

De Brigard, Felipe. "If You Like It, Does It Matter If It's Real?" *Philosophical Psychology* 23, no. 1 (2010): 43–57.

DeMul, Jos. "Awesome Technologies." In *Art and Social Change. International Yearbook of Aesthetics*, Volume 13, edited by Curtis Carter, 120–39. Milwaukee: Marquette University, 2009.

DeMul, Jos, introduction to *Plessner's Philosophical Anthropology. Perspectives and Prospects*, edited by Jos DeMul, iv–xxii. Amsterdam: Amsterdam University Press, 2014.

Dennett, Daniel C. "Why You Can't Make a Computer That Feels Pain." *Synthese* 38, no. 3 (1978): 415–56.

Descartes, René. *Meditations on First Philosophy.* Translated by Donald A. Cress. Indianapolis: Hackett Classics, 1993.

Dibbell, J. "A Rape in Cyberspace." In *High Noon on the Electronic Frontier: Conceptual Issues in Cyberspace*, edited by Peter Ludlow, 375–96. Cambridge, MA: MIT Press, 1996.

Dibbell, J. "The Life of a Chinese Gold Farmer." *New York Times Magazine*, June 17, 2007, 200.

Dick, Philip K. *Do Androids Dream of Electric Sheep?* New York: Doubleday, 1968.

Dijksterhuis, Eduard J. *The Mechanization of the World Picture: Pythagoras to Newton.* Princeton, NJ: Princeton University Press, 1986.

DiSilvestro, Russell. "The Arc of the Moral Universe Is Long, But It Bends Toward Mercy and Grace: And Other Delightful Surprises of a Distinctively Christian Bioethics." *Christian Bioethics* 21 (2015): 262–81.

Dretske, Fred. *Knowledge and the Flow of Information.* Cambridge, MA: The MIT Press, 1981.

Dretske, Fred. *Perception, Knowledge and Belief: Selected Essays.* Cambridge, UK: Cambridge University Press, 2000.

Dreyfus, H. "Nihilism on the Information Highway: Anonymity versus Commitment in the Present Age." In *Community in the Digital Age: Philosophy and Practice*, edited by A. Feenberg and D. Barney, 69–82. Oxford: Rowman & Littlefield, 2004.

Dreyfus, H. *On the Internet*, 2nd edition. New York: Routledge, 2009.

Dworkin, Ronald. *Law's Empire.* Cambridge, MA: Harvard University Press, 1986.

Edmundson, William. *Three Anarchical Fallacies.* New York: Cambridge University Press, 1998.

Egan, Greg. *Permutation City.* London: Gollancz, 2008.

Eiben, C., J. Siegel, J. Bale, S. Cooper, F. Khatib, and B. Shen, et al. "Increased Diels-Alderase Activity through Backbone Remodeling Guided by Foldit Players." In *Nature Biotechnology* 30, no. 2 (2012): 190–92.

Ellison, N. B., C. Steinfeld, and C. Lampe. "The Benefits of Facebook 'Friends': Social Capital and College Students' Use of Online Social Network Sites." *Journal of Computer-Mediated Communication* 12, no. 4 (2007): 1143–68. Accessed December 11th, 2016. http://onlinelibrary.wiley.com/doi/10.1111/j.1083-6101.2007.00367.x/full.

Fassone, Riccardo. "Every Game Is an Island: Borders, Endings, Extremities in Video Games." 2013. Doctoral thesis, University of Turin. Accessed December 11, 2016. https://www.academia.edu/14263064/Every_Game_Is_an_Island._Borders_Endings_Extremities_in_Video_Games_-_Ph.D_Thesis_Introduction?auto=download.

Feldman, Fred. "The Good Life: A Defense of Attitudinal Hedonism." *Philosophy and Phenomenological Research* 65, no. 3 (2002): 604–28.

Feldman, Fred. *Pleasure and the Good Life.* Oxford: Oxford University Press, 2004.

Feldman, Fred. "On the Philosophical Implications of Empirical Research on Happiness." *Social Research: An International Quarterly* 77, no. 2 (2010a): 625–58.

Feldman, Fred. *What Is This Thing Called Happiness?* Oxford: Oxford University Press, 2010b.

Feldman, Fred. "What We Learn from the Experience Machine." In *The Cambridge Companion to Nozick's Anarchy, State, and Utopia*, edited by J. Meadowcroft and R. Bader, 59–88. Cambridge: Cambridge University Press, 2012.

Flanagan, Mary. *Critical Games: Radical Game Design*. Cambridge, MA: The MIT Press, 2009.

Floridi, Luciano. "On the Intrinsic Value of Information Objects and the Infosphere." *Ethics and Information Technology* 4, no. 4 (2002): 287–304.

Floridi, Luciano. *The Philosophy of Information*. Oxford, UK: Oxford University Press, 2011.

Floridi, Luciano, and Jeff W. Sanders. "On the Morality of Artificial Agents." *Minds and Machines* 14, no. 3 (2004): 349–79.

Frankfurt, H. G. *The Reasons of Love*. Cambridge: Cambridge University Press, 2004.

Fratiglioni, L., H. X. Wang, K. Ericsson, M. Maytan, and B. Winblad. (2000). "Influence of Social Network on Occurrence of Dementia: A Community-Based Longitudinal Study." *The Lancet* 355, no. 9212 (2000): 1315–19.

Fröding, B., and M. Peterson. "Why Virtual Friendship Is Not Genuine Friendship." *Ethics and Information Technology* 14, no. 3 (2012): 201–7.

Gans, Chaim. *Philosophical Anarchism and Political Disobedience*. Cambridge, UK: Cambrdge University Press, 1992.

Gaut, Berys. *A Philosophy of Cinematic Art*. Cambridge: Cambridge University Press, 2010.

Gibson, J. J. "The Theory of Affordances." In *Perceiving, Acting and Knowing: Toward and Ecological Psychology*, edited by R. Shaw and J. Bransford, 67–82. Hillsdale, NJ: Lawrence Erlbaum, 1977.

Gitelman, Lisa. *Always Already New*. Cambridge, MA: The MIT Press, 2006.

Glover, Jonathan. *What Sort of People Should There Be?* London: Penguin, 1984.

Goldsworthy, Jeffrey. "Well-Being and Value." *Utilitas* 4 (1992): 1–26.

Grau, Christopher. "There Is No 'I' in 'Robot': Robots and Utilitarianism." In *Machine Ethics*, edited by Michael Anderson and Susan Leigh Anderson, 461–64. New York: Cambridge University Press, 2011.

Grodzinsky, F. S., K. W. Miller, and M. J. Wolf. "Developing Automated Deceptions and the Impact on Trust." *Philosophy & Technology* 28, no. 1 (2015): 91–105.

Gualeni, Stefano. "ENLARGE YOUR MESOSCOPY: A Philosophical Reflection on Projectual Ontologies and the Human Scale." Paper presented at the 2015 euSLSA conference in Furjana, Malta, June 15–18, 2015a.

Gualeni, Stefano. *Virtual Worlds as Philosophical Tools: How to Philosophize with a Digital Hammer*. Basingstoke: Palgrave Macmillan, 2015b.

Gualeni, Stefano. "Self-Transformation through Game Design." Paper presented at the 2015 Philosophy of Computer Games conference, held at the BTK University of Art and Design of Berlin, Germany, October 14–17, 2015c.

Gunkel, David J. "A Vindication of the Rights of Machines." *Philosophy & Technology* 27, no. 1 (2014): 113–32.

Haferkamp, N., and N. C. Krämer. "Social Comparison 2.0: Examining the Effects of Online Profiles on Social-Networking Sites." *Cyberpsychology, Behavior, and Social Networking* 14, no. 5 (2011): 309–14.

Harman, Graham. *Weird Realism: Lovecraft and Philosophy*. Washington, DC: Zero Books, 2012.

Harris, Paul L. *The Work of the Imagination*. London: Wiley-Blackwell, 2000.

Hart, H. L. A. "Are There Any Natural Rights?" *Philosophical Review* 64 (1955): 175–91.

Hatfield, Elaine, J. T. Cacioppo, and R. L. Rapson. "Emotional Contagion." *Current Directions in Psychological Sciences* 2 (1993): 96–99.

Hatfield, Elaine, J. T. Cacioppo, and R. L. Rapson. "Primitive Emotional Contagion." *Emotions and Social Behavior: Review of Personality and Social Psychology* 14, edited by M. S. Clark, 153–54. Newbury Park, CA: Sage, 1992.

Heidegger, Martin. "The Question Concerning Technology." In *Basic Writings*. Translated by David Farrell Krell, 307–42. San Francisco: Harper Collins, 1972.

Heim, Michael. *Virtual Realism*. New York: Oxford University Press, 1998.

Heller, Joshua, and Jon Cogburn. "Meillassoux's Dilemma." Accessed November 22, 2015. https://www.academia.edu/18797280/MEILLASSOUX_S_DILEMMA_PARADOXES_ OF_TOTALITY_AFTER_THE_SPECULATIVE_TURN.

Hermosillo, C. "Pandora's Vox." In *High Noon on the Electronic Frontier: Conceptual Issues in Cyberspace*, edited by Peter Ludlow, 437–44. Cambridge: MIT Press, 1996. Article published under the name "humdog."

Hewitt, Sharon. "What Do Our Intuitions about the Experience Machine Really Tell Us about Hedonism?" *Philosophical Studies: An International Journal for Philosophy in the Analytic Tradition* 151, no. 3 (2010): 331–49.

Hick, John. *Evil and the God of Love*. Houndsmill: Palgrave Macmillan UK, 2010.

Hickey, Lance. "The Brain in a Vat Argument." *Internet Encyclopedia of Philosophy*. Accessed June 22, 2015. http://www.iep.utm.edu/brainvat/.

Hintikka, Jaakko. *Socratic Epistemology: Explorations of Knowledge-Seeking by Questions*. Cambridge, UK: Cambridge University Press, 2007.

Holland, Greg J. "An Analytic Model of the Wind and Pressure Profiles in Hurricanes." *Monthly Weather Review* 108 (1980): 1212–8.

Horton, John. *Political Obligation*, 2nd Edition. London: MacMillan, 2010.

Huizinga, Johan. *Homo Ludens: A Study of the Play Element in Culture*. Boston: Beacon Press, 1955.

Hume, David. *Treatise of Human Nature*. Edited by L. A. Selby-Bigge. Oxford: Clarendon Press, 1978.

Hume, David. *An Enquiry Concerning the Principles of Morals*. Indianapolis: Hackett, 1983.

Hume, David. "Of the Original Contract." In *Hume, Political Essays*. Cambridge, UK: Cambridge University Press, 1994.

Hurka, Thomas. *Best Things in Life: A Guide to What Really Matters*. Oxford: Oxford University Press, 2011.

Husserl, Edmond. *The Crisis of European Sciences and Transcendental Phenomenology: An Introduction to Phenomenological Philosophy*. Translated by David Carr. Evanston, IL: Northwestern University Press, 1954.

Huxley, Aldous. *Brave New World*. London, UK: Chatto & Windus, 1932.

Ihde, Don. *Technology and the Lifeworld*. Bloomington, IN: Indiana University Press, 1990.

Ito, M., H. A. Horst, M. Bittanti, D. Boyd, B. Herr-Stephenson, P. G. Lange, C. J. Pascoe, and L. Robinson. 2008. Accessed December 11, 2016. *Living and Learning with New Media: Summary of Findings from the Digital Youth Project*. http://digitalyouth.ischool.berkeley. edu/report.

Jahoda, M. "Current Concepts of Positive Mental Health." *Journal of Occupational and Environmental Medicine* 1, no. 10 (1959): 565.

Jørgensen, Kristine. *Gameworld Interfaces*. Cambridge, MA: The MIT Press, 2013.

Juul, Jesper. *Half-Real: Video Games Between Real Rules and Fictional Worlds*. Cambridge, MA: The MIT Press, 2005.

Kagan, Shelly. "Me and My Life." *Proceedings of the Aristotelian Society* 94 (1994): 309–24.

Kahneman, D., J. L. Knetsch, and R. H. Thaler. "Anomalies: The Endowment Effect, Loss Aversion, and Status Quo Bias." *The Journal of Economic Perspectives* 5, no. 1 (1991): 193–206.

Kaliarnta, S. "Using Aristotle's Theory of Friendship to Classify Online Friendships: A Critical Counterview." *Ethics and Information Technology* 18, no. 1 (2016): 65–70.

Kant, Immanuel. *Lectures on Ethics*. Translated by Louis Infield. London: Methuen & Co. Ltd., 1930.

Kapp, E. *Grundlinien einer Philosophie der Technik: Zur Entstehungsgeschichte der Cultur aus neuen Gesichtspunkten*. Braunschweig: Westermann, 1877.

Kawall, Jason. "The Experience Machine and Mental State Theories of Well-Being." *Journal of Value Inquiry* 33, no. 3 (1999): 381–87.

Kelly, Heather. "Do Video Games Cause Violence?" CNNTech, August 17, 2015. Accessed December 14, 2016. http://money.cnn.com/2015/08/17/technology/video-game-violence/.

King, Barbara J. "A Virtual View of a Slaughterhouse." *Cosmos and Culture: Commentary of Science and Society* 13, no. 7, NPR 2/4/16. Accessed May 5, 2016. http://www.npr.org/sections/13.7/2016/02/04/465530255/a-virtual-view-of-a-slaughterhouse?utm_source=facebook.com&utm_medium=social&utm_campaign=npr&utm_term=nprnews&utm_content=20160204.

Klein, Ezra. "Elon Musk Believes We Are Probably Characters in Some Advanced Civilization's Video Game." *Vox.com*, June 2, 2016. Accessed December 14, 2016. http://www.vox.com/2016/6/2/11837608/elon-musk-simulation-argument.

Klosko, George. *The Principle of Fairness and Political Obligations.* Savage, MD: Rowman & Littlefield, 1992.

Klosko, George. *Political Obligations.* Oxford, UK: Oxford University Press, 2005.

Kolber, A. J. "Mental Statism and the Experience Machine." *Bard Journal of Social Sciences* 3 (1994): 10–17.

Korsgaard, Christine. *The Sources of Normativity.* Cambridge, UK: Cambridge University Press, 1996.

Kretzmann, Norman. "Omniscience and Immutability." *Journal of Philosophy* 63 (1966): 409–21.

Kripke, Saul. *Naming and Necessity.* London: Wiley-Blackwell, 1991.

Kross, E., P. Verduyn, E. Demiralp, J. Park, D. Lee, N. Lin, N., et al. "Facebook Use Predicts Declines in Subjective Well-Being in Young Adults." *PLoS ONE* 8. no. 8 (2013): e69841.

LaBossiere, Michael. "The Unbreakable Skeptic." In *What Don't You Know?* 38–40. New York: Continuum, 2008a.

LaBossiere, Michael. "Virtual Violence and Moral Purpose." In *What Don't You Know?* 84–86. New York: Continuum, 2008b.

LaBossiere, Michael. "Saving Dogmeat." *Talking Philosophy: The Philosophers' Magazine Blog*, June 28, 2010. Accessed December 14, 2016. http://blog.talkingphilosophy.com/?p=1843.

Lee, Patrick, and Robert P. George. *Body-Soul Dualism in Contemporary Ethics and Politics.* Cambridge: Cambridge University Press, 2009.

Leibniz, Gottfried Wilhelm. *The Monadology.* Translated by Robert Latta. Accessed May 21, 2016. http://sqapo.com/completetext-leibniz-monadology.htm.

Lévy, Pierre. *Qu'est que le Virtuel?* Paris: La Découverte, 1998.

Locke, John. *An Essay Concerning Human Understanding.* Edited by Peter H. Nidditch. Hong Kong: Oxford University Press, 1987.

Lopes, Dominic McIver. "The Ontology of Interactive Art." *The Journal of Aesthetic Education* 35, no. 4 (2001): 65–81.

Lopes, Dominic McIver. *A Philosophy of Computer Art.* Oxford: Routledge, 2009.

Lovecraft, H. P. "The Whisperer in Darkness." In *Lovecraft Tales*, 415–80. New York: Literary Classics of the United States, 2005.

Ludlow, Peter, ed. *High Noon on the Electronic Frontier: Conceptual Issues in Cyberspace.* Cambridge, MA: MIT Press, 1996.

Ludlow, Peter, ed. *Crypto Anarchy, Cyberstates, and Pirate Utopias.* Cambridge, MA: MIT Press, 2009.

Ludlow, P., and M. Wallace. *The Second Life Herald: The Virtual Tabloid That Witnessed the Dawn of the Metaverse.* Cambridge, MA: MIT Press, 2009.

Luhman, Nathan. "Trust: A Mechanism for the Reduction of Social Complexity." In *Trust and Power: Two Works by Niklas Luhman.* Chichester, UK: John Wiley & Sons, 1979.

Mackenzie, Robin, and John Watts. "Robots, Social Networking Sites and Multi-User Games: Using New and Existing Assistive Technologies to Promote Human Flourishing." *Tizard Learning Disability Review* 16, no. 5 (2011): 38–47.

Mackie, J. L. "Evil and Omnipotence." *Mind* 64, no. 254 (1955): 200–12.

Martin, Paul. "The Pastoral and the Sublime in Elder Scrolls IV: Oblivion." *Game Studies* 11, no. 3 (2011). Accessed December 12, 2016. http://www.gamestudies.org/1103/articles/martin.

Martinez-Conde, S., S. Macnik, and D. Hubel. "The Role of Fixational Eye Movements in Visual Perception." *Nature Reviews* 5 (2004): 229–40.

Mason, Elinor. "Do Consequentialists Have One Thought Too Many?" *Ethical Theory and Moral Practice* 2, no. 3 (1999): 243–61.

McGonigal, Jane. *Reality Is Broken: Why Games Make Us Better and How They Can Change the World*. London: Cape, 2011.

McKim, Robert. *Religious Ambiguity and Religious Diversity*. Oxford; New York: Oxford University Press, 2001.

Meadows, M. S., and P. Ludlow. "A Virtual Life. An Actual Death." *H+*, September 2, 2009. Accessed December 12, 2016. http://hplusmagazine.com/2009/09/02/virtual-life-actual-death/.

Meskin, Aaron, and Jonathan Cohen, "Photographs as Evidence." In *Photography and Philosophy: Essays on the Pencil of Nature*, edited by Scott Walden, 70–90. West Sussex: Blackwell Publishing Ltd., 2010.

Mill, J. S. *Utilitarianism*. Indianapolis, IN: Hackett, 2001.

Millikan, Ruth. *Clear and Confused Ideas: An Essay on Substance Concepts*. Cambridge, UK: Cambridge University Press, 2000.

Minnesota Department of Corrections. *Characteristics and Behavioral Indicators of Adults who Molest Children*. 2009. Accessed May 30, 2016. http://www.doc.state.mn.us/pages/files/4313/8695/0043/05-09Characteristics_newlogo.pdf.

Misselhorn, C., U. Pompe, and M. Stapleton. "Ethical Considerations Regarding the Use of Social Robots in the Fourth Age." *GeroPsych: The Journal of Gerontopsychology and Geriatric Psychiatry* 26, no. 2 (2013): 121.

Mumford, Lewis. *Technics and Civilization*. London (UK): Routledge, 1934.

Munn, N. J. "The Reality of Friendship within Immersive Virtual Worlds." *Ethics and Information Technology* 14, no. 1 (2012): 1–10.

Nietzsche, Friedrich. *Daybreak*. Translated by R. J. Hollingdale. Cambridge, UK: Cambridge University Press, 1997.

Nadelhoffer, T. "How the Experience Machine Works." *Experimental Philosophy Blog*, 2011. Accessed May 8, 2016. http://philosophycommons.typepad.com/xphi/2011/02/how-the-experience-machine-works.html.

Neely, Erica L. "Machines and the Moral Community." *Philosophy & Technology* 27, no. 1 (2013): 97–111.

Nissenbaum, H. "Securing Trust Online: Wisdom or Oxymoron?" *Boston University Law Review* 81, no. 3 (2001): 101–131.

Nozick, Robert. *Anarchy, State, and Utopia*. New York: Basic Books, 1974.

Nozick, Robert. *Philosophical Explanations*. New York: Belknap Press; Reprint edition, 1983.

Nozick, Robert. *The Examined Life: Philosophical Meditations*. New York: Simon and Schuster, 1989.

Nozick, Robert. "The Pursuit of Happiness." *Forbes Magazine*, October 2, 2000.

Obama, B. 2010. "Speech to the Graduating Class at Hampton University." Presentation at Hampton University Graduation Ceremonies, Hampton, Virginia, May 12, 2010.

Ong, A. D., and M. H. M. Van Dulmen. *Oxford Handbook of Methods in Positive Psychology*. Oxford, UK: Oxford University Press, 2007.

Parekh, Bhikhu. "A Misconceived Discourse on Political Obligation." *Political Studies* 41 (2003): 236–51.

Parfit, Derek. "On Doing the Best for Our Children." In *Ethics and Population*, edited by Michael D. Bayles. Cambridge, MA: Schneckman, 1976.

Parfit, Derek. *Reasons and Persons*. Oxford, UK: Oxford University Press, 1984.

Parks, J. A. "Lifting the Burden of Women's Care Work: Should Robots Replace the 'Human Touch?'" *Hypatia* 25, no. 1 (2010): 100–20.

Parks, M. R., and K. Floyd. "Making Friends in Cyberspace." *Journal of Computer-Mediated Communication* 1, no. 4 (1996): 80–97.

Patridge, Stephanie. "Is It Only a Game? The Ethics of Video Game Play." In *Aesthetics: A Reader in the Philosophy of the Arts*, edited by David Goldblatt and Lee B. Brown, 386–90. Upper Saddle River, NJ: Prentice Hall, 2011a.

Patridge, Stephanie. "The Incorrigible Social Meaning of Video Game Imagery: Making Ethical Sense of Single-Player Video Games." *Ethics and Information Technology* 14, no. 4 (2011b): 303–12.

Pereboom, Derek. "The Problem of Evil." In *The Blackwell Guide to the Philosophy of Religion*, edited by William E. Mann, 148–70. Oxford, UK: Blackwell, 2005.

Pérez-Montoro, Mario. *The Phenomenon of Information: A Conceptual Approach to Information Flow*. Plymouth, UK: Scarecrow Press, Inc., 2007.

Peterson, C. *A Primer in Positive Psychology*. Oxford, UK: Oxford University Press, 2006.

Phillips, Whitney. "LOLing at Tragedy: Facebook Trolls, Memorial Pages and Resistance to Grief Online." *First Monday*, December 16, 2011.

Plantinga, Alvin. *God, Freedom, and Evil*. New York: Harper & Row, 1974.

Plato. *Philebus*. In *The Dialogues of Plato*, translated by Benjamin Jowett, 343–403. New York: Random House, 1937.

Plato. *Republic*. Translated by Benjamin Jowett. The Internet Classics Archive. Accessed June 3, 2016. http://classics.mit.edu/Plato/republic.11.x.html.

Ponte, E. "Recent FDA Medical Device Regulation and Its Relevance to Robotics." *Tech Policy Lab*, January 27, 2014.

Postman, Neil. *Amusing Ourselves to Death: Public Discourse in the Age of Show Business*. London: Penguin Books Ltd., 1986.

Priest, Graham. *Beyond the Limits of Thought*. Oxford, UK: Oxford University Press, 2002.

Putnam, Hilary. "The Meaning of Meaning." *Minnesota Studies in the Philosophy of Science* 7 (1975): 131–93.

Putnam, Hilary. *Reason, Truth, and History*. Cambridge, UK: Cambridge University Press, 1981.

Putnam, Robert D. *Bowling Alone: The Collapse and Revival of American Community*. New York: Simon and Schuster, 2000.

Rachels, Stuart. "Is It Good to Make Happy People?" *Bioethics* 12, no. 2 (1998): 93–110.

Rainie, L., J. Horrigan, B. Wellman, and J. Boase. "The Strength of Internet Ties." *Pew Internet and American Life Project*. 2006. Accessed December 12, 2016. http://www.pewinternet.org/2006/01/25/the-strength-of-internet-ties/.

Rawls, John. "Legal Obligation and the Duty of Fair Play." In *Law and Philosophy*, edited by S. Hook, 3–18. New York: New York University Press, 1964.

Rawls, John. *A Theory of Justice*. Cambridge, MA: Harvard University Press, 1971.

Raz, Joseph. "The Problem of Authority: Revisiting the Service Conception." *Minnesota Law Review* 90 (2006): 1003–44.

Rotenstreich, N. "On Confidence." *Philosophy* 47, no. 182 (1972): 348–58.

Rowe, William L. "The Problem of Evil and Some Varieties of Atheism." *American Philosophical Quarterly* 16, no. 4 (1979): 335–41.

Rowe, William L. "Ruminations About Evil." *Philosophical Perspectives* 5 (1991): 69–88.

Rowe, William L. "Reply to Plantinga." *Noûs* 32, no. 4 (1998): 545–52.

Rowe, William L. "Friendly Atheism, Skeptical Theism, and the Problem of Evil." *International Journal for Philosophy of Religion* 59, no. 2 (2006): 79–92.

Ryan, Marie-Laure. *Possible Worlds, Artificial Intelligence, and Narrative Theory*. Bloomington, IN, Indiana University Press, 1991.

Ryan, Marie-Laure. *Avatars of Story*. Minneapolis, MN, University of Minnesota Press, 2006.

Ryberg, J. "Is the Repugnant Conclusion Repugnant?" *Philosophical Papers* 25 (1996): 161–77.

Saenz, A. "Entrepreneur Anshe Chung Makes a Fortune Selling Virtual Land, Banking and Fashion." *SingularityHUB*, August 23, 2011. Accessed June 6, 2016. http://singularityhub.com/2011/08/23/entrepreneur-anshe-chung-makes-millions-selling-virtual-land-banking-and-fashion/.

Salvini, Pericle, W. Yu, G. Ciaravella, G. Ferri, A. Manzi, B. Mazzolai, C. Laschi, S. Oh, and P. Dario. "How Safe Are Service Robots in Urban Environments? Bullying a Robot." Paper resented at the 19th International Symposium in Robot and Human Interactive Communication, Pisa, September 13–15, 2010.

Samuelson, W., and Zeckhauser, R. "Status Quo Bias in Decision Making." *Journal of Risk and Uncertainty* 1, no. 1 (1988): 7–59.

Schermer, Maartje. "Health, Happiness and Human Enhancement—Dealing with Unexpected Effects of Deep Brain Stimulation." *Neuroethics* 6 (2013): 9097–95.

Schwartz, Barry. *The Paradox of Choice: Why More Is Less.* New York: Harper Perennial, 2005.

Searle, J. R. *The Construction of Social Reality.* New York: Free Press, 1995.

Searle, J. R. "Social Ontology: Some Basic Principles." *Anthropological Theory* 6, no. 1 (2006): 12–29.

Seligman, M. E. P. *Authentic Happiness: Using the New Positive Psychology to Realize Your Potential for Lasting Fulfillment,* 1st edition. New York: Atria Books, 2004.

Shannon, Claude. "A Mathematical Theory of Communication." *Bell Systems Technical Journal* 27 (1948): 379–423, 623–56.

Sharkey, A. "Robots and Human Dignity: A Consideration of the Effects of Robot Care on the Dignity of Older People." *Ethics and Information Technology* 16, no. 1 (2014): 63–75.

Sharkey, N., and A. Sharkey. "Living with Robots: Ethical Tradeoffs in Eldercare." In *Close Engagements with Artificial Companions: Key Psychological, Social, Ethical and Design Issues,* edited by Yorick Wilks, 245–256. Amsterdam: John Benjamins, 2010.

Sharkey, A., and N. Sharkey. "Granny and the Robots: Ethical Issues in Robot Care for the Elderly." *Ethics and Information Technology* 14, no. 1 (2012): 27–40.

Shaw, Philip. *The Sublime.* New York: Routledge, 2006.

Shelley, Mary. *Frankenstein.* New York: Dover Publications, 1994.

Sherman, N. "The Virtues of Common Pursuit." *Philosophy and Phenomenological Research* 53, no. 2 (1993): 277–99.

Silver, J. (Producer). *The Matrix.* DVD. Directed by Lana Wachowski and Lily Wachowski. United States–Australia: Warner Brothers, Roadshow Entertainment, 1999.

Silverstein, Matthew. "In Defense of Happiness." *Social Theory and Practice* 26, no. 2 (2000): 279–300.

Simmons, John. *Moral Principle and Political Obligations.* Princeton, NJ: Princeton University Press, 1979.

Simmons, J. *Justification and Legitimacy: Essays on Rights and Obligations.* Cambridge, UK: Cambridge University Press, 2001.

Simmons, J., and C. Wellman. *Is There a Duty to Obey the Law?* Cambridge, UK: Cambridge University Press, 2005.

Sinclair, Brendan. "Gaming Will Hit $91.5 Billion This Year—Newzoo." *Gameindustry.biz,* April 22, 2015. Accessed December 13, 2016. http://www.gamesindustry.biz/articles/2015-04-22-gaming-will-hit-usd91-5-billion-this-year-newzoo.

Skyrms, Brian. *Signals: Evolution, Learning, and Information.* Oxford, UK: Oxford University Press, 2010.

Smith, Quentin. "An Atheological Argument from Evil Natural Laws." *International Journal for Philosophy of Religion* 29, no. 3 (1991): 159–74.

Sober, Elliot. "Psychological Egoism." In *The Blackwell Guide to Ethical Theory,* edited by Hugh Lafollette and Ingmar Persson, 129–148. Malden, MA: Blackwell Publishers, 2000.

Søraker, J. H. "The Value of Virtual Worlds and Entities: A Philosophical Analysis of Virtual Worlds and Their Potential Impact on Well-Being." PhD diss. Enschede, Ipskamp, 2010.

Søraker, J. H. "Virtual Entities, Environments, Worlds and Reality: Suggested Definitions and Taxonomy." In *Trust and Virtual Worlds: Contemporary Perspectives,* edited by C. Ess and M. Torseth, 44–73. New York: Peter Lang, 2011.

Søraker, J. H. " How Shall I Compare Thee? Comparing the Prudential Value of Actual Virtual Friendship." *Ethics and Information Technology* 14, no. 3 (2012): 209–19.

Sorell, T., and H. Draper. "Robot Carers, Ethics, and Older People." *Ethics and Information Technology* 16, no. 3 (2014): 183–95.

Sparrow, R., and L. Sparrow. "In the Hands of Machines? The Future of Aged Care." *Minds and Machines* 16, no. 2 (2006): 141–61.

Suits, Bernard. *The Grasshopper: Games, Life and Utopia.* Toronto: Broadview Press, 1978.

Sumner, L. W. *Welfare, Happiness, and Ethics.* New York: Clarendon Press, 1996.

Sumner, Thomas. "Mystery at the Center of the Earth." *Science News* 188 (2015): 18–21.
Swinburne, Richard. *Providence and the Problem of Evil*. New York: Oxford University Press, 1998.
Swinburne, Richard. *The Existence of God*, 2nd edition. Oxford, UK: Clarendon Press, 2004.
Tamir, Yael. *Liberal Nationalism*. Princeton: Princeton University Press, 1993.
Tamura, T., S. Yonemitsu, A. Itoh, D. Oikawa, A. Kawakami, Y. Higashi, et al. "Is an Entertainment Robot Useful in the Care of Elderly People with Severe Dementia?" *Journals of Gerontology Series A Biological Sciences and Medical Sciences* 59 (2004): 83–85.
Tassi, Paul. "Can We Forgive Hillary Clinton for Her Past War on Video Games?" *Forbes*, February 5, 2016. Accessed June 4, 2016. http://www.forbes.com/sites/insertcoin/2016/02/05/can-we-forgive-hillary-clinton-for-her-past-war-on-video-games/ -32aac2a198d6.
Tavinor, Grant. *The Art of Videogames*. Malden: Wiley-Blackwell, 2009.
Toffler, Alvin. *Future Shock*, Reissue Edition. New York: Bantam, 1990.
Tooley, Michael. "The Problem of Evil." *The Stanford Encyclopedia of Philosophy*, s.v. "The Problem of Evil." Stanford, CA: The Stanford Encyclopedia of Philosophy, 2015. Accessed December 12, 2016. http://plato.stanford.edu/archives/fall2015/entries/evil/.
Torrance, Steve. "Ethics and Consciousness in Artificial Agents." AI & Society 22, no. 4 (2007): 495–521.
Trepte, Sabine, Leonard Reinecke, and Keno Juechems. "The Social Side of Gaming: How Playing Online Computer Games Creates Online and Offline Social Support." *Computers in Human Behavior* 28, no. 3 (2012): 832–39.
Turing, Alan. "Computing Machinery and Intelligence." *Mind* 236 (1950): 433–60.
Turkle, Sherry. *Alone Together*. New York: Basic Books, 2011.
Vallor, S. "Carebots and Caregivers: Sustaining the Ethical Ideal of Care in the Twenty-First Century." *Philosophy & Technology* 24 (2011): 251–68.
Vallor, S. "Flourishing on Facebook: Virtue Friendship & New Social Media." *Ethics and Information Technology* 14, no. 3 (2012): 185–99.
Van Binsbergen, Wim. *Virtuality as a Key Concept in the Study of Globalisation*. Den Haag (The Netherlands): WOTRO, 1997.
Van Inwagen, Peter. *The Problem of Evil*. New York: Oxford University Press, 2008.
Verbeek, Peter-Paul. *Moralizing Technology: Understanding and Designing the Morality of Things*. Chicago: The University of Chicago Press, 2011.
Wada, K., and T. Shibata. "Robot Therapy in a Care House: Its Sociopsychological and Physiological Effects on the Residents." *Ethical Issues in Robot Care for the Elderly: Proceedings of the 2006 International Conference on Robotics and Automation* (2006): 3966–71.
Waldron, Jeremy. "Special Ties and Natural Duties." *Philosophy & Public Affairs* 22 (1993): 3–30.
Walker, A.D.M. "Political Obligation and the Argument from Gratitude." *Philosophy & Public Affairs* 17, no. 3 (1988): 191–211.
Wallace, P. *The Psychology of the Internet*. Cambridge: Cambridge University Press, 1999.
Walton, Kendall. *Mimesis as Make Believe*. Cambridge, MA: Cambridge University Press, 1993.
Weckert, J. "Trust in Cyberspace." In *The Impact of the Internet on Our Moral Lives*, edited by R. J. Cavalier, 95–117. New York: SUNY Press, 2005.
Weijers, Dan. "The Experience Machine Objection to Hedonism." in *Just the Arguments*, edited by Michael Bruce and Steven Barbone, 229–31. Hoboken, NJ: Wiley-Blackwell, 2011a.
Weijers, Dan. "Reality Doesn't Really Matter." In *Inception and Philosophy*, edited by D. Kyle Johnson and William Irwin, 92–107. Hoboken, NJ: Wiley-Blackwell, 2011b.
Weijers, Dan. "We Can Test the Experience Machine." *Ethical Perspectives* 19, no. 2 (2012): 261–68.
Weijers, Dan. "Intuitive Biases in Judgements about Thought Experiments: The Experience Machine Revisited." *Philosophical Writings* 41, no. 1 (2013): 17–31.
Weijers, Dan. "Nozick's Experience Machine Is Dead, Long Live the Experience Machine!" *Philosophical Psychology* 27, no. 4 (2014): 513–35.

Weijers, Dan. *Internet Encyclopedia of Philosophy*, s.v. "Hedonism." Accessed October 20, 2016. http://www.iep.utm.edu/hedonism/.

Weijers, Dan, and Vanessa Schouten. "An Assessment of Recent Responses to the Experience Machine Objection to Hedonism." *Journal of Value Inquiry* 47, no. 4 (2013): 461–82.

Wellman, B., A. Haase, J. Witte, and K. Hampton. "Does the Internet Increase, Decrease or Supplement Social Capital? Social Networks, Participation, and Community Commitment." *American Behavioral Scientist* 45, no. 3 (2001): 436–55.

Wellman, C. "Liberalism, Samaritanism, and Political Legitimacy." *Philosophy & Public Affairs* 25 (1996): 211–37.

Wellman, C. "Toward a Liberal Theory of Political Obligation," *Ethics* 111 (2001): 735–59.

Westworld. "The Original." Episode 1. Directed by Jonathan Nolan. HBO. First Aired Octobr 2, 2016.

Whitby, Blay. "Do You Want a Robot Lover?" In *Robot Ethics: The Ethical and Social Implications of Robotics*, edited by Patrick Lin, Keith Abney, and George A. Bekey, 233–49. Cambridge, MA: The MIT Press, 2011.

Williams, Bernard. "The Makropulos Case: Reflections on the Tedium of Immortality." In *Problems of the Self: Philosophical Papers 1956–1972*, 82–100. Cambridge, UK: Cambridge University Press, 1973.

Williams, B. "Persons, Character, and Morality." In *Moral Luck*, 1–19. Cambridge: Cambridge University Press, 1981.

Wilson, R. S., et al. "Loneliness and Risk of Alzheimer Disease." *Archives of General Psychiatry* 64 (2007): 234–40.

Winner, L. "Cyberlibertarian Myths and the Prospects for Community." *ACM Sigcas Computers and Society* 27, no. 3 (1997): 14–19.

Wolf, Mark J. P. "Video Games, Cinema, Bazin, and the Myth of Simulated Lived Experience." *G|A|M|E—The Italian Journal of Game Studies* 4, no. 1 (2015): 2280–7705. Accessed December 12, 2016. http://www.gamejournal.it/wolf_lived_experience.

Wolf, Susan, Stephen Macedo, John Koethe, Robert M. Adams, Nomy Arpaly, and Jonathan Haidt. *Meaning in Life and Why It Matters*. Princeton, NJ: Princeton University Press, 2012.

Wolff, J. "Political Obligation: A Pluralistic Approach." In *Pluralism: The Philosophy and Politics of Diversity*, edited by M. Baghramian and A. Ingram, 179–96. London: Routledge, 2000.

Wright, Crispin. "On Putnam's Proof That We Cannot Be Brains in a Vat." In *Reading Putnam*, edited by P. Clark and Bob Hale, 216–41. Oxford: Blackwell, 1994.

Young, Garry, and Monica Whitty. *Transcending Taboos: A Moral and Psychological Examination of Cyberspace*. London: Routledge, 2012.

Zarkadakis, George. *In Our Own Image: Will Artificial Intelligence Save or Destroy Us?* London: Rider Books, 2015.

LUDOGRAPHY

Artoon. (2002). *Blinx: The Time Sweeper*. Microsoft Xbox.

Atari Inc. (1979). *Asteroids*. Arcade.

Cancer Research UK. (2014). *Play to Cure: Genes in Space*. Windows.

Crytek. (2016). *The Climb*. Oculus Rift.

Mark Johnson. (2012). *Ultima Ratio Regum*. Windows.

Mojang. (2011). *Minecraft*. Various platforms.

Mossmouth. (2013). *Spelunky* (remake). Various platforms.

Number None. (2008). *Braid*. Various platforms.

Rockstar San Diego. (2010). *Red Dead Redemption*. Various platforms.

Santa Ragione. (2012). *Mirrormoon*. Various platforms.

Sensory Acumen, Inc. *Game Skunk*. (2016). Peripheral.

UbiSoft Montreal. (2003). *Prince of Persia: The Sands of Time*. Sony PlayStation 2.

University of Washington's Center for Game Science. (2008). *Foldit*. Windows.

Valve Corporation. (2007). *Portal*. Various platforms.

Index

achievement machine, 105, 109, 110

algorithms, 19, 105, 108, 128, 149

animals (nonhuman), 80, 97, 148, 150; Kant on, 170–172

artificial intelligence (AI), 125, 140–141, 142, 153n4–153n5, 175–176; virtual agents/beings, 138–152, 169–177, 180–181, 192

autonomy, 2, 4, 9, 75, 78, 140, 146, 147, 153n4, 217n27

avatars, 17, 18, 56n2, 164, 168n11, 200

brains in vats, 57, 58, 60, 61, 64–65, 68, 70

computer games. *See* video games

Dungeons and Dragons (game), 103, 105, 179

experience machine argument, 1, 13, 15, 33, 37, 41n3, 43, 44, 52–53, 70, 76, 87, 100, 105, 113–114, 118, 121, 132n10, 137–139, 155, 156–157, 169, 186, 204, 212

external world, problem of, 4, 70, 177–179

fantasy, 7, 29, 66, 67, 71n6, 130, 210, 215

free will, 78, 146–148

friendship, 26, 28, 54, 87–98, 137, 170, 182n4, 193, 195, 196, 213

gedankenexperiments. See thought experiments

God, 10n5, 67, 76, 144, 146–147, 148–150, 154n7, 154n9, 176, 197, 201n9; hiddenness of, 151, 199–200

hedonism, 2, 4, 14–15, 30, 43, 70, 78, 113, 114, 117, 153n1; attitudinal, 44–49, 55, 56n3; hedonic treadmill, 103

identity (personal), 75, 78, 85, 89–90, 111, 137, 139–140, 153n6, 208

illusion, 14, 27, 35, 41n2, 44, 58, 75, 77, 80, 81–80, 100, 116, 199

imagination, 7, 37, 41n3, 78, 85n3, 106

information, 17, 55, 56n5, 93, 129, 151, 155–156, 159–162, 165

instrumental value, 45, 91, 97, 102, 108, 109, 117, 198, 207

interactivity, 7, 56n2, 91, 104–107, 114, 115, 126–129, 162, 163, 179

interfaces, 117, 155–156, 162–167, 166, 168n13–168n17, 203

internet, 1, 2, 26, 27, 94, 128, 158, 159, 197

intrinsic value, 10n5, 33, 44–48, 97, 109, 110

loneliness, 85n2, 91, 197, 199

love, 26, 27, 28, 51, 54, 56n1, 81, 85n2, 153n2, 189, 191, 197, 212, 214

231

About the Authors

Jon Cogburn is associate professor in the Louisiana State University Department of Philosophy. He's published papers on aesthetics, epistemology, philosophy of logic, metaphysics, and the philosophy of popular culture. He has cowritten (with Mark Silcox) *Philosophy Through Video Games* (2009), coedited (with Mark Silcox) *Dungeons and Dragons and Philosophy* (2012), cotranslated with (Mark Ohm Tristan Garcia) *Form and Object: A Treatise on Things* (2014), and is the author of the forthcoming *Garcian Meditations: The Dialectics of Persistence in Form and Object* (2017).

E. M. Dadlez has a PhD in philosophy from Syracuse University and is professor of philosophy at the University of Central Oklahoma. Her work is mainly on the philosophy of art and literature, and on topics at the intersection (sometimes, more accurately, the collision) of aesthetics, ethics, and epistemology. She is the author of various articles on aesthetics and applied ethics, as well as *What's Hecuba to Him?* (1997) and *Mirrors to One Another* (2009).

Russell DiSilvestro is an associate professor and chair of the Department of Philosophy at Sacramento State. He received his PhD from Bowling Green State University. Professor DiSilvestro works on the intersection between metaphysics and ethics, especially as it relates to contemporary bioethical issues involving the nature and moral status of human beings. He is the author of *Human Capacities and Moral Status* (2010).

Alexis Elder is an assistant professor of philosophy at the University of Minnesota Duluth. Her research involves the nature of friendship, ethical issues involving social technologies (from robots, to social media, to computer-mediated communication), and the intersection of these topics. More information about her publications and research in progress can be found at http://www.alexiselder.net.

Trained as an architect, **Stefano Gualeni** is a philosopher and videogame designer who is best known for creating the videogames *Tony Tough and the Night of Roasted Moths* (1997) and *Gua-Le- Ni; or, The Horrendous Parade* (2012). He is a senior lecturer at the Institute of Digital Games, University of Malta (Malta). His work takes place at the intersection between continental philosophy and the design of virtual worlds. Both a philosopher who designs videogames and a game designer who is passionate about philosophy, he studies virtual worlds in their role as mediators of thought: as interactive, artificial environments where philosophical ideas, world-views, and thought-experiments can be explored, negotiated, and communicated.

Emiliano Heyns, MSc., is a recent graduate in philosophy of science, technology and society at the Department of Philosophy, University of Twente. His graduation thesis argued for the viability of hedonism as a theory of well-being with a special focus on friendship in a highly mediated world. He intends to branch out by pursuing a doctorate degree in the field of philosophy of expertise, intrigued by the changing role of knowledge and experts in a world increasingly driven by algorithms.

Michael LaBossiere, PhD, is a philosophy professor at Florida A&M University. Originally from Maine, he earned his doctorate from Ohio State University while also writing for gaming companies such as GDW, TSR, R. Talsorian Games, and Chaosium. His first philosophy book, *What Don't You Know*, was published in 2008. He blogs for *A Philosopher's Blog*, *Talking Philosophy*, *The Creativity Post*, and *Philosophical Percolations*. When not writing, he enjoys running, gaming, and the martial arts.

Peter Ludlow has written widely on topics ranging from metaphysics and epistemology to issues in cyberculture and virtual worlds. His publications include *Our Future in Virtual Worlds* (2010) and (with Mark Wallace) *The Second Life Herald: The Virtual Tabloid That Witnessed the Birth of the Metaverse* (2007). He has also written a number of popular articles on issues ranging from hacktivism to life online, including (with Mark Stephen Meadows) "A Virtual Life, An Actual Death," *H+ Magazine*, September 2, 2009. He lives in Playa del Carmen, Mexico.

James McBain is associate professor of philosophy at Pittsburg State University. His research and publications focus on issues in epistemology, metaphilosophy, moral philosophy, and the philosophy of video games.

Steven Montgomery is a doctoral candidate at Birkbeck College, University of London. His research examines questions of authority, obligation, and disobedience in a political context. Previously he spent fifteen years working for international campaigning organizations, including Friends of the Earth, Liberty, and Global Witness. He lives in London with his wife.

Daniel Pietrucha has a BS from the University of Virginia and an MA from the University of Victoria.

Brendan Shea, PhD, is a philosophy instructor at Rochester Community and Technical College and a resident fellow at the Minnesota Center for the Philosophy of Science. His research and teaching interests include the philosophy of science, applied ethics, logic, and the philosophy of religion. Recent publications include articles in *Prolegomena, Reason Papers*, and the *Journal for Cognition and Neuroethics*, as well as the "Karl Popper: Philosophy of Science" entry for the *Internet Encyclopedia of Philosophy.* He's also published a number of book chapters on popular culture and philosophy. He lives in Rochester, Minnesota, with his wife, Anne.

Mark Silcox is chair of the Humanities and Philosophy Department at the University of Central Oklahoma. His other academic books are *Philosophy Through Video Games* (coauthored with Jon Cogburn; 2009), and *Dungeons & Dragons and Philosophy: Raiding the Temple of Wisdom* (coedited with Jon Cogburn; 2012). His science fiction novel *The Face on the Mountain* was published in 2015.

Dr. **Johnny Hartz Søraker** is assistant professor of philosophy of technology at the Department of Philosophy, University of Twente. Although he is inspired by all kinds of philosophy, his main research interests lie in the intersections between information technology, on the one hand, and both theoretical and practical philosophy, on the other. He often grounds his work in psychological research, especially work in the field of positive psychology, and is developing this toward both a theory of the good life and a corresponding framework intended to help engineers design for well-being.

Grant Tavinor is senior lecturer in philosophy at Lincoln University in New Zealand and has a PhD from Auckland University. He is author of *The Art of Videogames* (2009) as well as a number of articles and book chapters on video games and aesthetics.

Dan Weijers is lecturer (equivalent of U.S. assistant professor) at the University of Waikato in New Zealand, and a coeditor of the *International*

Journal of Wellbeing. Dan has written extensively on the experience machine in his PhD thesis and in several papers, including "Nozick's Experience Machine Is Dead, Long Live the Experience Machine!" in *Philosophical Psychology* 27, no. 4 (2014): 513–35; "An Assessment of Recent Responses to the Experience Machine Objection to Hedonism with Vanessa Schouten," in *Journal of Value Inquiry* 47, no. 4 (2013): 461–82; and "Intuitive Biases in Judgements about Thought Experiments: The Experience Machine Revisited," in *Philosophical Writings* 41, no. 1 (2011): 17–31.